FREEDOM OF RELIGION, APOSTASY AND ISLAM

Debate on freedom of religion as a human right takes place not only in the Western world but also in Muslim communities throughout the world. For Muslims concerned for this freedom, one of the major difficulties is the 'punishment for apostasy' – death for those who desert Islam.

This book argues that the law of apostasy and its punishment by death in Islamic law is untenable in the modern period. Apostasy conflicts with a variety of foundation texts of Islam and with the current ethos of human rights, in particular the freedom to choose one's religion. Demonstrating the early development of the law of apostasy as largely a religio-political tool, the authors show the diversity of opinion among early Muslims on the punishment, highlighting the substantial ambiguities about what constitutes apostasy, the problematic nature of some of the key textual evidence on which the punishment of apostasy is based, and the neglect of a vast amount of clear Qur'anic texts in favour of freedom of religion in the construction of the law of apostasy.

Examining the significant challenges the punishment of apostasy faces in the modern period inside and outside Muslim communities – exploring in particular how apostasy and its punishment is dealt with in a multi-religious Muslim majority country, Malaysia, and the challenges and difficulties it faces there – the authors discuss arguments by prominent Muslims today for an absolute freedom of religion and for discarding the punishment of apostasy.

Freedom of Religion, Apostasy and Islam

ABDULLAH SAEED
and
HASSAN SAEED

ASHGATE

Published by
Ashgate Publishing Limited   Ashgate Publishing Company
Gower House   Suite 420
Croft Road   101 Cherry Street
Aldershot   Burlington
Hants GU11 3HR   VT 05401-4405
England   USA

Ashgate website: http://www.ashgate.com

British Library Cataloguing in Publication Data
Saeed, Abdullah
   Freedom of religion, apostasy and Islam
   1.Freedom of religion 2.Apostasy – Islam 3.Apostasy (Islamic law) 4.Freedom of religion – Malaysia
   I.Title II.Saeed, Hassan
   297.2'72

Library of Congress Cataloging-in-Publication Data
Saeed, Abdullah.
      Freedom of religion, apostasy and Islam / Abdullah Saeed and Hassan Saeed.
         p. cm.
      Includes bibliographical references and index.
      ISBN 0-7546-3082-X (alk. paper) — ISBN 0-7546-3083-8 (pbk. : alk. paper)
         1. Liberty of conscience (Islam) 2. Apostasy—Islam. 3. Religious
tolerance—Islam. 4. Freedom of religion—Islamic countries. 5. Freedom of
religion (Islamic law) I. Saeed, Hassan, 1970– II. Title

BP173.65.S26 2002
297.2'72—dc21

                                                          2002066448

ISBN   0 7546 3082 X Hardback
       0 7546 3083 8 Paperback

Typeset in Times New Roman by SetSystems Ltd, Saffron Walden, Essex
Printed and bound in Great Britain by MPG Books Ltd, Bodmin, Cornwall

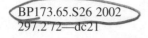

Contents

Part IV

Introduction

Apostasy (*riddah*), desertion of Islam or converting from Islam to another religion, is today vigorously debated among Muslims. High-profile apostasy cases, and an increasing number of publications affirming the punishment of death for apostasy, have brought this once largely ignored pre-modern Islamic law to life. In the recent past, several high-profile cases of apostasy have emerged in Muslim societies and made headlines in the international media. It is these cases that have led Muslims, particularly intellectuals, to look at the question of apostasy and its place in a modern Muslim society.

One of the most famous recent apostasy cases is related to Ayatollah Khomeini's *fatwa* (1989) declaring Salman Rushdie, the British-Indian novelist, an apostate. Since then Egypt, for example, has seen several high-profile cases of apostasy. In 1992, an Egyptian intellectual, Farag Foda, was gunned down by extremists who had accused him of apostasy. In 1993, a case of apostasy was filed against Nasr Hamid Abu Zayd, a professor of Islamic philosophy at Cairo University, asking the Egyptian courts to declare him an apostate. Similarly, a case of apostasy was filed in 2001 against Nawal al-Saadawi, the Egyptian feminist writer. Apart from these high-profile cases, a number of cases of apostasy or blasphemy that did not make international headlines were brought against converts, intellectuals, journalists and writers in a variety of Muslim nations including Egypt, Jordan, Algeria, Yemen and Saudi Arabia. Under Pakistan's blasphemy law, which functions like an apostasy law as far as Muslims are concerned, hundreds of people have been accused since the law's promulgation in 1986. Several Muslim heads of state remain accused of apostasy by their extremist opponents. While the majority of Muslim states have no death penalty for apostasy, states like Saudi Arabia, Yemen and Sudan are exceptions.

Though apostasy has a long history in texts on Islamic law, its treatment has not differed essentially from its conceptualization in the second century of Islam. Even in the modern period, Muslim scholars have remained, on the whole, faithful to the law of apostasy as it exists in the pre-modern Islamic legal texts. Since the law of apostasy had been considered by many Muslims to be one of the 'immutable' laws in Islamic law, no attempt was made until the modern period to question its basis or debate its validity. The law of apostasy had become one of the non-negotiable aspects of Islamic law, much like the prescribed punishments (*hudud*) specified in the Qur'an for theft or fornication. However, those punishments at least have

1

Qur'anic support, whereas the punishment of apostasy does not, as this book argues. It is largely based on a number of isolated traditions of the Prophet (*hadith ahad*) or their interpretations.

Muslim questioning of the basis of the apostasy law stems only from the late nineteenth and early twentieth centuries. Muslim modernists of this period such as Ahmad Khan, Muhammad Abduh, Rashid Rida and Muhammad Iqbal were among the earliest to provide the basic framework within which it became possible to question the pre-modern conception of apostasy and its punishment. Gradually, in the twentieth century, several thinkers of a more 'liberal' persuasion also began to highlight the problematic nature of the law. In the late twentieth century, even a number of leading Islamists joined the call for rethinking of the law of apostasy.

Among those who contributed significantly to the debate from a 'liberal' perspective was S.A. Rahman, the retired Chief Justice of Pakistan, who examined the textual basis of the law in detail and highlighted the weakness of the foundations on which the law of apostasy was based. Others included Hasan al-Turabi, Rashid al-Ghannushi, Mohammad Hashim Kamali, Mohammed Salim el-Awa and Abdullahi An-Na'im. Their views have been vigorously challenged by scholars of a more traditionalist persuasion.

One of the important aspects of the debate is the punishment for apostasy, that is, death for those who turn away from Islam. This punishment, specified in pre-modern Islamic law, is seen by many Muslims today as a tool for preventing Muslims from converting to another religion, or for forcing intellectuals, thinkers, writers and artists to remain within the limitations of the established orthodoxy in a given Muslim state. The death penalty is staunchly defended by a significant number of Muslims, but equally strongly opposed by an increasingly vocal group that includes some prominent Muslim thinkers and even Islamists. Its defenders, however, dominate the debate by drawing on ideas and views expressed in pre-modern Islamic law. They are armed with what they consider to be supporting texts from the the the Qur'an and *hadith*, the views of pre-modern Muslim scholars as well as *fatwas* from conservative religious leaders today. This leaves opponents of the law of apostasy largely defenceless against what appears to be unassailable and authoritative 'textual' evidence.

Many Muslims are uncomfortable with the law of apostasy and argue that it is outdated and should be abolished. They have attempted to reinterpret the associated texts, pointing out that there is no Qur'anic basis for the death penalty and that, in the practice of the Prophet (*sunnah*), the death penalty for apostasy was not for a simple change of faith but for a more political act such as high treason. These thinkers argue, on the contrary, that freedom of religion for all, Muslim and non-Muslim alike, is a fundamental principle of Islam and that the law of apostasy therefore goes against this fundamental principle and should be discarded.

This book is a contribution to the thinking that freedom of religion is a fundamental principle of Islam and that the death penalty for apostasy violates this principle. It argues that the death penalty conflicts with the foundation texts of Islam, the Qur'an and the *sunnah*, and with the current ethos of human rights, in particular the freedom to choose one's religion. The book demonstrates that the early development of the law of apostasy in general, and its punishment in particular, was in response to the socio-political situation of the Muslim community in the immediate post-prophetic period (in the seventh century CE). The Qur'anic texts used in support of the law are either not relevant or their interpretation conflicts with many other Qur'anic texts that emphasize religious freedom and the adoption of a faith as an individual choice. The book shows the diversity of opinion among early Muslims regarding the punishment and highlights an early lack of consensus on the issue. It highlights some of the many ambiguities associated with the meaning of apostasy and what constitutes it, as well as the problematic nature of key textual evidence in support of the death penalty. It also demonstrates the range of views among Muslims today on the question, and attempts to show why apostasy has become such a problematic issue.

The central task of this book is therefore to reread the relevant foundation texts of Islam and to show that the punishment of apostasy by death cannot be justified by an appeal to the Qur'an or the practice of the Prophet. It also places the punishment in the context of the current debate on human rights, particularly freedom of religion. It concludes that such a punishment conflicts with the ethos of the Qur'an and the practice of the Prophet, as well as with the needs of the modern period.

A feature of this book is the exploration of how apostasy and the debate on its punishment are dealt with in a multi-religious Muslim majority society, in this case Malaysia. We chose Malaysia for a variety of reasons. It is one of those countries where the punishment of apostasy has attracted the attention of both scholars and politicians. Its population profile is typical of many Muslims nations in that it is multi-religious. It has a secular constitution, which provides religious freedom for all citizens. Malaysia is also important because many Muslims see it as a role model, not only for its recent rapid economic development and its championing of an enlightened Islam, but also for its relatively harmonious management of its multiracial and multi-religious society. It has not only a strong non-Muslim minority totally opposed to the law of apostasy and the death penalty, but also a Muslim segment equally insistent on the implementation of that law, which presents the government with a dilemma. Any solution Malaysia may find to the issue of apostasy could well be copied by other Muslim countries, and any step Malaysia takes in this respect is also important from a human rights point of view as Malaysia is a relatively 'liberal' Muslim country.

Structure of the Book

The book has two main parts. Since the discourse on apostasy is really a global one, the treatment of the subject in the first part of the book does not focus on one particular region. The discourse in its pre-modern as well as modern formulations can be found in almost all Muslim communities; therefore it seemed appropriate to treat the issue from a global perspective and include examples of apostasy cases from several parts of the Muslim world. The second part of the book presents a case study on Malaysia.

Several Arabic terms occur in the book. In order to make the text more readable, we have used a simplified system of transliteration. Arabic words used in the Malay language are often transliterated somewhat differently. For example, the term *shari'ah* is written in Malay as *syariah*. In the second part of the book we have used the Malay transliteration of the word, rather than the standard one. For the sake of readability, we have kept footnotes and references to a minimum. Where dates are given, we have attempted to provide both the Islamic (*hijri*) and Gregorian dates. For instance, 1/622 means year 1 of the Islamic calendar and year 622 of the Gregorian calendar.

For quotations from the Qur'an, we have adopted Muhammad Asad's translation.[1] His is one of the most readable translations by a Muslim and his critical comments in the footnotes seem highly relevant to the topic. In a few instances where Asad's translation does not seem to do justice to the text, we have amended it.

Part I has eight chapters and focuses on the law of apostasy itself. Chapter One traces the historical development of the concept of freedom of religion. This also highlights the scope of Article 18 of the Universal Declaration of Human Rights of the United Nations (1948) on which various human rights conventions of today are based. It then traces the diversity of approaches to religious freedom in the Muslim world. Chapter Two outlines the religious and political context in which the law of apostasy developed. Chapter Three explores the definition of apostasy and related terms. It highlights the high degree of fluidity in the understanding of what constitutes apostasy. Chapter Four provides an overview of the law of apostasy in pre-modern Islamic law, and examines critically the textual basis for punishment. Chapter Five brings together the most important Qur'anic evidence against the death penalty for change of faith. It then explores other textual and historical evidence against the punishment. Chapter Six examines differing views among Muslims today on the issue of punishment. Chapter Seven highlights the potential for misuse of apostasy law, while Chapter Eight is an attempt to understand the reasons for apostasy and the level of fear of apostasy among Muslims.

Part II presents a detailed study of how some laws related to apostasy are debated, discussed and implemented, and the challenges these laws face in the Muslim-majority state of Malaysia. Chapter Nine provides a background to Malaysian society, including religion, the political and legal systems, and the constitutional guarantee of religious freedom. Chapter Ten explores the attitude of the two main political parties of Malaysia towards apostasy laws. Chapter Eleven looks at the question of jurisdiction in Malaysia regarding apostasy and related cases, and some of the legal problems involved. Chapter Twelve explores the future of apostasy laws in Malaysia, with particular reference to the two main political parties, UMNO and PAS, which have agendas for the further Islamization of Malaysian society.

Chapter Thirteen reflects on the need to rethink apostasy laws.

Many have made suggestions for improvements to the book: Rachel Butson, Jacky Angus, Christina Mayer, Donna Williams, Redha Ameur, Domenyk Eades, Alex Radovanovic and Abdul Ghafoor Abdul Raheem. Any errors are, of course, the responsibility of the authors. We trust that this book will contribute to the ongoing debate on the need to rethink this area of Islamic law.

Abdullah Saeed and Hassan Saeed

PART I

Chapter 1

The Context of the Debate on Apostasy: Freedom of Religion in the Modern Period

Although the term 'human rights' (*huquq al-insan*) has its equivalent in many languages, the understanding of what 'human rights' means is subject to debate and controversy. For some in non-Western societies, the discourse of human rights is a product of the West and Western civilization; it has a neo-imperialistic tone, and is used to dominate, control and restrict the progress of non-Western societies. For others in these societies, the concept of 'human rights' reflects the concerns and interests of the vast majority of people on earth; the fact that it began as a Western construct does not mean that it is specifically a Western idea, interest or concern.[1]

The discourse of human rights is based on the idea that 'individuals possess rights simply by virtue of being human'.[2] Freedom of religion is seen as one element of human rights addressed in the major religious traditions of Judaism, Christianity and Islam. Many of the rights referred to in the Universal Declaration of Human Rights can be found explicitly or implicitly in the Bible or the Qur'an (the Holy Scripture of Muslims). However, as a discourse, 'human rights' emerged relatively recently and developed gradually into its current form. The French Revolution of 1789 and the American Bill of Rights of 1791 are considered important landmarks of this discourse. The Universal Declaration of Human Rights by the United Nations (1948) was a result of this development, which was drafted by an international panel that included non-Western members. This Declaration was followed by a series of human rights conventions supported in varying degrees by Western as well as non-Western nations. For the purpose of our discussion on religious freedom, other relevant conventions include the European Convention for the Protection of Human Rights and Fundamental Freedoms (1950), the International Covenant on Civil and Political Rights (1966), the International Covenant on Economic, Social and Cultural Rights (1966), and the United Nations Declaration on the Elimination of All Forms of Intolerance and of Discrimination Based on Religion or Belief (1981).

Right to Freedom of Religion

The right to freedom of religion is perhaps the oldest human right recognized internationally. In the context of the West, the international document enshrining the Peace of Westphalia, which accorded international protection to religious groups, was signed in 1648. In the eighteenth century, the right of religious liberty added dynamism to the Commonwealth of Virginia's Bill of Rights of 1776, the Austrian Act of Religious Tolerance of 1781 and the Virginia Statute of Religious Liberty of 1786.[3]

In the USA, the First Amendment to the US Constitution emphasizes the free exercise of religion. It states that: 'Congress shall make no law respecting an establishment of religion, or prohibiting the free exercise thereof.' The second clause, containing the phrase 'free exercise', guarantees a citizen's right to express religious beliefs, and act in accord with those beliefs. As Thomas Jefferson noted: 'All men shall be free to profess, and by argument to maintain, their opinions in matters of religion. And the same shall in no wise diminish, enlarge or affect their civil liberties.'[4]

In Europe, two main conventions safeguard freedom of conscience and religion: Article 9 of the European Convention on Human Rights (ECHR), and Article 18 of the International Covenant on Civil and Political Rights. Both Articles are based, almost verbatim,[5] on Article 18 of the United Nations' Universal Declaration of Human Rights (UDHR) of 1948, which states:

> Everyone has the right to freedom of thought, conscience and religion; this right includes freedom to change his religion or belief, and freedom, either alone or in community with others and in public or private, to manifest his religion or belief in teaching, practice, worship and observance.

This right was included in the International Covenant on Civil and Political Rights (ICCPR, in force 23 March 1976). Article 18 of this covenant provides that:

1 Everyone shall have the right to freedom of thought, conscience and religion. This right shall include freedom to have or to adopt a religion or belief of his choice, and freedom, either individually or in community with others and in public or private, to manifest his religion or belief, observance, practice, and teaching.
2 No one shall be subject to coercion, which would impair his freedom to have or to adopt a religion or belief of his choice.
3 Freedom to manifest one's religion or beliefs may be subject only to such limitations as are prescribed by law and are necessary to protect public safety, order, health, or morals or the fundamental rights and freedoms of others.

Two key freedoms related to religion are specified above: freedom to maintain or to change religion or belief; and freedom to manifest religion or belief. In the case of the first freedom, it includes not only the 'inner freedom of an individual to maintain his religion or belief, but also his freedom to belong, or not to belong, to an organized religion or belief'.[6] The inner freedom, freedom of thought and conscience, is related to the mind. But simply having freedom of thought and conscience is of very little practical value unless freedom to express what is in the mind is also recognized. This does not mean, however, that the right to freedom of thought and conscience has no other benefits:

> It also guarantees that one cannot be subjected to a treatment intended to change the process of thinking – brainwashing and so on. It forbids any form of compulsion to express thoughts, to change an opinion or to divulge a religious conviction. It also means that no sanction may be imposed, either on the holding of any view whatsoever, or on the change of religion or conviction. It protects against indoctrination by the state.[7]

Article 18 of the UDHR or ICCPR does not permit any limitations whatsoever on the freedom of thought and conscience or on the freedom to have or adopt a religion or belief of one's choice. These freedoms are protected *unconditionally*. The freedom to have or to adopt a religion or belief 'necessarily entails the freedom to choose a religion or belief, including, *inter alia*, the right to replace one's current religion or belief'.[8]

Article 18 indicates that it is not just what is in the mind that is important. One ought to have the opportunity to put it into practice; that is, to be able to profess any religion and practise it privately or in community with others. This involves manifesting that religion in worship, teaching, practice and observance. The Article protects theistic, non-theistic and atheistic beliefs, as well as the right not to profess any religion.[9] However, Article 18 of the Universal Declaration, upon which other religious freedom-related instruments in the modern period have been based, requires interpretation in the light of the restrictions specified in Article 29(2), which reads:

> In the exercise of his rights and freedoms, everyone shall be subject only to such limitations as are determined by law solely for the purpose of securing due recognition and respect for the rights and freedoms of others and of meeting the just requirements of morality, public order and the general welfare in a democratic society.[10]

The limitations refer to what is contrary to morality, public order or general welfare. This includes practices such as human sacrifice, self-immolation, mutilation of oneself or others, and slavery or prostitution carried out in the service of, or under the pretext of, promoting a religion or belief. Similarly, activities aimed at the destruction of the state, such as rebellion or subversion, or the breach of international peace and security in the name of a religion are not allowed. In the application of this freedom, the state is also required to secure 'due recognition and respect for the rights and freedoms of others'.[11]

Thus, it is clear that Article 18 of the UDHR provides a high degree of freedom to adopt, maintain, change and manifest one's religion, or to not have a religion. Lee Boothby of the International Academy for Freedom of Religion and Belief indicates ways in which religious freedom should be protected in the spirit of Article 18.

According to him, the state should ensure the full equality before the law of all religious organizations, giving each, regardless of size or age, an equal opportunity to enter the religious marketplace, and to propagate their religious views. It should be prohibited from intruding into their internal affairs, and permit them to function fully without regard to national boundaries. Discrimination based on an individual's religious belief or membership should be prohibited. Individuals should (a) be permitted to manifest their religious beliefs in public and in private; (b) be unrestricted, fully protected with respect to their right to believe or not to believe, and be equally free to change their religious belief; (c) be permitted to worship, either individually or in community, with others. The varied religious beliefs and practices of all should be accommodated by the state, unless the state is able to demonstrate a legitimate state interest that cannot be otherwise served by actions less intrusive into religious belief and expression.[12] However, this level of freedom does not yet exist in most countries.

Universality of the Right: the Debate

The Universal Declaration promotes respect for the human rights and fundamental freedoms specified in it for all people regardless of religion, race or language. It is 'universal' in its orientation and several of its Articles convey this concept.[13] The idea of the universality of human rights has, however, been questioned by many, both Muslims and non-Muslims.[14] Cultural relativists, for example, condemn the notion that there are universal standards by which all cultures may be judged; that is, values taken from Western cultures should not be used to judge non-Western cultures, including Islamic ones.[15] From a non-Western perspective, universal values can be regarded as neo-colonialist, imperialist, and aimed at demonstrating superiority of Western values over other values.

There are varying Muslim views on the universality of human rights. Those Muslims who support it argue that the rights specified in the UDHR are not alien from a Qur'anic point of view and that, in fact, almost all the rights can be supported by the Qur'an and the practice of the Prophet. According to this view, the reservation Muslims have with regard to the right to change one's religion is based on a misreading of the relevant sections of the Qur'an and a reliance on pre-modern Islamic law. They do not see this pre-modern Islamic law as sacred or immutable; rather they see it as a human product constructed in a certain socio-historical context and therefore susceptible to change. A rereading of the Islamic tradition in the light of modern concerns, interests and needs will, in their view, come to the conclusion that much of the UDHR is in line with the fundamental objectives of the Qur'an and *sunnah*.

On the other hand, Muslims who oppose the universality of human rights argue that the UDHR and other similar human rights documents are a product of the secular West and therefore cannot be a basis for a Muslim understanding of human rights. For them, the UDHR is a 'human construct' and should not be privileged over 'Divine Law' (reflected in the Qur'an and *sunnah*) and the rights and freedoms covered by Divine Law. Some dismiss the UDHR as a relic of neo-colonialism while others argue that the United Nations, or any similar body, has no authority to legislate for Muslims. For the Muslims who oppose universality, Islam has a particular concept of human rights, including religious freedom, and these must be understood in the context of the Islamic law, which itself determines the scope of freedom available to a Muslim. They rely on ideas that exist in Islamic law in their rejection of freedom of religion as specified in Article 18.

In pre-modern Islamic law, as far as religious freedom is concerned, legal capacity is determined by the religion to which the person belongs. Non-Muslims, for example, are divided into two groups: (a) 'People of the Book' including Jews, Christians and Zoroastrians; (b) people without a revealed religion. While People of the Book are automatically granted certain privileges in the area of religious freedom, those who do not have a revealed religion pose a problem for pre-modern Islamic law. Differences of opinion exist among pre-modern Muslim jurists on whether this latter group should be 'forced' to convert to Islam if under Islamic rule. However, in Islamic history, these people were treated like the People of the Book (as was the case with Hindus and Buddhists in India), and the question remained largely theoretical. Non-Muslims within a Muslim state may practise their religion (with certain restrictions related to manifesting their religion) as long as they submit to the authority of the Muslim state. Similarly, Muslims may practise their religion freely as long as they are not in conflict with the local 'orthodoxy', where such is in place.

In most modern Muslim states, however, many restrictions on non-Muslims (as they exist in pre-modern Islamic law) have been virtually eliminated. Where religious pluralism exists, the state does not generally discriminate against non-Muslims. All are considered equal citizens of the Muslim state and equal before the law, although certain restrictions under family law will still be in place.

Muslim Nations and Religious Freedom

Today, the vast majority of Muslims subscribe to the idea of the 'nation-state', although various states have adopted different systems of government, including monarchies, democracies and dictatorships. An important result of the recognition of the nation-state is the place of national identity as a basis for social organization. This is critical to the life of Muslim communities, even at a practical level.[16] Constitutions exist in almost all Muslim states, and even where they do not in a formal sense, as in Saudi Arabia, the idea of a constitution as the basis for the state certainly exists. Saudi Arabia, for instance, argues that it has a 'constitution': the Qur'an and *sunnah*. In Oman, there is a Basic Charter that is akin to a constitution. Where constitutions exist in Muslim states, some declare that Islam is the religion of the state, as in Malaysia and Iran. Others prefer not to declare an official religion, as is the case in Mali.

In the case of religious freedom, there is no consensus among Muslims as to whether religious freedom includes the right to change religion. In 1948, for example, the representative of Saudi Arabia to the United Nations objected to Article 18, in particular to the freedom to change one's religion, as this was claimed to be prohibited under Islamic law. The Pakistani representative, Muhammed Zafarullah Khan, on the other hand supported the Article on the basis that the Qur'an allows a person to believe or not to believe. Interestingly, a number of Muslim nations have signed and ratified the United Nations Covenant on Civil and Political Rights,[17] which includes an article similar to Article 18 of the UDHR. These nations include Afghanistan, Albania, Algeria, Egypt, Iran, Iraq, Jordan, Lebanon, Libya, Mali, Morocco, Niger, Somalia, Sudan, Syria and Tunisia.

By ratifying such covenants, several Muslim states have indicated that they accept freedom of religion for all citizens, in principle. Moreover, freedom of religion is also declared in the constitutions of a number of Muslim states. The Constitution of Mali, for example, includes this, and declares Mali to be a secular state. The 1996 Basic Charter of Oman considers Islamic law as the basis for legislation, but preserves the freedom to practise traditional religious rites provided this does not breach public order. Discrimination against individuals, on the basis of religion or sect, is prohibited in Oman. The Constitution of Bangladesh establishes Islam as the state religion but also stipulates the right to follow the religion of one's choice, and the government respects this provision in practice.[18] Most Muslim states, particularly those with significant non-Muslim minorities, realize the importance of religious freedom. Thus, various Muslim states have endowed the right to believe, practise and express religious beliefs on minorities, as well as on the Muslim majority.

In the modern period, freedom of religion has therefore become an important question for Muslims themselves. In the second half of the twentieth century, an increasing number of Muslim contributors to the debate on freedom of religion argued in favour of retaining the pre-modern Islamic legal view of religious freedom, and produced several so-called 'Islamic human rights' instruments. From their point of view, these were developed on the basis that 'Islam provided fourteen centuries ago [what is referred to as] "human rights" comprehensively and in detail'.[19] These instruments generally tend to state in general terms that 'each person has the right to freedom of belief and worship according to one's religion' on the basis of the Qur'anic verse, 'To you your religion, to me my religion'.[20] Such documents do not specify anything about conversion of a Muslim to another religion. The question of change of religion is usually not addressed in these documents as it is still a sensitive issue for many Muslims.

While many Muslims would argue that freedom of religion was a right given by the Qur'an fourteen hundred years ago in the famous Qur'anic verse 'There shall be no coercion in matters of faith', they may still be uncomfortable with the phrasing of Article 18 of the UDHR. Sultanhussein Tabandeh of Iran is one of the few Muslims who has attempted to write a commentary on the UDHR from an Islamic perspective. In his commentary on Article 18, while saying that the Article is 'largely acceptable',[21] he lists several problems with it. First, he says that under an Islamic state, religious minorities who follow the one true God and the revelation given to one of His prophets – whether Jews, Christians or Zoroastrians – enjoy complete religious freedom within the limits of their faith. However, followers of a religion, the basis of which is contrary to Islam, have no official right to freedom of religion under an Islamic government.[22] A second difficulty is that Article 18 affirms the individual's freedom to change his religion.[23] One of the reasons for objecting to this is 'the decision to change religion may be forced on a person under pressure or duress, or again it may be induced by false motives like the desire to get a divorce under easier conditions of some other doctrine'.[24] More importantly, from Tabandeh's point of view, the fundamental objection to change of religion is that:

> No man of sense, from the mere fact that he possesses intelligence, will ever turn down the better in favour of the inferior. Anyone who penetrates beneath the surface to the inner essence of Islam is bound to recognize its superiority over the other religions. A man, therefore, who deserts Islam, by that act betrays the fact that he must have played truant to its moral and spiritual truths in his heart earlier.[25]

Both Sunni and Shi'i writers use these arguments when they object to the right to change one's religion. The argument of the superiority of Islam is ancient, found in classical sources of Islamic law, while the point about 'pressure' comes largely from experience of the missionary activities of Christians among Muslims. While Tabandeh reflects Shi'i thinking, Hassan Ahmad Abidin of Egypt is typical of many contributors to the debate within

Sunni Islam. Like other advocates of Islamic human rights proposals, Abidin states that 'belief is a fundamental human right', that 'Islam does not force anyone to profess it', and that, since Islam is from God, this right is in line with the nature (*fitrah*) of the human being.[26]

Although Abidin reiterates that Islam does not force anyone to profess it or any other religion, his 'sticking point' is the question of apostasy from Islam. He notes that apostasy was prohibited at the time of the Prophet because certain people professed Islam in order to harm the religion. To prevent this, Islam prohibited apostasy as a precautionary measure to safeguard the Muslim community.[27] He then raises the point that the Muslim community is strong today and is therefore not in need of such protection, and consequently there is no need to retain the ruling. However, despite this reasoning, Abidin returns to the classical argument of the superiority of Islam. Abidin goes on to claim that Judaism and Christianity are 'corrupted' and 'distorted' religions and that Islam is the only true religion from God:

> To which [religion] does the apostate convert? If he or she is going to convert to a better and more complete religion than Islam, it is not fair for Islam to punish [the apostate]. If the apostate is going to convert to a religion that will guarantee for him and others more and better rights than what Islam guarantees, there will be no one to support Islam's ruling on the punishment [of the apostate]. But the reality is that Islam is the most perfect and complete religion; it is the religion that gave rights which no human being ever thought of [in the pre-modern period].[28]

Thus, whether Sunni or Shi'i, many Muslims may find the 'right' to apostatize from Islam particularly challenging, difficult and problematic. For them, freedom of conscience and the rights to worship and practise religion are given in the Qur'an and the *sunnah*; the right of apostasy is not.[29] They strongly oppose the idea of apostasy as a universal right because Islam does not recognize this freedom or right. In line with the arguments advanced by classical Muslim jurists, many Muslims today argue that Islam is the true and final religion and that turning from this true religion to another which is, by definition, 'false' cannot be tolerated. Since salvation is the most important objective for a human being, all attempts should be made, in their view, to keep the person within the fold of Islam, the only path to salvation.

In 1990, the Organization of the Islamic Conference recognized the importance of engaging in mainstream international discourse on human rights, including freedom of religion, by adopting the Cairo Declaration on Human Rights in Islam. Earlier, in 1981, the Islamic Council of Europe had adopted with much fanfare what was termed the 'Universal Islamic Declaration of Human Rights'. Both declarations have articles dealing with religious freedom. On closer inspection, however, they do not reach the level of religious freedom guaranteed in the Universal Declaration of

Human Rights of 1948.[30] Instead, they follow the more conventional Muslim argument for limited 'freedom' as specified in the pre-modern Islamic law. For instance, Article 10 of the Cairo Declaration on Human Rights in Islam states:

> Islam is the religion of unspoiled nature. It prohibits any form of compulsion on Man or the exploitation of his poverty or ignorance in order to convert him to another religion or to atheism.

This Article does not specify that all citizens of a Muslim state have the right to religious freedom in the sense enunciated in Article 18 of the Universal Declaration. Rather, the Article in the Cairo Declaration restates the Islamic legal position with regard to coercion; that is, coercion is prohibited. It bans the exploitation of a Muslim's economic and social disadvantage as an incentive to change religion. Other related Articles of the Cairo Declaration such as 22(a) deal with the right to express one's opinion. Article 22(b) declares the right 'to advocate what is right, and propagate what is good, and warn against what is wrong and evil'. In the latter, a clear reference is made to Islamic law and therefore to the limitations it places on such matters. The Articles do not add any new freedoms, or expand the scope of religious freedom implicit in pre-modern Islamic law. The Cairo Declaration has no article that corresponds to Article 18 of the Universal Declaration of Human Rights.

The Universal Islamic Declaration of Human Rights (UIDHR) of 1981, however, appears to come somewhat closer to the Universal Declaration of Human Rights (UDHR) with regard to religious freedom. Article 13 of the UIDHR states: 'Every person has the right to freedom of conscience and worship in accordance with his religious beliefs'. However, even here the freedom is only of conscience and worship; what is in the conscience is not observable, and private worship is prohibited only in a few countries. The UIDHR does not address the right to change religion covered by the Universal Declaration. The UIDHR thus simply affirms the freedom that is given in general terms under pre-modern Islamic law. For instance, in Article 10 (Rights of Minorities), the UIDHR defines key concepts as follows:

a   The Qur'anic principle 'There is no compulsion in religion' shall govern the religious rights of non-Muslim minorities.
b   In a Muslim country religious minorities shall have the choice to be [*sic*] governed in respect of their civil and personal matters by Islamic Law, or by their own laws.

The English version of the UIDHR appears to be a document written for a largely non-Muslim Western audience. Arabic and English versions differ on significant points.[31] A number of the Articles regarding freedom of religion appear to be rather vague and over-qualified. The phrases used in the UIDHR such as 'according to the *shari'ah* [Islamic law]' or so long as one 'remains within the limits prescribed by the Law'[32] resonate with positions in pre-modern Islamic law which are restrictive of religious freedom.

With regard to religious freedom, the situation in modern Muslim states today varies greatly. Some states allow religious freedom with few restraints, while others severely restrict religious freedom, even for Muslims. This may range from not allowing Muslim legal or theological schools, other than those sanctioned by the government, to restricting proselytization, to enforcing the death penalty for apostasy. In a number of Muslim states, freedom of religion is guaranteed. For example, the Constitution of the Republic of Turkey (1982) states in Article 24:

Everyone has the right to freedom of conscience, religious belief and conviction. No one shall be compelled to worship, or to participate in religious ceremonies and rites, to reveal religious beliefs and convictions, or be blamed or accused because of his religious beliefs and convictions.

Similarly, the Constitution of Tunisia states in Article 5:

The Tunisian Republic guarantees the inviolability of the human person and the freedom of conscience, and protects the free exercise of beliefs, with the reservation that they do not disturb the public order.

The Constitution of the Federation of Malaysia also provides for religious freedom. Religious minorities there generally worship freely, but there are some anomalies (see Part II of this book).

In this context,[33] apostasy emerges as a significant problem for many Muslim states. In some, the proselytizing of Muslims is not allowed, and the abandonment of Islam is thus also prohibited and severely punished. In some states, proselytizing of Muslims is allowed and change of religion permitted. Others regulate 'religious propagation', as the Indonesian government attempted to do in the 1970s. According to the Joint Decree of the Minister of Religion and the Minister of Home Affairs No.1 of 1979:

Religious propagation should not be directed toward a group of [already] converted people by any means, such as:
a   Conducting [propogation] in a persuasive manner or by offering donations, money, clothing, food and beverages, medical service and other forms of gifts, so that the group of converted people might be persuaded to change to the religion that is propagated;
b   Distributing pamphlets, magazines, books, bulletins, and other publications in the locality of the converted people;
c   By way of door-to-door visits to the converted peoples' houses for whatever reasons.[34]

In Saudi Arabia, for instance, conversion by a Muslim to another religion is considered apostasy. Public apostasy is a crime under Islamic law and is punishable by death. Similarly in Sudan, while non-Muslims may convert to Islam, the 1991 Criminal Act makes all apostasy, including conversion to another religion by Muslims, punishable by death. Sudan introduced the death penalty for apostasy in 1983. Yemen also prohibits apostasy and imposes capital punishment.

In Malaysia, the right of a Muslim to leave Islam in order to adhere to another faith is a controversial question. In practice, it is somewhat difficult for a Muslim to change religion in Malaysia. Proposals for dealing with various punishments for 'apostates' have been floated within and beyond government circles (see Part II). Recently the Malaysian government appeared at times to take the position that apostates would not face punishment as long as they did not defame Islam after their conversion. Nonetheless, proselytizing of Muslims by adherents of other religions is strongly prohibited, while proselytizing of non-Muslims faces no obstacles.

In Iran, the Constitution allows religious freedom, although successive governments there have been highly suspicious of proselytizing of Muslims by non-Muslims. In Oman, the government prohibits non-Muslims from proselytizing Muslims. In Morocco, by contrast, voluntary conversion from Islam to other religions may pass unpunished. Here, although Islamic law and tradition call for strict punishment of any Muslim who converts to another faith, voluntary conversion is not a crime under the criminal or civil codes. Any attempt to induce a Muslim to convert is, however, illegal in Morocco. Pakistan maintains its 'blasphemy law' (1986), which effectively functions as a law of apostasy, since blasphemy is one dimension of apostasy if the blasphemer is Muslim.

It is clear that there are diverse approaches by Muslims to the question of religious freedom. While there is general consensus that coercion should not be used to convert someone to any religion, including Islam, the right of religious freedom is not extended to a Muslim who wants to change his or her religion to another. Significantly, pre-modern Islamic law states that coercion must be used to bring such a person back to Islam. If the person refuses, he or she should receive the ultimate penalty. However, as shall be seen in the following chapters, this position is now being challenged by some Muslims on a number of grounds.

Chapter 2

The Historical Context of the Debate on Apostasy and the Roots of Intolerance

On the eve of Islam in the sixth century CE, in the west of the Arabian peninsula, several religious traditions and religious communities were in existence, including idolatry, Christianity and Judaism. Christianity was widespread throughout Arabia. Nestorian and Jacobean communities were prominent in the north and north-east of the Peninsula. In the south, one of the most important Christian communities was in Najran.[1] Jewish communities also existed in relatively large numbers, in particular in Tayma', Fadak, Khayber, Wadi al-Qura and Yathrib (Medina).[2]

Within Mecca itself, the birthplace of Islam, there existed several religious traditions. The Meccans had interacted with other Arabs coming to Mecca for trade or religious reasons. Mecca had two key advantages over other towns in the region: it was on the trade route from the south of Arabia to the north, and it possessed the Ka'bah,[3] the sanctuary that many Arabs visited to perform pilgrimage (a practice that existed well before Islam). According to early Muslim historical sources, it seems that people in Mecca were comfortable with religious diversity as long as this did not challenge the dominant political, religious and commercial interests of the Meccan community. It was in this environment that Islam emerged in 610 CE.

Towards the end of the Prophet's mission in Medina, Islam increasingly came to dominate the religious scene in Arabia, especially in the Hijaz. It gradually replaced existing religious traditions, in particular Arab idolatry. Many tribes adopted Islam en masse. Where tribes did not become fully Muslim, many of them preferred to have some form of peace agreement or a pact of non-aggression with the Prophet. The year 9/630 is in fact referred to as the 'Year of Delegations'. According to Ibn Hisham (d.213/828 or 218/833), 'When Mecca was conquered and the Thaqif tribe professed Islam, Arab delegations came to him [the Prophet] from all directions.'[4] Some individuals converted to Islam and then either migrated to Medina or remained among their tribespeople. Other tribes remained hostile to the Prophet and Islam, and used any available means to inflict maximum harm on the Muslim community. These circumstances are important in any understanding of developments in the area of freedom of religion in the practice of the Prophet, particularly in the last two years of his mission.

Tolerance of the Religious 'Other'

The Qur'an recognized the diversity of religion, religious traditions, institutions and values among the people to whom the Prophet was sent. It also recognized that certain religions functioning within Arabian society, namely Judaism and Christianity, were God-sent and therefore to be considered valid, at least in principle. Indeed, the Qur'an gave a relatively prominent place to Judaism and Christianity. They were recognized as bona fide religious traditions as well as communities. There are references to them, containing both praise and criticism, in the Qur'an.[5] In its criticism of their beliefs and practices, the Qur'an often addressed a group of Jews or a group of Christians.[6] The Qur'an did not ever criticize the religions of Judaism or Christianity as such, nor the status of their Scriptures represented by the Torah (*Tawrah*) and the Gospel (*Injil*). Both Judaism and Christianity were respected as religions of the 'Book' alongside Islam. The Qur'an, however, saw itself as the Scripture that had come to 'confirm' what was in the Torah and the Gospel,[7] and as the determiner (*muhayminan*)[8] of what was genuine of the earlier revelations.

As far as Judaism and Christianity were concerned, the Qur'an made a distinction between the religious community and the religion itself; between the historic community and the contemporaries of the Prophet Muhammad. These monotheistic religions were thought to have come from God through recognized prophets and revelation (*wahy*), and were considered preserved to some extent in scriptures and sacred texts. However, from a Qur'anic point of view, certain ideas and institutions in Judaism and Christianity were not consistent with what was regarded as the 'true' teachings of the prophets. The Jewish belief that Jews were a 'chosen' people and their view of their place with God in the life after death,[9] as well as the Christian concept of the Trinity, were criticized and rejected[10] as inconsistent with the original religious teaching of the Jewish prophets or of Jesus, respectively.

For the Qur'an, revealed religion is sacred and each scripture must be approached with respect. When the Qur'an criticized the Jewish and Christian communities of the time of the Prophet Muhammad it seemed to be asking them primarily to rectify specific problems and to recognize and accept the prophethood of Muhammad. However, the same degree of tolerance was not afforded to non-revealed religions that involved practices such as idolatry, then widespread in Arabia. There was no recognition of such beliefs, practices or values. Despite this non-recognition, the Qur'an urged Muslims to deal with all people, including idolaters, with respect, as long as they too showed respect. Indeed, the Muslims were commanded not to abuse or slander even the deities of idolaters.[11]

On many occasions, however, those who professed the new religion, Islam, faced harassment, opposition, hostility and war from idolaters, well up to the year 9/630. By then, Muslims were politically in control of the Hijaz and surrounding regions, and Islam held sway. From 9/630 onwards, idolaters, as well as Jews and Christians who remained hostile and refused to live at peace with Muslims, were warned that they should desist from their hostilities or face open war.[12] Muslims were not to tolerate their hostility any further. Non-Muslims who were not hostile to Muslims were to retain their religious traditions and no threat was directed against them.

The adversaries of Muslims, however, were to be brought under *political control*, perhaps to eliminate any potential threat to the nascent Muslim community. The Qur'an rejects the idea of forced conversion as against its principle of freedom of belief. The perceived threat from idolaters and those People of the Book (Jews and Christians) who were collaborating with them was a political-military threat. Consequently the aim was to bring to a halt the hostilities coming from that quarter. The harsh and uncompromising texts of the Qur'an from 9/630 in relation to followers of other religions (in particular, idolatry) flow directly from this context. Thus the religious tolerance demonstrated by the Qur'an from the beginning of Islam onwards remained unchanged. Under no circumstances did the Qur'an tolerate forced conversion to Islam or the initiation of hostilities towards any with whom Muslims had peaceful relations.

There is substantial evidence that, during the post-prophetic period, the degree of tolerance that had been demonstrated in the Qur'an and by the Prophet in his lifetime was continued by the Prophet's political successors, from the first Caliph Abu Bakr (d.13/634) to the fourth Caliph ʿAli b. Abi Talib (d.40/661).[13] In the Muslim conquests (of the Sassanid and Byzantine empires) that began in the caliphate of Abu Bakr, the people of the conquered regions were given the right to maintain their own religions, whether Christianity, Judaism, Zoroastrianism or any other. In return, they were obliged to recognize Muslim political rule. Payment by non-Muslims of a tax (*jizyah*) earned them protection against internal or external threat and security for their people and property. This practice was considered among the acceptable norms of relations between conquerors and conquered at that time. The non-Muslims were thus allowed to govern their lives by the rules and norms of their religions without Muslim interference. Thus Jewish law remained operative among Jewish communities, while Christians had their own laws to govern their affairs. When Islam came into contact with Zoroastrianism and Hinduism, their adherents were accorded the same rights as Jews and Christians.

Freedom was thus accorded to each religious community under Muslim political rule up until the abolition of the last remaining Islamic caliphate, the Ottoman Empire, in 1342/1924. That non-Muslims should have this freedom was regarded as a fundamental principle under Islamic law. However, during certain periods, some rulers, such as the Fatimid Caliph al-Hakim bi-Amr Allah (d.411/1021) in Egypt, occasionally contravened religious freedom and committed atrocities against non-Muslims. Such instances, however, were relatively few and are considered exceptions, not the norm. Even in these cases, Islamic law upheld religious freedom for non-Muslims. In general, this principle of religious tolerance remained an important aspect of the historical relationship between Muslims and the adherents of other religious traditions.

Intra-Islamic Intolerance in the Pre-Modern Period

The success of Muslims in establishing a caliphate and conquering large parts of the Near East and North Africa in the thirty years after the death of the Prophet led to the dispersal of Arab Muslims to Iraq, Syria (*Sham*) and Egypt (*Misr*). These conquests provided religious challenges. Muslims, many of them from Arab Bedouin backgrounds, came face to face with many different cultures, traditions and customs outside Arabia. Military success brought enormous wealth for these Arab Muslims, never seen before in Arabia. The development of *mawali* or client relations with non-Arabs, and the growing interaction with people of other religious traditions, in part led to the emergence of significant theological debates between Muslims and others, in particular Christians. On the political front, prominent Arab Muslim families, such as the Umayyads, made dynastic claims to leadership of the Muslim community (*ummah*). This soon led to conflict, and even to military confrontation between opposing Muslim groups. For example, the fourth Caliph ʿAli clashed with his opponent, Muʿawiyah b. Abi Sufyan (d.60/680), the then Umayyad Governor of Syria, a clash which represented the first major military confrontation among Muslims on the issue of political leadership of the expanding community.

The first thirty years after the death of the Prophet was therefore a period of major upheaval within the body politic of the Muslim community. It precipitated a high degree of social and political tension. Problems among Muslims were not simply about political leadership but also about what and who represented religious 'authority'. The horror with which some pious Muslims viewed *nouveaux arrivés* and their resultant 'un-Islamic' practices, such as the spread of alcohol consumption, appear to have led to major debates about what was or was not acceptable in Islam. In these circumstances, some Muslims wanted to remain faithful to the letter and spirit of the religion and to avoid the debilitating disputes in the community by remaining politically neutral. Some were eager to be part of the emerging material affluence of the society and to take sides in the political disputes. It was natural therefore that differences of opinion among Muslims should emerge as to who was right and who was wrong, and who was most faithful to the religious precepts and values. These developed into debates on the political leadership of the Muslim community as to who was a true Muslim and who was not. In fact, binary options of this nature were among the earliest questions posed in Muslim theological discourses in the first century of Islam. Many were later to become key questions of Islamic theology.

It was in this context of upheaval during the Umayyad period (41/661–132/750) that several groups with diverse theological or religio-political orientations emerged in Arabia, Syria and Iraq. Among these were the Kharijis (*khawarij*), the Shi'is (*shi'ah*), the Qadaris (*qadariyyah*), the Jabris (*jabriyyah*) and the Murji'is (*murji'ah*).

The Kharijis, the earliest of these groups, emerged even before the establishment of the Umayyad caliphate in 41/661. Their beginning goes back to the aftermath of the Battle of Siffin in 37/657, which had brought the fourth Caliph 'Ali into confrontation with the governor Mu'awiyah.[14] The Kharijis seceded from 'Ali's army, and formed a group that later became a radical puritanical group who believed that they were the only true Muslims. The Kharijis believed that other Muslims, by engaging in war against each other and by committing major sins, became apostates or unbelievers. Two principles were implicit in their political activity. The first was that there should be no decision but God's (*la hukma illa li-Allah*), meaning that questions such as the selection of the caliph should be decided by principles based on the Qur'an. The second was that the grave sinner (*sahib al-kabirah*) was to be excluded from the community.[15]

During this initial period, the Kharijis opposed both the party of 'Ali and the party of Mu'awiyah and also remained opposed to the mainstream Muslim community, maintaining their militant activities against the state and against other Muslims who did not share their views. Extremists among them had no mercy on fellow Muslims whom they regarded as unbelievers or apostates. During conflict, Kharijis went to extreme lengths in providing protection to non-Muslims, but that protection did not extend to those they considered unbelievers or apostates. To them, many of those who had participated in major disputes in early Islam, for example the Battle of Camel in 36/656, were to be considered unbelievers. Similarly, those who arbitrated in the aftermath of the Battle of Siffin between 'Ali and Mu'awiyah, or those who accepted the arbitration (*tahkim*) between these two, were also condemned.[16]

The Kharijis believed that any Muslim, regardless of ethnic background or social status (including non-Arabs and slaves), could become the political leader of the Muslims simply on the basis of their religious virtue and refusal to compromise in matters of religion.[17] They also believed that Muslims should rebel against any unjust ruler. For many Muslims, early Kharijis were the first intransigent group to emerge among Muslims. They initiated heated debates on notions of 'Muslim', 'believer' (*mu'min*), 'unbeliever' (*kafir*) and 'idolater' (*mushrik*). Like any social or religious movement, Kharijis had their share of divisions, extremists and moderates.[18] Today, only a moderate Khariji group, the Ibadis, exist in Oman and in parts of North Africa. Their views on many theological matters are very close to those of mainstream Muslims.

The Shi'is, another movement to emerge during this early period, believed that the family of the Prophet should be given priority over any other Muslim in political succession to the Prophet. They argued that 'Ali, the Prophet's cousin and son-in-law, should have been his immediate political successor. All political leadership of the community should thus have remained within the Prophet's family. From this basic position the Shi'is developed a distinctive theological system over the first three centuries of Islam. Due to their views on the leadership (*imamah*) they were considered political enemies by the Umayyads, who persecuted them up to the beginning of the Abbasid period (132/750–656/1258). The Shi'is believed that al-Hasan b. 'Ali (d.49/670), the grandson of the Prophet and their second imam, was poisoned by the Umayyads. Al-Husayn b. 'Ali, also a grandson of the Prophet, became the third imam but was killed with a number of his family members at Karbala in 61/680. This, too, occurred at the hands of the Umayyads during the caliphate of Yazid b. Mu'awiyah (d.64/683). This was followed by the death of yet another Shi'i imam, Zayd b. 'Ali b. al-Husayn (d.122/740), who was killed during the reign of the Umayyad Caliph Hisham b. 'Abd al-Malik (d.126/743).

This bloody history set the pattern of Shi'i perception of their place in Islam. They consider the first three caliphs to be usurpers of political power that should have legitimately fallen to 'Ali. Unlike the Sunnis, they do not see the Companions of the Prophet *collectively* as good Muslims, but strongly criticize many of them. The Sunni reaction to such beliefs about political leadership and perceptions of the Companions was to associate many of the Shi'is with heresy and even apostasy. For their part, the Shi'is direct the same charges against Sunnis. It is a conflict that continues to this day, though with less intensity.

Beyond the Kharijis and Shi'is, several new trends of thought emerged during the first/seventh and second/eighth centuries. Some of these reflected the refinement of positions adopted by earlier groups on theological or religio-political matters. The Murji'is emerged in opposition to the Khariji view that anyone who commits a major sin is a *kafir*.[19] This was not really a movement or distinct group, but rather an intellectual trend followed by a large number of Muslims. The Murji'is held that a person's belief should be judged not on their actions but on their words. If a person says they are a Muslim, then they are. If they commit major sins, it is up to God to decide their fate, not human beings. For the Murji'is someone ceases to be a believer 'only if he falls into the sin of idolatry or polytheism (*shirk*), expressed in Arabic as "associating other beings (or deities) with God"'.[20]

Such a position enabled early Muslims to minimize division within the community. It also kept the Companions who were engaged in early military confrontations against one another within the fold of Islam. This idea of 'postponement' of judgement enabled Umayyad caliphs, governors and generals who perpetrated crimes against other Muslims to escape condemnation as unbelievers. The Murji'i position provided some protection for early

Muslims from the extremism advocated by the early Kharijis, as it enabled the Kharijis, Shiʿis and Umayyads all to be defined as believers (*muʾminun*). The idea was that it was God alone who would determine their fate on the Day of Judgement in the Hereafter.[21]

Closely related to the Murjiʾis in the Umayyad period were the Jabris. According to the Jabris, human beings do not have control over what they do: their actions are all predetermined by God. As a number of Umayyad rulers committed heinous crimes like the wanton killing of Muslim subjects, according to the Khariji view these rulers should have been ousted as unbelievers (*kafirun*) and unsuitable rulers of the Muslim community. However, in the Jabri view, they could not be labelled unbelievers as they had no real control over their actions and so their legitimacy remained relatively untarnished. Thus, in conjunction with the Jabri doctrine of predetermination, it was argued that the crimes the Umayyads had committed were in a sense 'sanctioned' by God, since they must have been 'predetermined' by Him. Moreover, the Umayyad ruler must also have been predetermined by God to rule and therefore any attempt to overthrow the ruler must be tantamount to going against God's will. Since Umayyad rule was predetermined by God, Muslims could not change the Umayyads' behaviour or hold them accountable for it; they had no option but to wait patiently for God to help them. Not surprisingly, the Umayyads appear to have used 'religion' and the religious ideas of the Jabris and Murjiʾis to justify their decisions and legitimate their rule.

It is in this context that the Qadaris, a trend that challenged the Jabris and Umayyads, emerged. According to the Qadaris, God does not 'create' or pre-ordain what people do. Human beings are free and can choose between right and wrong. This position implied that it was possible to challenge and even change the status quo. Such a radical view, if supported by the Khariji militancy, which labelled anyone who committed a major sin an unbeliever, posed a potentially powerful threat to the Umayyad political elite.

An important development in the theological sphere following the Qadari position was the rise of the Muʿtazilis, who accepted some of the Qadari views on human freedom. They also agreed with some of the Khariji views, while disagreeing with the Kharijis on the definition of 'true believer' and the status of those who committed major sins. The Muʿtazilis seem to have adopted views that were largely aimed at preserving the strict monotheism (*tawhid*) of the Qurʾan by emphasizing the uniqueness of God. In this, they rejected the idea that the Qurʾan, as speech of God, was an actual attribute of God. For them, the Qurʾan was 'created' by God. The Muʿtazili ideas were, in a sense, an extension of earlier theological developments, and quite moderate in comparison with some of the earlier views. However, some of their ideas, in particular that of the 'creation of the Qurʾan', led to the famous inquisition of the early Abbasid period, which has left its mark on the collective psyche of Muslims to the present day.

It was in this theological and religio-political context, as well as in the aftermath of the political and intellectual developments of the first/seventh and second/eighth centuries, that Sunnism (*ahl al-sunnah*) developed in the third/ninth and fourth/tenth centuries. Early debates gave way to a synthesis of sorts. Certain positions adopted by all the groups referred to above were refined and developed into what may be considered the 'mainstream' outlook of the majority of Muslims which came to be known as 'Sunnism'. In the third/ninth and fourth/tenth centuries, Sunnism came to accept a set of creeds and legal schools (*madhahib*). Coupled with this was the consolidation of a number of Islamic disciplines such as interpretation of the Qur'an (*tafsir*), *hadith*, Islamic law (*fiqh*) and early Islamic history (*tarikh*). Given that this Sunnism reflected the position of the majority of Muslims, it came to be conceived of as 'orthodoxy'. Other groups that did not adhere to the Sunni positions on theological, religio-political or legal matters continued to exist and develop in their own ways. Some of these groups came to be labelled 'heretical', 'unorthodox' or 'innovators' by their Sunni opponents, while others came to be considered 'acceptable' from a Sunni point of view.

In addition to the legal, theological and religio-political groupings, Islamic mysticism (*sufism*) also emerged in the second century of Islam and gradually developed into Sufi orders throughout the Muslim regions. Unlike the other groupings, Sufis tended to be more accommodating and inclusive:

> Because Sufis cared only for the heart's inner disposition, they were not conformists who required that true Muslims should everywhere submit to the same outward modes. They tolerated local differences, even between Christianity and Islam.[22]

By wholeheartedly accommodating diversity, Sufis were doing what others were not. Others were keen to differentiate themselves from the rest in order to demonstrate their superiority in the authenticity and truth of what they professed. The accommodation of the Sufis, coupled with their appropriation of elements from other religious traditions, as well as their influence and views on religion, ensured that they remained the target of non-Sufi scholars. At times this meant persecution and even the execution of some leading Sufis by the political authorities.

In this theological fluidity, elements of intolerance among Muslims developed and grew. Sunnis charged Shi'is with extremism and at times with heresy. Shi'is accused Sunnis of the same. Sunnis accused Kharijis of heresy and even unbelief, and seem to have supported their views by inventing a number of *hadith*. Jabris accused Qadaris of heresy, and vice versa. Sunni traditionalists labelled their long-standing Mu'tazili opponents heretics, and the Mu'tazilis responded in kind. Sufis were considered heretics by their opponents. These charges and counter-charges of heresy, apostasy and even unbelief (*kufr*) continued into the modern period, with varying degrees of intensity.

Exacerbating Intra-Islamic Intolerance: State Involvement in Theological Matters

State involvement in theological matters began in the Umayyad period. Some rulers took a particularly harsh stand against thinkers with a Qadari orientation. Ma'bad al-Juhani, for instance, was executed for his views on free will by order of the Umayyad Caliph 'Abd al-Malik b. Marwan (d.86/705). Ghaylan b. Muslim al-Dimashqi was put to death for the same reason by Caliph Hisham b. 'Abd al-Malik.[23] Involvement by the state in various theological causes succeeded in wreaking havoc in the Muslim community from the earliest times. Some rulers played a major role in reducing the scope available for discussion and debate on theological matters where certain views appeared to be incompatible with state ideology. However, the state was generally indifferent to the development of Islamic disciplines, such as law, *hadith*, *tafsir* and philosophy, as it considered these areas to be politically neutral, on the whole; but it gave theological issues close scrutiny.

The best-known example of state involvement in theological matters occurred during the Abbasid period. This took the form of an attempt by the Abbasids to impose their particular preferences in theological matters on the *ummah*, first during the reign of Caliph Ma'mun (d.218/833), who initiated an inquisition to force the Muslims to accept certain theological positions. This continued up to the reign of Caliph Mutawakkil (d.247/861), who renounced the inquisition which had been instituted to ensure public official adherence to the Mu'tazili doctrine of a created Qur'an.[24] During the inquisition, substantial pressure was put on the *ulama* (scholars) to adopt the official view. Some accepted it, while others vehemently rejected it, and for that they suffered greatly.

As this state interference occurred at the height of Abbasid power, the impact of this policy on vast regions of the Islamic world was felt significantly. Large numbers of *ulama* were forced to conform. Many who refused to submit had to flee their towns or remain in hiding for a long time, while others attempted to confront what they considered to be a heresy. As a result of this opposition, several *ulama* were imprisoned, tortured and persecuted. This produced one of the most difficult periods in terms of freedom of belief within Islam, and left a lingering air of resentment for a long time to come. The dominant personality to emerge from this period of persecution was Ahmad b. Hanbal (d.241/855), a traditionalist scholar who eschewed the rationalist approach of the Mu'tazilis to theological questions and argued for a somewhat literal reading of the foundation texts wherever possible. Consequently, he suffered greatly during the period of caliphs Ma'mun, Mu'tasim (d.228/842) and Wathiq (d.235/849).

The Mu'tazilis suffered a setback, however, during the caliphate of Mutawakkil, who adopted the traditionalist position and turned against the

Mu'tazilis. When Ahmad b. Hanbal was released from prison after a long period of torture and persecution, he became the rallying point that opponents of the Mu'tazilis had been waiting for. It was now the traditionalists, under the symbolic guidance of Ahmad b. Hanbal and his followers, who set out to impose their own brand of orthodoxy.

Ahmad b. Hanbal and his fellow traditionalists adopted a somewhat literalistic approach to the foundation texts, particularly those that were related to theological issues. They dismissed as innovation (*bid'ah*) the linguistic analysis adopted by the Mu'tazilis in reading the foundation texts to justify their theological views. They also treated literally the metaphorical expressions used in the Qur'an in relation to God and God's attributes. Similarly they frowned upon philosophy and philosophical speculation. This reaction against Mu'tazili rationalism heralded a resurgence of a strong literalist traditionalism, which later came to dominate much of the Islamic world, with Islamic theology adopting many of the views of the traditionalists. To a large extent this traditionalist approach was anti-rationalist and anti-philosophical speculation. Once Ahmad b. Hanbal and his fellow traditionalists gained ascendancy, Mu'tazili views were denounced and the Mu'tazilis, in turn, were subjected to persecution in regions where traditionalists were influential. To hold Mu'tazili views was sufficient to condemn even a prominent scholar (*'alim*) to obscurity, imprisonment or exile. Scholars had to publicly declare their 'abhorrence' or disavowal of Mu'tazili views and beliefs. For example, Ibn 'Aqil (d.513/1119), even though he was a Hanbali theologian, was accused of holding some Mu'tazili views. In 465/1072 he had to make a public retraction in which he repented of following such doctrines.[25] The precedent of persecution for theological beliefs had been well-established.

Meanwhile, the Ash'ari school had emerged in the fourth/tenth century. This sought a middle ground between the Mu'tazilis and the traditionalists. Seeking to combine a degree of rational enquiry with conservative theology, Ash'arism came to be accepted as 'orthodox', and became largely the norm in Sunni Islam. The 'official' *ulama* retained a watchful eye on behalf of the state to monitor what people believed, and thus became the guardians of 'orthodoxy'. Nonconforming *ulama* were at times persecuted for their refusal to co-operate with the state or simply because they were opposed to the political aspirations of the ruling family of the time. In this, even some of the prominent religious leaders (*imams*) were not spared.

There was, however, no *universally* recognized single authority in Islam to determine what 'orthodoxy' was and who represented it. Consequently, each group claimed to be the representative of true Islam, and those who did not share their views were readily labelled heretics, apostates or unbelievers. The 'truest' representative of Islamic teaching appears to have been settled by those who had the most power at the time. It was thus the political authority in collaboration with the official *ulama* that represented the local orthodoxy. Once the Muslim *ummah* was divided, never to be re-united, after the second/eighth century, multiple 'orthodoxies' co-existed in the Muslim world. Where religious leaders had political power in a particular locality, they could not only label nonconformists as heretics, apostates and unbelievers, but also eliminate them with the support of the political authorities. In this the collaboration of both the political and religious establishment was essential.

Many well-known and highly respected Islamic scholars were accused of apostasy, unbelief or heresy because of the school they belonged to, or because of their intellectual orientation. Many of these scholars are respected and revered by Muslims today. However, in their own time, some of the official *ulama* who were in charge of the protection of 'local orthodoxy' accused some of these scholars of 'denying' Islam and at times considered them to be outside the bounds of faith.

Scholars accused in this way include the following:

- Abu Hanifa (d.150/767), the *imam* of the Hanafi school of law, was imprisoned and tortured, and died in custody. After his burial, his remains were reportedly exhumed and burnt.[26]
- Muhammad b. Isma'il al-Bukhari (d.256/870), the famous Sunni traditionist who composed the most important Sunni *hadith* collection, *Sahih al-Bukhari*, was labelled an unbeliever by a number of *ulama*.[27]
- Ahmad b. Hanbal, *imam* of the Hanbali school of law and a great traditionist, was imprisoned and forced to walk in heavy chains in the heat of summer. He was also beaten and tortured for his refusal to say that the Qur'an was created.[28]
- Al-Husayn b. Mansur al-Hallaj (d.309/922) was accused of apostasy by the vizier of Caliph Muqtadir (d.320/932), Hamid b. al-'Abbas, in 309/932. He was convicted, then flogged, executed and burned.[29]
- Dhu al-Nun al-Misri (d.246/861), an Egyptian Sufi, was imprisoned and persecuted by the Mu'tazilis for his belief that the Qur'an was uncreated.[30]
- Abu al-Husayn al-Nuri (d.295/907), a Sufi, is regarded as the greatest representative of the idea of the pure love of God, which had been introduced by Rabi'ah al-'Adawiyyah, the mystic. He, with several well-known Sufis of Baghdad, were accused of heresy and charged. When they were about to be executed, Nuri offered his life to save his companions. The caliph, touched by such magnanimity, investigated the case, found the Sufis to be good Muslims, and set them free.[31]
- Abu al-'Abbas al-Sufi, a leading Sufi teacher (*shaykh*), died, reportedly, as a result of a beating on the order of the vizier Hamid b. al-'Abbas.[32]
- Abu Hamid Muhammad al-Ghazali (d.505/1111), the theologian, Sufi and philosopher, was accused by opposing *ulama* of being a

freethinker and apostate and of writing books that opposed the pious ancestors. His books were ordered to be burned, and Muslims were prohibited from reading them.[33]

- Ibn Hazm (d.456/1064), the great Zahiri scholar and philosopher, was persecuted at the hands of the *ulama* of his time.[34]
- Muhyi al-Din b. ʿArabi (d.638/1240), a Sufi, was labelled by the *ulama* of his time as an unbeliever, apostate and sinner (*fasiq*). He was called the 'Great Apostate'.[35]
- Shihab al-Din Abu al-Futuh Yahya al-Suharawardi's (d.587/1191) attempt to formulate a theosophy of illumination (*ishraq*) caused scandal. He was accused of unbelief and apostasy, which led to his execution by the Ayyubid ruler of Aleppo.[36]
- Abu al-Hasan al-Shadhli and ʿIzz b. ʿAbd al-Salam were both well-known scholars but they were labelled heretics or apostates.[37]
- Ibn Taymiyyah (d.728/1328) was persecuted and imprisoned for his theological views and died in prison.[38] Similarly his student, Ibn al-Qayyim, was accused of heresy.[39]
- Shah Waliullah translated the Qur'an into Persian. Since a Muslim had not translated the Qur'an, some *ulama* conspired to eliminate him.[40]

Easy targets for this intolerance were thinkers and philosophers who, at different times, were harassed or oppressed by authorities, both religious and political. Many of the philosophers respected and recognized today as major contributors to Islamic civilization had their books confiscated or burnt. They were often forced to flee their homes. From Farabi (d.339/950) and Ibn Sina (d.428/1037) to Ghazali and Ibn Hazm, the story is repeated. For instance, Sarakhsi (d.286/899), a student of the philosopher Kindi (d.252/866), was executed after being accused of heresy (*zandaqah*) during the reign of Caliph Muʿtadid (d.289/903).[41] Ibn al-Rawandi (d.245/860), considered a freethinker, was also accused of heresy and unbelief,[42] as was Abu Bakr al-Razi (d.313/925), another self-declared freethinker who was accused of heresy and *ilhad*.[43] Ibn Rushd (d.595/1198), a student of Ibn Tufayl, was accused by many of unbelief. His books were burnt, he was driven out of Cordoba, and an order was issued warning against the teaching of philosophy and theology (*kalam*).[44]

The Concept of the *Firqah Najiyah*: from Individual Apostasy to Group Apostasy

The debate on apostasy, although initially related to the apostasy of the individual, gradually led to the idea of the apostasy of a group. This was facilitated by the emergence and consolidation of the concept of 'the group that will be saved from Hell' (*al-firqah al-najiyah min al-nar*). This concept

provided the basis for classifying Muslims into two main camps: the party
that would be saved from Hell and the party that was damned. The first are
the true Muslims while the second are not. Creeds were effectively used to
classify Muslims into one or another group, and became one of the most
important ways of defining Islamic orthodoxy. On the basis of this, those
who adopted the creed of the local orthodoxy were considered true
believers, while others would be labelled heretics, apostates or unbelievers,
or at best Muslims of doubtful quality.

Whereas the Qur'an and the Prophet seem to have taken a fairly broad
view of what a believer or a Muslim was, the theological, legal, philosophical, mystical and religio-political differences among Muslims in the first
three centuries of Islam resulted in the community finding it necessary to
identify which group belonged to the 'true' Islam and which did not. from
a Sunni point of view crystallization of early *kalam* (theological) debates
into Sunnism provided the basis for the first major attempt to unify the
outlook and views of the 'true' representatives of Islam, the Sunnis.

This brand of Islam rejected Shi'is, Mu'tazilis, Jahmis, Jabris, Kharijis
and philosophers. Nonetheless, what emerged as Sunnism in fact incorporated ideas and concepts from all of these, and refined and synthesized
them, but it remained unclear as to who qualified as a Sunni. To bring
better clarity to the issue, creeds came to be developed that became the
basis for the belief of Sunnism. The notion of a state-imposed theological
creed was given a major boost during the reign of the Abbasid Caliph
Qadir (d.422/1031). He demanded repentance from the Mu'tazili jurists and
a statement that they no longer held Mu'tazili views or views opposed to
the prevalent 'orthodoxy'. During this period, Mu'tazilis, Shi'is, Jahmis and
anthropomorphists were at times executed, crucified, imprisoned or exiled.[45]

Attempts were made to tighten the definition of the truest representative
of Islam by Muslim heresiographers such as Shahrastani (d.548/1153), Ibn
Hazm and Baghdadi (d.429/1037). The heresiographical work was largely
conducted on the understanding that Muslims, like Jews and Christians
before them, had diverged from the path of the Prophet, and that a large
number of groups had emerged that no longer represented the Islam of the
Qur'an and the Prophet. From their point of view, given that there was only
one true path, and that all others were by definition not true, the heresiographers attempted to identify the many groups and their sub-divisions who
were not on the true path. According to a *hadith*, Muslims would be divided
into 73 groups. All of them but one would go to Hell. The group that
would be saved, according to the *hadith*, consisted of those who followed
the Prophet and his Companions. Thus, each group attempted to declare
itself as the *firqah najiyah* and thus the true Muslims.

Several other names were used for this *firqah najiyah*. Among them
were people of the *sunnah* and 'true community'[46] (*ahl al-sunnah wa al-
jama'ah*); people of the *sunnah* (*ahl al-sunnah*); people of the true community (*ahl al-jama'ah*); the pious ancestors (*al-salaf al-salih*); people who

follow the Qur'an, *sunnah* and traditions of the pious ancestors (*ahl al-ittibaʿ*); and the group supported by God (*al-taʾifah al-mansurah*).[47] The result was that each group claimed the legitimacy of being the true Muslims, although the most dominant group politically was usually the most successful. Such a group, therefore, had the necessary power to label others as heretics, apostates or unbelievers on the basis that it was the true follower of the Islam of the Qur'an and the Prophet.[48]

Sources of Intra-Islamic Intolerance in the Modern Period

Blind following of one's *imam* or school (theological or legal) remained a prominent feature of Islam from the fourth/tenth century right up to the modern period. Historically each locality decided which school of law it would adopt. Thus, for instance, the Ottoman Empire adopted the Hanafi school of law. In the twentieth century, Saudi Arabia adopted the Hanbali school, while Malaysia adopted the Shafiʿi school. Until recently, one had to follow one's school of law in matters related to rituals and other areas of Islamic law such as family law. In some communities, even mosques were at times classified as Hanafi, Maliki, Shafiʿi, Hanbali or Shiʿi (Jaʿfari). Efforts were made during the twentieth century to bring these schools of law together. Concerned scholars therefore sought to emphasize the commonalities and similarities among them and that they all represented 'orthodox' Islam. Today, schools of law do not appear to be a major point of conflict and intolerance in most parts of the Muslim world; however, other forms of intolerance have replaced them.

The modern period has witnessed the emergence of tensions other than legal or theological. Intolerance appears to be primarily focused on five main trends: Islamists, Puritans, Traditionalists, Ijtihadis and Secularists. Accusations of heresy and apostasy against one's opponents are common in the debates.

Islamists are concerned with developing an Islamic socio-political order in the Muslim community. They reject, at least in theory, the modern ideologies of nationalism, secularism and communism. They also reject 'Westernization'. Islamists argue for reform and change in Muslim communities, emphasizing 'Islamic' values and institutions over what they see as Western counterparts. They are interested in establishing an Islamic state. Some argue for a revolutionary approach to what they consider 'non-Islamic' governance of Muslim states even if this means using violence. Others argue for a gradual approach through education, beginning at the grassroots level. The main proponents of Islamism are the Muslim Brotherhood in the Arab world, the Jamaʿat Islami of the Indian sub-continent, and the revolutionary Islam of Iran. Typical opponents include Muslim secularists, nationalists, liberals, modernists, Westernized Muslims and some puritans.

Puritans are concerned primarily with theological matters such as 'correct belief'. They seek to purify society of what they consider practices antithetical to Islam, such as reverence for saints and saint-worship, magic, certain Sufi practices and what they call innovation (*bid'ah*). They emphasize the literal affirmation of God's attributes without any interpretation. They rely heavily on the teachings of figures such as Muhammad b. 'Abd al-Wahhab (d.1207/1792) and Ibn Taymiyyah and the modern proponents of their teachings. Their hallmark is a degree of puritanism and literalism, coupled with accusations against other Muslims of being engaged in *bid'ah*. Their key opponents include the Shi'is, Mu'tazilis, Sufis, Muslim 'orientalists', 'innovators' and liberal Ijtihadis.

Traditionalists tend to follow strictly the pre-modern schools of Islamic law and associated theological teachings. They uphold solutions arrived at by pre-modern jurists and theologians of the relevant school, and view calls for reform of Islamic law and criticism of traditionalism with a degree of horror. This trend is dominant in the traditionalist seminary system (*madrasah*) across the Islamic world, for instance in the Middle East, Africa, the Indian subcontinent and the Malay world. Typical opponents tend to be those who call for reform (*ijtihad*) in Islamic law, including modernists, neo-modernists, Western-educated Islamic scholars and 'liberal' Muslims.

Ijtihadis argue for major changes in the methodology of Islamic law and for the reform of Islamic law itself. For them, many areas of traditional Islamic law require substantial change and reform to meet the needs of Muslims today. They perceive some areas of traditional Islamic law as not relevant today, or in need of replacement with legislation more in keeping with the needs of contemporary Muslims. This trend includes Muslim modernists, liberals and even 'secular' Muslims and reform-minded traditionalists. Typical opponents include traditionalists, some puritans and Islamists.

Secular Muslims see Islam as largely confined to the domain of personal belief and a relationship between God and the individual. Many value personal piety. They do not see any need for an Islamic state, nor the implementation of what is referred to as Islamic law. Typical opponents include anyone calling for establishing an Islamic state or an Islamic socio-political order, or those seeking the implementation of pre-modern Islamic law in society.

Chapter 3

Apostasy and Related Concepts

This chapter deals with the definition of apostasy (*riddah*) and related terms such as blasphemy (*sabb Allah* and *sabb al-rasul*), heresy (*zandaqah*), hypocrisy (*nifaq*) and unbelief (*kufr*). It will highlight the differences between these concepts and explore their relationship to the concept of apostasy. An examination of four 'apostasy lists' will demonstrate the fluid nature of apostasy as understood in the modern period.

Apostasy and its punishment, death, existed well before Islam in other Semitic religions such as Judaism. Early Jewish law prescribes death as a punishment for apostasy. In Christianity, in the medieval period, the punishment for apostasy and heresy was often death. The biblical basis for this punishment appears to be the following:

> If your brother, the son of your mother, or your son, or your daughter, or the wife of your bosom, or your friend who is as your own soul, entices you secretly, saying, 'Let us go and serve other gods,' which neither you nor your fathers have known, some of the gods of the people that are round about you, whether near you, or far off from you, from the one end of the earth to the other, you shall not yield to him or listen to him, nor shall your eye pity him, nor shall you spare him, nor shall you conceal him; but you shall kill him; your hand shall be first against him to put him to death, and afterwards the hand of all the people.[1]

On blasphemy, a concept closely associated with apostasy, the Bible says:

> He who blasphemes the name of the LORD shall be put to death; all the congregation shall stone him; the sojourner as well as the native, when he blasphemes the Name shall be put to death.[2]

There are frequent biblical allusions to the evils and the dangers of apostasy. It is described as departure from the faith (1 Timothy 4:1–3) and as being carried away by the error of lawless men (Hebrews 3:12).[3]

Through its conquests and contacts with Judaism and Christianity, early Islam found itself amid adherents of religions that had adopted the concept of apostasy and believed in its punishment by death. This, combined with Qur'anic and *hadith* references to *riddah* (apostasy) as well as experiences of the community with the problem of apostasy and rebellion against the central authority of the caliph, paved the way for Muslim jurists in the early history of Islam to construct a law that prohibited apostasy and punished it by death.

Riddah (Apostasy)

There is no doubt that several derivatives of the term *riddah* are used in the Qur'an. The usages that appear closest to 'apostasy' are:

> Truly, those who turn their backs [on this message] (*irtaddu 'ala adbarihim*) after guidance has been vouchsafed to them, [do it because] Satan has embellished their fancies and filled them with false hopes . . .[4]

> O you who have attained to faith! If you ever abandon your faith (*man yartadda minkum 'an dinihi*), God will in time bring forth [in your stead] people whom He loves and who love Him – humble towards the believers, proud towards all who deny the truth . . .[5]

> . . . [Your enemies] will not cease to fight against you till they have turned you away from your faith, if they can. But if any of you should turn away from his faith (*wa man yartadid minkum 'an dinihi*) and die as a denier of the truth – these it is whose works will go for naught in this world and in the life to come; and these it is who are destined for the fire, therein to abide.[6]

Riddah literally means 'turning back'. *Murtadd*, the active participle from *irtadda* (to turn back, to renounce), means 'one who turns back'. In Islamic law, *riddah* is understood to be reverting from the religion of Islam to *kufr*, whether by intention, by an action that would remove one from Islam, or by a statement, be it in the form of mockery (*istihza'*), stubbornness (*'inad*) or conviction (*i'tiqad*).[7]

The majority of Muslim jurists argue that once a person becomes a Muslim, it is not permissible to change religion.[8] To flout this is to commit the 'crime' of apostasy, and a person so doing should be put to death. In Islamic law, apostasy is defined as:

> unbelief of a Muslim who had earlier accepted Islam by confessing the unity of God and prophethood of Muhammad of his [or her] own free-will, after having acquired knowledge of the fundamentals [of Islam] and made a commitment to abide by the rules of Islam.[9]

Thus an apostate is a Muslim who rejects Islam and/or converts to another religion.[10] Islamic law lists many ways in which this may occur. Among these are:[11] the denial of the existence of God, or the attributes of God; the denial of a particular messenger or that a messenger is truly a messenger of God; the denial of one of the fundamentals of religion, for instance, the denial that there are five obligatory prayers (*salat*) in a day or that a particular prayer, say 'late afternoon prayer' (*'asr*), requires four units of prayer (*rak'ah*); declaring prohibited (*haram*) what is manifestly permitted (*halal*) or vice versa; or worshipping an idol.[12]

Jurists of the four Sunni legal schools – Hanafi, Maliki, Shafi'i and Hanbali – classify apostasy in three categories: belief-related, action-related and utterance-related. Each is divided into many subdivisions.

The first, that is, belief-related, covers many cases, including doubts about the existence of Allah and/or about the message of the Prophet Muhammad or any other prophet; doubts about the Qur'an, the Day of Judgement or the existence of Paradise and Hell; doubt about the eternity of God; and doubt on any fundamental point of belief such as the attributes of God on which there is consensus (*ijma'*) among Muslims. Where such agreement does not exist, doubts are not generally considered apostasy.[13] Included in this first category are making permissible what is considered prohibited (in Islamic law) by consensus, or vice versa.

The second category concerns actions. These may include prostrating oneself before an idol, the sun or the moon, or any other created being as a form of worship, and deliberately throwing a copy of the Qur'an into a dirty place such as a rubbish bin.

The third category is that of utterances, whether the utterance was made in anger or not. Examples in this category are innumerable and they include cursing Allah, any prophet or angel; declaring a Muslim an unbeliever (*kafir*) without a valid reason; attributing to Allah human attributes such as age, time, body, place, organs, colours, shapes, or attributing a child to Allah.

Apart from the explicit term *riddah* to cover apostasy, there are a number of associated terms and concepts such as blasphemy, heresy, hypocrisy and unbelief that amplify the notion and clarify its scope. There is a substantial amount of overlap between them; at times apostasy appears to be almost synonymous with them. According to a contemporary scholar, Mohammad Hashim Kamali, early jurists did not generally attempt to differentiate between these concepts. Consequently, they attempted to use the broader category of *riddah* (apostasy) and to subsume the other concepts within it.[14] A Muslim accused of apostasy could thus be referred to as a 'blasphemer', 'heretic', 'hypocrite' or 'unbeliever'. In fact, when we look at modern-day 'apostasy lists' (see later in this chapter), we find that those who compile the lists often do not make any distinction between these terms and concepts and instead lump them all together, simply labelling them 'apostasy'. In the following, we will explore a number of such terms and concepts.

Sabb Allah and *Sabb al-Rasul* (Blasphemy)

In the discussion on apostasy there is a special category in which the jurists explore the use of foul language primarily with regard to the Prophet. This is known as *sabb al-rasul*. Later on this was considered to include the use of foul language with regard to Allah (*sabb Allah*) or any of the angels or other prophets. Anyone using such language in relation to any of these is considered among the greatest of sinners. If the person is a Muslim, they are considered apostate and condemned to death, according to most jurists.[15] For some jurists, if a Muslim blasphemes, they remain a Muslim and do not become an apostate, but may be executed in punishment for committing the offence of blasphemy. Other jurists consider that committing the offence of blasphemy automatically removes the person from the fold of Islam.[16] If this offence is committed by a non-Muslim the question of apostasy does not arise, but will still incur the punishment of death for blasphemy.

Evidence for punishment for blasphemy appears to be based on certain reported incidents in the lifetime of the Prophet, there being no clear Qur'anic instruction on the matter. When the Qur'an uses the term *sabb*, it only commands Muslims not to revile the deities of non-Muslims lest they revile Allah. There is no reference to a temporal punishment in that context:

> But do not revile those [beings] whom they invoke instead of God, lest they revile God out of spite, and in ignorance . . .[17]

During the time of the Prophet, some Muslims reportedly killed a number of non-Muslims who reviled the Prophet, God or Islam and thus apparently committed the offence of blasphemy. Some of those killed, such as the poet Ka'b b. al-Ashraf, composed poems denigrating the person of the Prophet and also incited others to revile him. In other cases abuse was perpetrated through fabricated stories about the Prophet, or through verbal attacks on Islam and the Muslim community in general.

Several reports in the *hadith* literature indicate that when such people were killed, the Prophet declared that their blood was spilt in vain.[18] No compensation or punishment was imposed in relation to those who killed such people, as in the case of war, where a Muslim is permitted to kill another person from enemy ranks without being subject to retaliation, payment of blood money or to any form of punishment. It seems that by using foul language against the Prophet, God or Islam, the transgressors were putting themselves on a war footing against Muslims. Despite this, neither the Qur'an nor the Prophet stated clearly the existence of an offence called 'blasphemy' or a specific temporal punishment for it.

This 'offence' was constructed and legitimated by Muslim jurists in the post-prophetic period. They based this on their understanding of reports in the *hadith* literature at a time when Islam was politically, militarily and economically strong. It held sway over vast territories from North Africa, the Iberian Peninsula, to China. Non-Muslims living in these territories acknowledged the political supremacy of Islam and Muslim peoples. As 'protected minorities' (*ahl al-dhimmah*), it was expected that the non-Muslims under Islamic rule would not denigrate the religion of Islam, nor cast aspersions on its major figures or institutions. The jurists saw any such denigration as a hostile act, not to be tolerated. The law also had another function: to silence dissenting voices among Muslims, such as Kharijis or Shi'is, who were intent on reviling leading figures of the early Muslim community, including the first four caliphs. Thus, largely from relevant reports in the *hadith* literature, Muslim jurists have argued that reviling the Prophet, or God or Islam and using foul language in relation to any of them constitutes a serious offence: blasphemy. Later, this offence was extended to cover using foul language against the Companions of the Prophet.

In Islamic law, some distinction has been made between the person who uses foul language in relation to the Prophet and the one who uses such language in relation to God. This distinction is based on the concept of 'right of God' and 'right of Man'. Reviling God appears to have been understood in Islamic law as a violation of the 'right of God' (*haqq Allah*), while reviling the Prophet is a violation of the 'right of Man' (*haqq al-'abd*).[19] In the case of reviling the Prophet, Islamic law takes a more severe view than in the case of reviling God.[20] As the Prophet is not in a position to avenge this abuse, it is seen to be the responsibility of the Muslim community to seek vengeance on his behalf by imposing the death penalty on the offender.

One might think that reviling God should be considered the more serious offence, but Islamic law does not generally appear to share this view, at least as far as punishment is concerned. For offences relating to the 'right of God' one can seek forgiveness through repentance. Offences relating to the 'right of Man' can be forgiven only if the person affected forgives. In the case of the Prophet, the Muslim community as a whole is considered to be under obligation to avenge the offence on his behalf, not to forgive as the Prophet is the only one who can forgive. Since the Prophet is not alive today, forgiving the offender is simply not possible.[21]

Zandaqah (Heresy)

The term heretic (*zindiq*) is often used in Islamic criminal law to describe *inter alia* a person whose teaching becomes a danger to the state, a crime liable to capital punishment.[22] This term does not exist in the Qur'an, but appears to have come to Arabic from Persian in the very early period of Islam. According to the *Shorter Encyclopaedia of Islam*, it was used for the first time in connection with the execution of Ja'd b. Dirham in 125/742.[23] As the Encyclopaedia states, 'In practice, the polemics of the conservatives describe as a zindik [*sic*] or a "free thinker" anyone whose external profession of Islam seems to them not sufficiently sincere.' The jurists made heresy (*zandaqah*) an intellectual rebellion insulting to the Prophet's honour.[24] On this basis, a number of figures in early Islamic history were labelled as heretics, such as the poets Bashshar b. Burd and Salih b. 'Abd al-Quddus, both of whom were executed, and thinkers such as Ibn al-Rawandi, al-Tawhidi and al-Maʿarri, who also died as 'heretics'.[25]

As with other terms associated with apostasy, it is difficult to find a unanimous view among Muslim jurists on the definition of *zindiq*. One meaning associated with the term *zindiq* is the outward show of Islam while in fact remaining faithful to one's former religion.[26] There are also references in early Islamic literature to the fact that some of those who were accused of heresy were claiming, for example, that there were two forces in the universe, light and darkness, a reference to a different conception of God to the one Muslims knew. Heresy also included questioning the fundamentals of Islam, such as the prophethood of Muhammad or the authenticity of parts of the Qur'an. Some jurists include in the definition those who advocate engagement in various acts prohibited in Islam such as adultery and fornication (*zina*) or consumption of wine.

In early Islamic history, heretics (*zindiq*s) were often associated with some Persian converts to Islam from their previous religions such as Zoroastrianism. In the first and second centuries of Islam, a large number of non-Muslims converted to Islam in the central regions of the Islamic caliphate, particularly in Iraq.[27] It seems that some of those who converted did so not out of any conviction, but in order to achieve economic, political and social goals. Living within the Muslim community, sharing the same space as other Muslims, their conversion enabled them to influence the political elite to a large extent and thus to play a significant role in the administration of the early Islamic caliphate and its decision-making processes. This gave them an important advantage over non-Muslims, who were often denied such a role.

From a socio-political point of view, *zandaqah* was seen as an infiltration of non-Muslims into the body politic of Islam and the use of Islam for personal gain. It also implied working in collaboration with the 'enemies' of Muslims. At another level, the fact that *zindiq*s could not be easily identified as a religious 'other' meant that there was a danger of them spreading 'heretical' views within the Muslim community, and in the process encouraging other Muslims to adopt such ideas. Muslim rulers of both the Umayyad and Abbasid periods, in tandem with the official religious establishment, worked hard to suppress this tendency and used various means to eliminate such people and groups. At times, caliphs and governors dealing with this problem were apparently motivated by the possibility of eliminating their political opponents in the name of fighting heresy. Thus a particular ruler may have turned against a group of so-called heretics for political gain and persecuted them with the support of the religious establishment. At times, some *ulama* who were interested in eliminating others who belonged to rival schools of theology or law appear also to have used this tactic.[28] Accusation of heresy could easily be exploited by political or religious opponents, given that a general accusation could be difficult to disprove.

What is noticeable in the literature on *zandaqah* is that the jurists viewed heresy more harshly than they did apostasy. Many jurists gave the apostate the opportunity to repent over a specified period of time. According to jurists such as Abu Hanifa and Malik, no such repentance was available for the heretic. While the Hanafis and Malikis were the most strict on this point, other schools of law, for instance the Shafi'is, considered a heretic an apostate with rights to repentance and eventual restitution to the faith.

Nifaq (Hypocrisy)

Nifaq, understood as religious hypocrisy, dates from the time of the Prophet. In the Medinan period of the Qur'an, there were many references to hypocrites (*munafiqun*) and hypocrisy (*nifaq*). Referring to the hypocrites, the Qur'an says:

> And there are people who say, 'We do believe in God and the Last Day,' the while they do not [really] believe. They would deceive God and those who have attained to faith – the while they deceive none but themselves, and perceive it not. In their hearts is disease, and so God lets their disease increase; and grievous suffering awaits them because of their persistent lying.[29]

The Qur'an repeatedly warns Muslims of the danger that these hypocrites posed to their community. Although the Qur'an does not order Muslims to kill them, it keeps warning that hypocrites are among the most dangerous elements within the community. In one verse, the Qur'an commands the Prophet to engage in *jihad* against hypocrites and unbelievers,[30] while in others it warns them of punishment in Hell.[31] However, in this context, it never clearly spells out a punishment of death in the mundane realm.

In spite of this, the jurists justified the death penalty for hypocrites,[32] perhaps on the basis of their understanding that *zandaqah* and *nifaq* had strong resemblances. It was difficult to see a significant difference from a legal point of view between a hypocrite and a heretic: both professed Islam outwardly and hid their true beliefs inwardly. In contrast to the influence of the heretics (*zindiqs*), the hypocrites of Medina during the Prophet's time did not have the capacity to inflict significant harm on the Muslim community as they had relatively little political clout. In Medina, where the hypocrites remained something of a threat, Muslims (including the Prophet himself) were aware of their presence. The leaders would have been well known. Any threat they posed remained restricted to a limited sphere.

However, for the jurists, the hypocrites of the post-prophetic period were more than a 'minor' threat. Large numbers of Christians and Zoroastrians professed Islam by the second/eighth century of Islam, and they began to play a role in the political system of the caliphate[33] and at least some of them were considered heretics. Even powerful caliphs such as the Abbasid

Caliph Harun al-Rashid (d.193/809) tended to rely heavily on converts to Islam. As a result, the power some of these converts and their families wielded was enormous. From the jurists' point of view, the potential threat to the state as a result of widespread *nifaq* and *zandaqah* among the converts was great. It was in this context that many jurists saw a need to equate *nifaq* with *zandaqah* and impose the punishment of death without differentiating between them.

Kufr (Unbelief)

Another term associated with apostasy is 'unbelief' (*kufr*). At a simple level, *kufr* denotes unbelief where, for example, a person does not recognize the existence or unity of God, or the prophethood of Muhammad. This is a rejection of the concept of God and prophethood that Muslims believe in. If a person takes the position that there is no God, that He is not One, or that Muhammad was not a prophet, then that person is considered an unbeliever (*kafir*).

Although the Qur'an often uses the terms *kufr* (unbelief), *iman* (faith or belief) *kafir* (unbeliever) and *mu'min* (believer) it does not provide a clear definition of who is a *kafir* and who is a *mu'min*, though it does set out some basic characteristics associated with these terms. *Iman* (faith), for instance, includes belief in the existence and unity of God and acknowledgement of the prophethood of Muhammad. At this level one can make a distinction between a believer and an unbeliever. A person who subscribes to the key beliefs of Islam will be considered a believer. In contrast, someone who does not subscribe to them will be viewed as an unbeliever.

However, there are other issues related to the adoption of Islam. It is not simply a question of a person declaring belief in the unity of God and the prophethood of Muhammad. It is also of putting that belief into practice in their personal life. Historically, there were major differences among Muslims on the place of 'action' or 'deed' (*'amal*) within the definition of *iman*. Some Muslim scholars argued that what mattered was belief and words (declaration of that belief), and not actions. Some felt that to be a *mu'min* (believer) a person must not only believe, but must also translate that belief into words and deeds.[34] This three-dimensional view of a *mu'min* was certainly a refinement of the earlier theological discussions about the definition of a *mu'min* and represents a later development. From this perspective, when a *mu'min* did not put into practice what *iman* demanded, that person no longer remained a *mu'min* but had become something else. For many Kharijis, for example, when a person committed grave sins and did not put into practice the requirements of the *shahadah* (declaration of faith in Islam: there is no god but Allah and Muhammad is the Messenger of Allah), they no longer remained within the bounds of Islam and could be labelled *kafir* (unbeliever).[35] Other Muslims disagree with this interpretation and are keen to de-emphasize the *'amal* (deeds) of a Muslim.

Early Fluidity in the Understanding and Use of these Terms

The debates explored in this chapter demonstrate the substantial degree of fluidity that exists in the understanding of these terms and concepts. Given that the Qur'an and *sunnah* left some doubt as to the specific definition of such terms, it would be extremely difficult to reach specific or clear definitions without a substantial amount of guesswork and *ijtihad*. On the basis of such *ijtihad* and soul-searching, many Muslim scholars of the early period were naturally reluctant to declare other Muslims to be unbelievers and to exclude them from the community.

Differences of opinion among early Muslims on the understanding of these terms and concepts provided the basis for later jurists and theologians to explore them at a more sophisticated level. These Muslims sought to refine early ideas surrounding these terms and arrive at reasonably clear definitions. Contemporary definitions of these terms are therefore the result of a long process of development and refinement.

This early fluidity led, however, to some rather negative developments. One was that Muslim jurists, scholars and ordinary Muslims who felt that their own position on Islam was the only authentic and true one, began to characterize fellow Muslims as apostates, blasphemers, hypocrites or unbelievers. Where there were differences of opinion among Muslims on legal or theological matters, it was easy for one Muslim to denigrate another by declaring that person an unbeliever.[36] For instance, the Sunni view of the Qur'an as uncreated and the Mu'tazili view of the Qur'an as created is a theological matter that did not arise at the time of the Prophet. With the rise of Mu'tazilism and its interest in this matter, however, the Muslim community was polarized between those who believed that the Qur'an was the created word of God and those who believed that the Qur'an was the uncreated word of God. Both sides were quite comfortable labelling the other as deviant Muslims or, in some cases, unbelievers or heretics. Labelling of opponents as unbelievers, heretics or apostates was an easy way of disposing of them, either through political means or by inciting other Muslims to act against them.

Since unbelievers, heretics or apostates by definition did not belong to the Muslim community, a Muslim who acted against such a person would be supported by the community, even if he took the law into his hands and killed the alleged offender. Political authorities who feared a prominent person with politically unacceptable views of a theological or legal nature could eliminate that person simply by accusing them of *kufr*, *zandaqah* or *riddah*. If the political authority was supported by the religious establishment, it would be easy to eliminate such a person on religious grounds.

Indicators of Apostasy: Contemporary Apostasy Lists and their Problems

I have noted the diversity of views on apostasy and how a person comes to be regarded an apostate. These views appear to combine – and even collapse – the concepts of apostasy, hypocrisy, heresy and unbelief into apostasy. Though in the early Islamic period a clear-cut idea of what might remove a person from Islam did not exist, it seems that from the second and third centuries of the Islamic era, Islamic law made the process of differentiation and exclusion relatively easy from a legal point of view.

For the purpose of illustrating the fluid nature of the concept of apostasy in the modern period, I have chosen four 'apostasy lists'. One is from a pre-modern scholar, Ahmad b. Naqib al-Misri (d.769/1368). The other three are from the modern period: Abu Bakr al-Jaza'iri, ʿAli al-Tamimi and ʿAbd al-ʿAziz b. ʿAbd Allah b. Baz. Given that there are innumerable apostasy lists circulating among Muslims, it is not possible to cover all or even most of them. The four lists below, however, will illustrate the point.

List 1: Ahmad b. Naqib al-Misri

The commission of certain acts, as provided in this list, by a Muslim would mean that they had left Islam. The acts are grouped together as follows: those considered to be generally accepted fundamentals of Islam (points 1–9) and those that are not (points 10–20):

1   To prostrate oneself before an idol, or to an object such as the sun or the moon.
2   To speak words that imply unbelief such as 'I am Allah' or 'Allah is the third of three'.
3   To deny the existence of Allah, His eternality without beginning or end, or to deny any of the attributes that the consensus of Muslims ascribes to Him.
4   To revile Allah or His messengers.
5   To be sarcastic about Allah's name, His command, His interdiction, His promise, or His threat.
6   To deny any verse of the Qur'an or anything that by scholarly consensus belongs to it, or to add a verse that does not belong to it.
7   To hold that any of Allah's messengers or prophets are liars, or to deny their being sent.
8   To deny the obligatory character of something that by the consensus of Muslims is part of Islam, when it is well known as such, like prayer (*salat*) or even one *rakʿah* from one of the five obligatory prayers.
9   To deny the existence of angels or *jinn* or heaven.
10 To intend to commit unbelief (*kufr*).
11 To revile the religion of Islam.

12 To mockingly say 'I don't know what faith is'.

13 To reply to someone who says, 'there is no power or strength save through Allah' by saying for example 'your saying there is no power or strength will not save you from hunger'.

14 For a tyrant, after an oppressed person says 'this is through the decree of Allah', to reply, 'I act without the decree of Allah'.

15 To say that a Muslim is an unbeliever (*kafir*) in terms that cannot be interpreted as merely meaning he or she is an ingrate towards Allah for divinely-given blessings.

16 When someone asks to be taught the testification of faith, *shahadah*, and a Muslim refuses to comply.

17 To describe a Muslim or someone who wants to become a Muslim in terms of unbelief (*kufr*).

18 To believe that things in themselves or by their own nature have any causal influence independent of the will of Allah.

19 To be sarcastic about any ruling of the sacred law.

20 To deny that Allah intended the Prophet's message to be the religion followed by the entire world.[37]

Comment Whereas points 1–9 above are largely related to matters on which there is consensus among Muslims and related to the fundamentals of Islam, the remaining examples are somewhat problematic. This is not to deny that the actions specified in points 10–20 are and can be major sins. Some of these are susceptible to different interpretations and are thus fluid in their signification. While some examples, such as point 16, constitute 'sins' from a religious point of view, perhaps they cannot be said to actually constitute apostasy.

List 2: Abu Bakr al-Jaza'iri

A contemporary scholar, Abu Bakr al-Jaza'iri, summarizes various ways a Muslim may become an apostate. His list covers *inter alia* the following:

1 Slandering God or a prophet or an angel.

2 Refusal to recognize that Allah is the true God or the prophethood of a prophet, or to hold the belief that a prophet may come after Muhammad.

3 Rejection of an Islamic obligation (*faridah*) on which there is unanimous agreement, such as prayer, *zakat*, fasting, pilgrimage, kindness to parents, or *jihad*.

4 Belief that an unlawful act such as adultery, consumption of alcohol, theft, murder, or the practice of black magic is lawful.

5 Rejection of a chapter of the Qur'an or a verse, or even a letter, of it.

6 Denial of an attribute of God such as His life, hearing, seeing or mercy.

7 Throwing a copy of the Qur'an into a dirty place or stepping on it.

8 Belief that there is no resurrection or punishment or reward in life after death.

9   Belief that punishment and reward are merely spiritual.
10 Belief that saints (*awliya'*) are better than prophets or that saints do not
    have to perform various acts of worship.[38]

Comment   The list concentrates first on the fundamentals of religion on
which there is consensus, particularly points 1–5. It then focuses on what
are theologically difficult issues such as the rejection of a 'letter' of the
Qur'an, 'denial of an attribute of God', 'belief that punishment and reward
are merely spiritual', or beliefs associated with so-called 'saints' in mystical
circles. There are significant differences in interpretation among Muslims
on some of these matters and it would not be easy to label Muslims who
hold a variety of views related to these matters apostates.

List 3: ʿAli al-Tamimi

Another contemporary Muslim, ʿAli al-Tamimi, provides his own list of
what leads to or constitutes apostasy, and indicates supporting Qur'anic
evidence (given in square brackets):

1   To commit *shirk* (polytheism) [4:48; 5:72]. There are four types of *shirk*:
    shirk through one's prayers [29:65]; *shirk* through one's intent in acts of
    worship [11:15–16]; *shirk* through one's obedience [9:31]; *shirk* through
    one's love [2:165; 9:24].
2   Denial of the finality of prophethood with the Prophet Muhammad. Whoever
    claims prophethood or believes the claim of a false prophet has left the fold
    of Islam. For example, those who believe the claims of prophethood by
    Ghulam Ahmad have left the fold of Islam.
3   Denial of the binding nature of the *sunnah*. For example, those who claim
    that Islam is based only on the Qur'an have left the fold of Islam.
4   To judge by other than the *shariʿah* that Allah sent down to the Prophet
    Muhammad, for example, those who believe that the systems and laws
    devised by men are better than the *shariʿah*, or that it is permissible to judge
    by other than the *shariʿah* even if one does not believe that judgement to be
    better than that of the *shariʿah*, or that Islam should be restricted to a private
    relationship between an individual and His Lord without entering into the
    other aspects of life.
5   To ridicule or make fun of any aspect of Islam [9:65–66].
6   To hate any aspect of Islam [47:9].
7   To perform sorcery or to be pleased with the performance of sorcery, such
    as bringing a man and a woman to love or hate one another [2:102].
8   To believe that one may obtain salvation by following other than the religion
    of Islam or by refusing to call the infidels, such as Jews and Christians,
    infidels, or to doubt their unbelief, or to say their religion is still valid [3:19;
    2:135].
9   To turn away from the religion of Islam by neither learning it nor acting
    upon it [32:22; 14:27].[39]

Comment This list perhaps is the most problematic in that it does not limit itself to the denial of the fundamentals of religion but goes into non-fundamentals. The list is dangerously ambiguous. For instance, according to this list, those Muslims who have some doubts about the authenticity of a significant part of the documented *sunnah* (*hadith*) could be considered apostates. According to point 4, perhaps the large number of Muslims who are not supportive of the idea of 'implementing *shari'ah*', as it is used in modern Islamist discourse, could be considered apostates. Point 6 is vague and any action or utterance could be interpreted as indicating apostasy. Point 8 is also problematic. If a Muslim believes that the scriptures of Jews and Christians are not 'corrupted' as understood in Muslim discourse, he or she could also come under the category of apostasy. Point 9 would put the vast majority of Muslims who are illiterate, or are Muslims by name, or Muslims who have a minimalist approach to Islamic practices, in the category of apostates. According to this list, only a few million of the world's 1.3 billion Muslims should be called believers.

List 4: *'Abd al-'Aziz b. 'Abd Allah b. Baz*

The late Shaykh 'Abd al-'Aziz b. 'Abd Allah b. Baz, Saudi Arabia's Grand Mufti and Chairman of the Council of Senior Islamic Scholars until his death in 1999, provides a list of acts that would make a Muslim an apostate and which, according to him, would 'nullify' a person's Islam. The evidence he cites from the Qur'an is in square brackets.

1 Associating partners with Allah (*shirk*) [5:72]. Calling upon the dead, asking for their help, or offering them gifts or sacrifices are all forms of *shirk*.
2 Setting up intermediaries between oneself and Allah, making supplication to them, seeking their intercession with Allah, and placing one's trust in them is unbelief (*kufr*).
3 Anyone who does not consider the polytheists (*mushrikun*) to be unbelievers, or who has doubts concerning their unbelief, or considers their way to be correct, is himself an unbeliever (*kafir*).
4 Anyone who believes that any guidance or a decision other than that of the Prophet to be more perfect or better, is an unbeliever. This applies to those who prefer the rule of 'evil' to the Prophet's rule. Some examples of this are:

- To believe that systems and laws made by human beings are better than the *shari'ah* of Islam; for example, if one believes (i) that the Islamic system is not suitable for the twentieth century, (ii) that Islam is the cause of the backwardness of the Muslims, or (iii) that Islam is merely a relationship between Allah and the individual, and that it should not interfere in other aspects of life.
- To say that enforcing the punishments prescribed by Allah, such as

amputation of the hand of a thief or stoning of an adulterer, is not suitable for this day and age.

- To believe that it is permissible to implement laws which Allah did not reveal. Although a person may not believe such things to be superior to the *shari'ah*, he or she in effect affirms such a stand by declaring a thing that Allah has totally prohibited, such as adultery, drinking alcohol or usury, to be permissible. According to the consensus of the Muslims, one who declares such things to be permissible is an unbeliever (*kafir*).

5	Anyone who hates any part of what the Messenger of Allah has declared to be lawful has nullified his Islam, even though he may act in accordance with it [47:9].
6	Anyone who ridicules any aspect of the religion of the Messenger of Allah, or any of its rewards or punishments, becomes an unbeliever [9:65–66].
7	The practice of magic. Included in this is, for example, causing a rift between a husband and wife by turning his love for her into hatred, or tempting a person to do things he dislikes by using magic. A person who engages in such activity or condones it is outside the fold of Islam [2:102].
8	Supporting and aiding polytheists against the Muslims [5:51].
9	Anyone who believes that some people are permitted to deviate from the *shari'ah* of Prophet Muhammad is an unbeliever.
10	To turn completely away from the religion of Allah, neither learning its precepts nor acting upon it [32:22].[40]

Comment	In his list Shaykh Ibn Baz does not seem to differentiate between major and minor forms of *shirk* (polytheism). Indeed, some of the practices of Sufis will come under points 1 and 2 (which would take them out of the fold of Islam). Point 4 is particularly problematic. There are various ways in which 'implementing Islamic law' can be understood. There are varying interpretations among Muslims of how this should proceed and if one took point 4 literally, it would probably remove a large proportion of Muslims from the fold of Islam. Point 5 can also be interpreted so as to categorize as an apostate any person who makes critical comments on some of the 'lawful' things mentioned in the *hadith*, for example, slavery. Points 8, 9 and 10 are all vague and have the potential to render the majority of Muslims unbelievers.

Conclusion

The above discussion indicates the rather fluid nature of the definitions of the terms associated with apostasy as well as the high degree of overlap among them. A Muslim may be accused of apostasy, blasphemy, hypocrisy, heresy or unbelief on the basis of the same action or utterance. Different Muslims may use different terms to express what such an action or utterance entails. In cases where a Muslim is accused of one of these offences, the punishment, generally speaking, is death as specified in pre-modern Islamic legal texts. Obviously a non-Muslim cannot meaningfully be accused of apostasy, hypocrisy or heresy; they are by definition 'unbelievers'. But a non-Muslim can be accused of blasphemy, and if found guilty within the jurisdiction of an 'Islamic' state their punishment is also death, according to classical Muslim jurists.

The problem of fluidity of definition is apparent when we look at some 'apostasy lists'. The first impression one gets from these lists is that they were drawn up by Muslims who consider themselves to be Sunnis emphasizing *their* version of established dogma. Some of the items are related to early controversies between Sunnis and their opponents, which in turn shaped Sunni theology. For instance, items include: the Mu'tazili controversy over God's attributes, the Muslim philosophers' controversy over the nature of punishment in the Hereafter, the early Shi'i dispute over the alleged omission of certain verses of the Qur'an, and the Sufi conception of 'saint'. What some Sunni scholars regard as apostasy may not be regarded as apostasy by their opponents.

These lists cover the whole gamut of a Muslim's sphere of beliefs, practices and actions within the purview of apostasy, and hence limit the spiritual freedom and space available to Muslims. Such lists can be used as a basis for total control over their beliefs and actions without making any distinction between 'major sins', 'minor sins', idolatry or unbelief. In their eagerness to prevent Muslims from 'misbehaving', the *ulama* who have constructed these elaborate lists have significantly constrained the degree of flexibility demonstrated by the Qur'an and the *sunnah* on the questions of human weakness, and the extent of disobedience to God or to the Prophet tolerable within Islam. Such lists would allow the *ulama* many an opportunity to declare a Muslim an apostate. Since the punishment of apostasy in Islamic law is a severe one, accusation of this offence can, as we saw in Chapter 2, be a powerful weapon in the hands of unscrupulous *ulama* or political authorities enabling them to eliminate their theological or political opponents.

These modern apostasy lists do not reflect the earliest period of Islam in which the *ulama's* careful approach to the declaration of other Muslims as unbelievers or apostates adhered to the limits imposed within the Qur'an. Today, there is a plethora of apostasy lists which can only be described as fluid, ambiguous and highly problematic. The rather individualistic nature of these lists seems to stem from the fact that each scholar develops their own list, based on their training and interests. Working from such lists, it is relatively easy to declare one's opponents to be apostates.

To illustrate this, we will also look briefly at a modern attempt to define a Muslim. One of the most famous investigations into the issue of apostasy by a Muslim government is one undertaken in Punjab-Pakistan. The 387-page Munir Report was the result of an enquiry into disturbances instigated by prominent religious figures in their demand that the Ahmadis be declared a non-Muslim minority in Pakistan. In this *Report of the Court of Inquiry Constituted under Punjab Act II of 1954 to Enquire into the Punjab Disturbances of 1953*, Justice Muhammad Munir and Justice Kayani explored the basic definition of a 'Muslim' and found that the definitions provided by various *ulama* in Pakistan differed significantly, each scholar giving a definition which was in line with his own school of thought, and which led to the declaration of others as either non-Muslims, heretics or unbelievers. According to the Report, 'considerable confusion exists in the minds of our *ulama* on such a simple matter'[41] (that is, definition of a 'Muslim'). It went on to say:

> Keeping in view the several definitions given by the *ulama*, need we make any comment except that no two learned divines are agreed on this fundamental. If we attempt our own definition as each learned divine has done and that definition differs from that given by all others, we unanimously go out of the fold of Islam. And if we adopt the definition given by any one of the *ulama*, we remain Muslims according to the view of that *alim* but *kafirs* according to the definition of every one else.[42]

According to this Report, each group accused another of unbelief (*kufr*) and labelled their opponents non-Muslims or heretics. If one follows the position of the *ulama*, there would be no Muslims except for those in one's own group:

> The net result of all this is that neither Shi'as nor Sunnis nor Deobandis nor Ahl-i-Hadith nor Barelvis are Muslims and any change from one view to the other must be accompanied in an Islamic State with the penalty of death if the Government of the State is in the hands of the party which considers the other party to be *kafirs*. And it does not require much imagination to judge of the consequences of this doctrine when it is remembered that no two *ulama* have agreed before us as to the definition of a Muslim.[43]

If the *ulama* of Pakistan could not agree on the definition of a Muslim, the difficulties of arriving at a universally acceptable definition of 'apostasy' and 'apostate' are obvious. Though this example is from Pakistan, the situation is not much different elsewhere in the Muslim world.

Chapter 4

Punishment for Apostasy in Islamic Law and the Evidence

There is no doubt that apostasy is regarded as a grievous sin in Islam. In Islamic law, almost all early jurists took a hard line, believing that apostasy was to be punished by death. Indeed, a surface reading of some of the verses of the Qur'an and of *hadith* texts could lead to the conclusion that anyone who turns away from the faith should be punished in this world. Close reading, however, reveals that there is no temporal punishment specified in the Qur'an. The Prophet did not take it on himself to punish people for this offence. His mission was to persuade, not coerce, people into professing Islam.

Overview of Apostasy in Pre-Modern Islamic Law

In pre-modern Islamic law, there is general agreement among the jurists that the punishment for apostasy is death (*qatl*), and that the implementation of this penalty is obligatory on Muslims.[1] This is largely based on the *hadith* 'Whoever changes his religion, kill him.'[2] Other textual evidence is also cited to support the view that it is obligatory on Muslims to impose the death penalty on apostates (see later in this chapter). The following will provide an overview of key aspects of the apostasy law as it exists in pre-modern Islamic law. Broadly speaking, there is substantial agreement among pre-modern jurists, even on some of the details.

Conditions for the Validity of Apostasy

The jurists state that certain conditions must be met in determining whether a Muslim has become an apostate. First, the person who commits apostasy should not have been compelled to do so, but should have committed it voluntarily.[3] Second, the person should be sane (*'aqil*) and not legally insane (*majnun*).[4] The apostasy of a legally insane person is not valid. In the case of insanity, questions of religious allegiance do not apply, nor does abandonment of religious duty.[5] There is some dispute among jurists as to whether an act committed by a drunken person can lead to apostasy. For Hanafis, the apostasy of a drunken person is not valid, neither is their

51

Islam. Malikis, Shafiʿis and some Hanbalis believe that the apostasy of a drunken person is valid under certain conditions.[6]

There is unanimous agreement among the jurists that the apostasy of a minor who does not comprehend the meaning of apostasy is not valid.[7] If a minor who can comprehend the meaning of apostasy and of Islam commits any of the designated offences leading to apostasy, there are two views. For Shafiʿis, the minor's apostasy is not valid. For the apostasy to remain valid, Shafiʿi (d.205/820) said that maturity or puberty (*bulugh*) would need to be evident. Even if the minor could distinguish between right and wrong, a judgement about their apostasy would be deemed invalid.[8] For Malikis, Hanbalis and some Hanafis the apostasy of a minor is valid. Their argument is that if the profession of Islam of such a minor is valid, so is their apostasy.[9] However, according to the Hanafi jurists Abu Hanifa (d.150/767) and Muhammad b. al-Hasan al-Shaybani (d.189/805), a minor should not be executed or beaten, but instead be instructed to accept Islam.[10]

Apostasy of a Woman

All jurists believe that both men and women can become apostates. As to punishment, the Hanafis argue that an apostate woman should not be put to death but instead forced to accept Islam. If she refuses, she should be beaten and imprisoned until she returns to Islam or dies.[11] To support their view that an apostate woman should not be executed, the Hanafis claim that there is a general prohibition by the Prophet that instructs Muslims not to kill women.[12] For the Malikis, Shafiʿis and Hanbalis, the apostate woman must repent within three days; otherwise she faces the death penalty. However, Malikis believe that the death penalty may be delayed due to specific circumstances such as breast-feeding.[13]

Ascertaining Apostasy

Whether or not a Muslim has become an apostate can be ascertained in two ways. First, confession is the most important form of evidence in Islamic law. If a person confesses that they have committed apostasy, that confession is sufficient to convict them. Second, the testimony of two upright witnesses is also sufficient. With regard to testimony relevant to determine apostasy, the Hanafis maintain that the testimony of two upright witnesses is acceptable, but the witnesses are to be interrogated and investigated by the judge to ensure they have correctly interpreted statements by the accused.[14] Others say that the testimony of the witnesses should be more fully investigated. The Malikis maintain that only a fully investigated testimony is acceptable due to the seriousness of the offence.[15] The Shafiʿis believe that the testimony regarding apostasy should be accepted prima facie. The judge need then only require the accused to utter the 'declaration of faith' (confession that there is no god but Allah and that Muhammad is the messenger of Allah) in order to confirm further whether or not there is a case of apostasy.[16] If two upright Muslims give evidence to the effect that a person has committed the offence of apostasy but the person denies this, the majority of jurists believe that the denial is not sufficient. The accused must pronounce the declaration of faith.

Impact of Apostasy on Property Ownership

Malikis, some Shafi'is and Hanbalis believe that the ownership of property by the apostate should be suspended until their situation becomes clear. The apostate will be prevented from disposing of their property until such time. If the apostate dies or is executed, ownership of the property ceases with death. The property becomes like 'spoils of war' (*fay'*) and is transferred to the public purse (*bayt al-mal*). If the apostate reverts to Islam, the right to ownership of property remains. Some Hanafis, such as Abu Yusuf and Shaybani, believe that the apostate's right to ownership of property remains even after apostasy. Some jurists believe that the apostate's property becomes 'spoils of war' from the time the offence is committed. Even if the person reverts to Islam, it cannot be regained.[17]

If the apostate dies as an apostate, according to the majority of jurists – that is, Malikis, Shafi'is and Hanbalis – their property is regarded as 'spoils of war'. For the Hanafi jurists Abu Yusuf and Shaybani, if the apostate refuses to revert to Islam and is executed, their property should be distributed among the heirs (*warathah*) according to the prescribed shares specified in Islamic law.[18] For Abu Hanifa, any income earned by the apostate whilst in the state of apostasy is automatically transferred to the public purse, but what the apostate earned as a Muslim can be inherited by the person's heirs.[19]

Impact of Apostasy on Marriage

If one of the spouses becomes an apostate, the couple should be separated, according to Malikis and Hanafis. If both spouses commit apostasy, according to Shafi'is and Hanbalis they should be separated, while for the Hanafis they remain married.[20] As for any children born before the parents' apostasy, they are considered Muslim and cannot be allowed to follow their parents in their apostasy.[21]

Impact of Apostasy on Various Forms of Worship (ʿibadat)

The majority of jurists believe that the prayers, fasting, and the obligations of the *zakat* that were not performed during the period of apostasy must be performed after reverting to Islam. Malikis believe there is no need to do this. As for pilgrimage, some jurists believe that if the apostate had undertaken the pilgrimage before apostasy, it should be repeated.[22]

Repentance

There are differences among the jurists on whether apostates should be asked to repent. Some jurists, particularly the Hanafis, argue that the apostate's return to Islam should be proposed, and repentance sought. Once this is done, the apostate may revert to Islam. This, according to the Hanafis, is a recommended option but not an obligatory one, because the apostate is already familiar with Islam as the true religion.[23] According to Hanafis, it is up to the apostate to consider their position, and revert to Islam. If they refuse to do this, death should follow. For Malikis it is essential to demand repentance; only if apostates remain obdurate should they be put to death. Views attributed to Shafiʿis and Hanbalis indicate that seeking repentance is obligatory.[24]

Since the majority of jurists regard the offering of an opportunity for repentance as essential before an apostate is put to death, it is reasonable to assume that a period of time should be allowed for the apostate to reconsider and to revert to Islam.[25] In Islamic law, a period of three days is the majority view. For the Hanafis, the death penalty should follow immediately unless the apostate asks for time to reconsider. Only then is the apostate granted three days, after which time either the apostate must revert to Islam or face the death penalty. The Shafiʿis believe that an apostate should automatically be granted three days to reconsider, even if this is not requested. Thereafter, the apostate either repents or is put to death. For the Malikis, an apostate should be granted three days from the day the judge pronounces the condemnation of apostasy. Then, either the apostate reverts to Islam or faces death. The Hanbalis have two stances on this issue: (a) an apostate must be given three days to reconsider; (b) an apostate must accept a return to Islam immediately on request, or face death.[26]

Apostates whose Repentance is not Accepted

The general view among the jurists is that the apostate's repentance is to be accepted. There are, however, differences of opinion among jurists on whether the repentance of some categories of apostates can be accepted or not:

1 A *zindiq* (heretic) who outwardly professes Islam but hides his unbelief (*kufr*). According to some jurists, this was the case with the hypocrites (*munafiqun*), who also professed Islam outwardly. For Malikis and some Hanafis, if the *zindiq* confesses to the heresy (*zandaqah*) and announces their repentance before their heresy becomes public knowledge, the repentance is accepted by the judge. If the heresy becomes known in any way before the repentance is announced, the person is executed and the repentance not accepted. According to Shafi'is, who are somewhat lenient on this matter, the heretic should be asked to repent and, if this is complied with, the repentance is accepted. The Hanbalis are stricter and their position is that the repentance of the heretic is not acceptable and the person should be executed.[27]

2 A Muslim who repeatedly apostatizes and repents. For Hanafis and Shafi'is, the repentance of a repeat offender will be accepted, but they specify discretionary punishments such as imprisonment. The Hanbalis do not accept the repentance of such a person; they condemn this type of apostate to death.[28]

3 A Muslim who uses foul language towards or reviles a prophet or an angel (that is, who commits the offence of blasphemy) is generally considered an unbeliever (*kafir*). For Hanafis, Hanbalis and Malikis, this person should be executed with no repentance sought. Even if the person repents, they should be executed. If the blasphemer repents, the execution is punishment for committing the offence in the first place, not for unbelief (*kufr*). The reason given is that blasphemy is a 'right of Man' (*haqq al-'abd*), and repentance by itself is not sufficient to absolve an offender of the consequences of reviling a prophet or an angel. Shafi'is believe that the repentance of such a person is acceptable.[29]

4 A Muslim who uses foul language towards or reviles God (that is, who commits the offence of blasphemy) is considered an unbeliever. According to Hanbalis, the person should be executed, with no repentance sought. Hanafis and Shafi'is believe that repentance should be accepted. The difference in treatment between blaspheming the prophets and blaspheming God is that the former is a 'right of Man', whereas the latter is a 'right of God' (*haqq Allah*). A right of God collapses upon repentance, whereas a right of Man does not by repentance alone.[30]

Authority to Impose Punishment

The jurists emphasize that the only authority that can impose the death penalty on an apostate is the ruler or his deputy; others may not take the law into their own hands. This position is weakened, however, by the general belief that the apostate's life is of no value, and is therefore forfeit. Thus, if the apostate is killed by a private individual there are no repercussions for the killer.[31] Nor does killing the apostate require redress or recompense.[32]

Is the Punishment Prescribed (hadd)*?*

There is a difference of opinion among jurists on whether the punishment for apostasy is prescribed (*hadd*) in the Qur'an or *sunnah*, or remains at the discretion of a judge (*ta'zir*). Shafi'is and Zahiris believe there are seven types of crime for which there is a *hadd* punishment, one of which is apostasy (*riddah*).[33] The Hanbalis do not consider the punishment for apostasy to be a *hadd* punishment.[34] Ibrahim al-Nakha'i (d.95/713) and Sufyan al-Thawri (d.161/777) were of the view that the apostate should be invited back to Islam and should never be put to death. Ibn Taymiyyah appears to hold the view that punishment for apostasy is a *ta'zir* (discretionary) punishment.[35] This difference of opinion indicates that there is no unanimous agreement among the jurists on the issue. If the punishment is a *hadd* punishment, it cannot be changed according to the generally accepted principles of Islamic law; the death penalty remains as the only penalty for apostasy. If it is at the discretion of the judge, it is a *ta'zir* punishment and can change from time to time.

The view that the punishment for apostasy is a *hadd* punishment has been challenged in the modern period. Awa, a contemporary jurist, questions whether it is a prescribed punishment like that for slander (*qadhf*), theft (*sariqah*) or fornication (*zina*).[36] According to him, unlike these prescribed punishments, which are clearly spelt out in the Qur'an, there is no clear text in the Qur'an which specifies a temporal punishment for the apostate:

> The Islamic penal system recognizes three kinds of punishment: *hadd* (fixed punishment), *qisas* (retaliation), and *ta'zir* (discretionary punishments). The second is certainly out of the question here, and since it cannot be proved that the punishment for apostasy pertains to the category of *hadd*, it can only be understood as a *ta'zir* punishment.[37]

Evidence for the Death Penalty for Apostasy

The overall picture that emerges from a variety of verses in different contexts in the Qur'an is that apostasy is a 'sin' for which there is no temporal punishment. It is only when apostasy is coupled with actual engagement in fighting against Muslims that it becomes a 'crime'. In the following, verses that are often quoted by the proponents of the death penalty for apostasy will be discussed first.

Qur'anic Verses Used by Proponents of the Death Penalty

Early jurists rarely attempted to demonstrate that the punishment for apostasy was based on the Qur'an. In almost all cases, they relied on the *hadith* to justify it. However, a number of Muslim thinkers of the modern period who support the death penalty for apostasy attempt to justify this by relying on Qur'anic texts. Muhammad Hamidullah,[38] for instance, refers to 'indirect verses of the Qur'an' that support the death penalty for apostasy, such as 5:54:

> O you who have attained to faith! If you ever abandon your faith [lit. whosoever from among you abandons his faith] God will in time bring forth [in your stead] people whom He loves and who love Him – humble towards the believers, proud towards all who deny the truth . . .

Yet despite clearly mentioning those who 'abandon' their faith (= apostasy), the verse does not specify any temporal punishment.

The Pakistani thinker Maududi relies *inter alia* on the following verse to support the death penalty:[39]

> Yet, if they repent, and take to prayer, and render the purifying dues, they become your brethren in faith: and clearly do We spell out these messages unto people of [innate] knowledge. But if they break their solemn pledges after having concluded a covenant, and revile your religion, then fight against these archetypes of faithlessness who, behold, have no [regard for their own] pledges, so that they might desist [from aggression].[40]

However, these verses were revealed in the context of encouraging Muslims to fight the unbelievers (*kuffar*) who reneged on their promises of non-aggression, who violated the terms of the treaties concluded with the Prophet, and were vilifying and slandering Islam. There is no indication that this verse has anything to do with apostasy or the death penalty.[41] The interpretation adopted by Maududi to support the death penalty is far-fetched and has no linguistic, contextual or historical basis. For instance, Muhammad al-Shawkani (d.1834), a well-known interpreter of the Qur'an from Yemen, having cited key reports and views relating to this verse, says: 'This verse [9:12] is general [in its application] to all leading figures of unbelief (*ru'asa' al-kuffar*).' He does not mention apostasy or its punishment at all.[42]

Another verse used by proponents of the death penalty is as follows:

> The recompense of those who make war on God and His apostle and spread corruption on earth shall but be that they shall be slain, or crucified, or that their hands and feet be cut off on opposite sides, or that they shall be banished from the land: such shall be their ignominy in this world.[43]

This verse refers specifically to those who are engaged in fighting against the Muslim community and 'spreading corruption on earth'. No reference is made here to apostasy or apostates who are not engaged in these acts of war and terror. Shawkani, having explored various opinions related to this verse, says that the verse applies to anyone who commits the crimes spelt out in it, be the person a Muslim or an unbeliever.[44] The focus is the crimes specified. He explains this further by saying that these crimes are related to aggression against people by injuring or killing them, or by misappropriating their property.[45] Hence, the crime referred to is a crime against life and property and has nothing to do with a person's belief.

Another Qur'anic verse cited at times in the modern period in support of the death penalty for apostasy is the following:

> As for anyone who denies God after having once attained to faith – and this, to be sure, does not apply to one who does it under duress, the while his heart remains true to his faith, but [only to] him who willingly opens up his heart to a denial of the truth – upon all such [falls] God's condemnation, and tremendous suffering awaits them . . .[46]

This verse specifically mentions the apostate ('anyone who denies God after having attained to faith') but again, like other similar verses, it does not mention any death penalty. The punishment it refers to is the 'tremendous suffering' that awaits them. Given that verse 16:109, which follows, says 'Truly it is they, they who in the life to come shall be the losers', this suffering is expected to be in the Hereafter, not in this world.

Shawkani refers to a verse about those whose belief is tested and found wanting:

> And there is, too, among people many a one who worships God on the borderline [of faith]: thus, if good befalls him, he is satisfied with Him; but if a trial assails him, he turns away utterly, losing [thereby both] this world and the life to come . . .[47]

This verse is used in support of the death penalty, but Shawkani makes it clear that, while this verse refers to an apostate, it makes no reference to temporal punishment. In his explanation of the phrase *inqalaba 'ala wajhihi* (he turns away utterly), Shawkani says: 'He reverts to apostasy and returns to what he was as an unbeliever'.[48] For him, the phrase 'losing this world' does not indicate a worldly punishment.[49]

Hadith *Used as Evidence for the Death Penalty*

'*Whoever changes his religion, kill him.*' The justification of capital punishment in the case of apostasy relies heavily on *hadith* such as 'The prophet reportedly said: Whoever changes his religion, kill him!'[50] This *hadith*, cited in the *Sahih* of Bukhari, is considered authentic (*sahih*), and for many is the primary evidence available on this issue for Muslim jurists. Bukhari mentions this *hadith* inter alia in the context of the fourth Caliph ʿAli's burning of some 'heretics' (*zanadiqah*). When news of this came to the Companion Ibn ʿAbbas, he is reported to have said that if he were ʿAli, he would not have burnt them because of the prohibition on punishing human beings by fire, 'the punishment of God'. Instead, Ibn ʿAbbas said that he himself would have executed them on the grounds of the Prophet's words, 'Whosoever changes his religion, kill him.'[51]

The *hadith* is, however, a rather general one. Taken literally, it could mean that, once a person accepts a religion, any religion, they cannot change it, whether it is Islam, Christianity, Judaism or any other. This, from the perspective of Islamic law, would be absurd, as changing one's religion to become a Muslim is considered among the most cherished actions. Thus, the meaning of the *hadith* should necessarily be restricted to changing one's religion from Islam to another.[52] Only a minority of Muslim jurists believe that the *hadith* refers to the change of any religion.[53] Given the general nature of this *hadith*, pre-modern jurists have allowed exceptions. In line with these exceptions, the following people cannot be executed: the hypocrite (*munafiq*) who outwardly professes Islam; one who commits apostasy while in a state of insanity or drunkenness; a minor or a woman (according to Hanafi jurists) who becomes an apostate; and anyone who professes Islam under duress, and then becomes an apostate. As an extension of these exemptions, a number of Muslim scholars of the modern period also argue that the apostate who simply changes their religion without engaging in 'war-like activities' against the Muslim community cannot be executed. According to them, the apostate to be executed is the one who commits 'treason', not the one who simply changes faith.

Also in making this *hadith* more specific, recourse is made to other *hadith* relevant to the issue. According to one such *hadith*, the person to be executed is one 'who reverts from Islam to unbelief'.[54] According to another, it is he 'who repudiates his religion and separates himself from the [Muslim] community' (*al-tarik al-islam al-mufariq li al-jamaʿah*).[55] In a related *hadith* this meaning is emphasized:

> The Prophet, peace be upon him, said: 'The blood of a Muslim who confesses that there is no god but Allah and that I am the messenger of Allah, cannot be shed except in three cases: a life for life; a married person who commits illegal sexual intercourse; and the one who turns renegade from Islam (apostate) and *leaves the community of Muslims* [author's emphasis].'[56]

A number of versions of this *hadith* exist. Shawkani gives several that explain what is meant by the phrase 'the one who turns renegade from Islam (apostate) and leaves the community of Muslims'. One version, known as ʿAʾishah's version, says, 'And a man who leaves Islam and engages in fighting against Allah and His Prophet shall be executed, crucified or exiled.'[57] This version makes a clear connection between apostasy and fighting against the Muslim community. In this context, it is also interesting to note that a number of scholars discuss the case of apostates along with that of those who take up arms against Muslims (*muharibun*), as the *hadith* scholar, Muslim b. Hajjaj, did in his collection of *hadith* (*Sahih Muslim*). The title of the chapter in the *Sahih* is 'Ruling relating to *muharibun* and apostates',[58] making a clear connection between apostasy and fighting against Muslims.

This evidence points to a strong connection between the punishment mentioned in the *hadith* and the reference to alienation from the Muslim community, and to rebelling and fighting against the community. This suggests that the punishment is meant for those who repudiate Islam, join the enemy and struggle to inflict harm upon the Muslim community and Islam. Thus the issue of apostasy could be said to be more of a political issue than a religious one.

The earliest Muslim community of Medina at the time of the Prophet was preoccupied with the threat to its survival from external and internal opponents. It was on this basis that some scholars believed that the person referred to in the *hadith* was to be considered a *muharib*; that is, someone who was in a state of war against Muslims. Under Islamic law, anyone – Muslim or non-Muslim – engaged in war against Muslims may be killed with impunity.[59] If this is the case, the person referred to in the *hadith* was not just committing the sin of apostasy but was joining the enemy ranks and using apostasy as a means to attack and inflict maximum harm on the Muslim community. In the political context of the Prophet's time, a person had to belong to one group or the other: the Muslims or their opponents. A person leaving one group was bound to join the other. The apostate, by leaving the Muslim community, automatically joined the non-Muslim side and thus posed a threat to the Muslims. Given the state of war that existed between Muslims and their non-Muslim opponents throughout much of the Prophet's time in Medina, the reported declaration that the apostate should be put to death seems reasonable *in that context*.

The nascent Muslim community required its members to express a strong sense of belonging to the community (*ummah*); to attest belief was not enough. After the migration of the Prophet to Medina, all Muslim converts in Mecca were expected to follow and to take part in struggles against their opponents. Failure to do so meant marginalization, even exclusion, from the community as expressed in the following verse in relation to the Muslims of Mecca who did not migrate to Medina. According to the Qurʾan:

> Those who believed, and emigrated and fought for the Faith with their property and their persons, in the cause of Allah, as well as those who gave them asylum

and aid, these are all friends and protectors of one another. As to those who believed but did not emigrate you owe no duty of protection to them until they emigrate.[60]

Disclaiming the duty of protection was another way of saying that those people were not part of the community. Arab custom of the time required and delivered such protection as a means of survival. The Prophet worked to strengthen this 'group-feeling' among the Muslims throughout his lifetime. The Qur'an, in turn, often warned Muslims of the dangers of division within the community, frequently stating that unity and mutual support were an important part of Islam.[61]

Moreover, the Qur'an considers that being a faithful member of the Muslim community is a spiritual virtue.[62] The Prophet reportedly said that those deliberately separating themselves from the community would die the death of a common pagan. Leaving the community and attempting to create division within its ranks was therefore regarded as sedition. As one *hadith* puts it: 'Let whoever intends to create division in a cohesive community be beheaded by a sword, regardless of who he may be.'[63]

This interpretation of the *hadith* 'Whoever changes his religion, kill him' as not declaring the death penalty for simple apostasy (that is, apostasy that is not accompanied by war-like activities against the Muslim community) is also supported by the Hanafi school's position on women apostates (see above, p. 52). According to the Hanafis, the justification for execution of the apostate is that the person is likely to join the enemy and fight against Muslims. According to this view, it is the socio-political consequences of apostasy that justify so severe a punishment. The Hanafis argue that, as women generally do not engage in such fighting, they should not be executed.[64] If we follow this Hanafi logic, the application of the *hadith* is to be restricted to a person who changes religion and then acts seditiously by siding with the enemy and threatening the Muslim community.[65]

The case of the 'Uraynah Other events reportedly attributed to the Prophet are used to support the death penalty for apostasy. The following *hadith* is one:

Anas b. Malik reported that some people belonging [to the tribe] of 'Uraynah came to the Prophet at Medina, but they found its climate uncongenial. So the Prophet said to them: If you so like, you may go to the camels belonging to the public purse and drink their milk and urine. They did so and were all right. They then fell upon the shepherds and killed them and turned apostates from Islam and drove off the camels of the Prophet. This news reached the Prophet and he sent [people] on their track, and they were [brought] and handed over to him. He [the Prophet] required their hands and their feet be cut off, and put out their eyes, and [they] were left on the stony ground to die.[66]

The use of this *hadith* in support of the punishment for apostasy is problematic. First, in the second version of the *hadith*, narrated by Muslim himself in his *Sahih*, there is no mention of apostasy. Instead it states only that the people of ʿUraynah killed the shepherds and drove away the camels.[67] Second, the punishment imposed on them is that of those 'who make war on God and His apostle', as in verse 5:33. In fact, Imam Muhy al-Din Yahya b. Sharaf al-Din al-Nawawi (d.676/1277) the jurist, in his explanation of the *hadith* in question, specifically refers to this verse and says that this ruling of the Prophet is in agreement with verse 5:33.[68] Obviously, Nawawi did not consider the punishment as simply a punishment for apostasy. The punishment is for their killing of the shepherds and their 'war against God and His apostle'.

Execution of Meccans at the time of the conquest of Mecca   Similarly, a reported order by the Prophet to execute certain people on the day of the conquest of Mecca (8/630) has been used to bolster the argument that the appropriate punishment for apostasy is death. The number of people on the list varies. They include: ʿAbd Allah b. Saʿd b. Abi al-Sarh; ʿAbd Allah b. Khatal; Hibar b. al-Aswad; Hind bint ʿUtbah; Miqyas b. Sababah; Huwayrith b. Naqid; Kaʿb b. Zuhayr; Wahshiy b. Harb; ʿAbd Allah b. al-Zibaʿra; ʿIkrimah b. Abi Jahl and Safwan b. Umayyah. The claim was that these people were to be rightly executed as apostates, and since the Prophet ordered it, this legitimates the death penalty for apostasy as a general rule.

There are serious flaws in this claim. Not all of those on the list were at the time Muslims who turned apostates. Some clearly were, while others never professed Islam, preferring to remain pagans. Interestingly, each of those listed had a background of persecution and oppression of Muslims and were considered a threat to the Muslim community. This apparently made them liable for capital punishment, without the added charge of apostasy. The Prophet, as the head of the community, was perhaps justified in declaring them *personae non gratae*, and to be executed following the custom of the time. ʿAbd Allah b. Saʿd b. Abi al-Sarh was one of those listed. He had been employed as a scribe to write down the revelation for the Prophet, but later reverted to his pagan religion and returned to Mecca to join the enemy forces.[69] He had boasted of corrupting the texts the Prophet dictated and because the Prophet had given him a position of trust, which he had breached, the Prophet imposed capital punishment. However, ʿAbd Allah was spared.

How this occurred is significant. After the Prophet entered Mecca in 8/630, a senior Companion, ʿUthman b. Affan (d.35/656), foster-brother of ʿAbd Allah, requested that the Prophet forgive ʿAbd Allah. The Prophet agreed, though somewhat reluctantly, as Ibn Ishaq indicates.[70] If this were a case of an obligatory punishment imposed by the Qurʾan, it is unlikely that the Prophet would have spared ʿAbd Allah. In another case involving punishment for theft, which is an obligatory punishment, the Companion Usama b. Zayd reportedly approached the Prophet requesting him to forgive the offender because she was part of the Meccan aristocracy. The Prophet angrily rejected this intercession, saying that, even if his own daughter, Fatimah, were convicted of theft, he would impose the punishment specified in the Qur'an, that is, the amputation of a hand.[71] It is clear that the Prophet was extremely concerned that obligatory punishments be implemented regardless of the social position of the culprit.

It is possible to continue with this list, and find justification for the execution of each person mentioned. Some of them had committed murder. For example, 'Abd Allah b. Khatal was a Muslim whom the Prophet sent, with another man from Medina, to collect the *zakat*. 'Abd Allah b. Khatal murdered the man and fled to Mecca. There, he began composing poems abusing the Prophet and slandering Islam.[72] The command to kill 'Abd Allah b. Khatal was thus in retaliation for murder.[73] Hibar, another of those to be put to death, attacked the camel carrying Zaynab, a daughter of the Prophet, and caused serious injuries to her as she travelled from Mecca to Medina. Huwayrith, another of those on the death list, was an accessory to this assault on Zaynab. Huwayrith also attacked a camel on which two other daughters of the Prophet, Fatimah and Umm Kulthum, were travelling.

The Prophet ordered the execution of Miqyas b. Sababah, a Muslim who reverted to idolatry and then murdered a Medinan Muslim.[74] Hind bint 'Utbah, not a Muslim at the time, was also under sentence of death for her role in the Battle of Uhud (3/625). She had mutilated the body of Hamzah b. 'Abd al-Muttalib, the Prophet's uncle. She reportedly chewed his liver in revenge for his killing of her relatives at the Battle of Badr in 2/624. Finally, Wahshiy b. Harb, not a Muslim at the time, was condemned to death for being an accessory to the killing of Hamzah. Yet in regard to the significance for apostasy of this famous event, it should be noted that not all the culprits were executed. Most on the list were forgiven by the Prophet, and later became Muslims.[75]

Execution of an apostate in Yemen One traditional account has the Companion Abu Musa al-Ash'ari sent by the Prophet to Yemen. The Prophet also sent another Companion, Mu'adh b. Jabal, to join him:

> When Mu'adh arrived [in Yemen] he declared: 'O people, I am the messenger of the Messenger of Allah (may peace be upon him) [sent] to you.' Abu Musa prepared a cushion for Mu'adh to sit on. A Jew who had become a Muslim and then reverted to unbelief was then brought to Mu'adh. Whereupon Mu'adh said, three times, 'I will not sit until this man is executed according to the judgement of Allah and His Prophet'. When the man was executed, he [Mu'adh] sat down.[76]

Mu'adh's action needs to be understood in the context of events in Yemen at the time. Towards the end of the career of the Prophet, a Yemeni named

Aswad al-ʿAnsi claimed prophethood and joined forces with other opponents of Islam. It seems that many who had previously been Muslims joined al-ʿAnsi. The Jewish presence in Yemen at that time was significant and several Muslim Yemenis appear to have been Jews by origin. The Jew to whom the *hadith* refers may well have been a Jewish convert to Islam who then joined the new prophet's movement. He was effectively becoming an enemy of the Prophet Muhammad, bent on destroying Islam and the Muslim community in Yemen. In this text, Muʿadh b. Jabal's decision to execute the Jew is said to have been based on the words of the 'Prophet and Allah'. Since there was no specific temporal punishment for apostasy as such in the Qur'an, it is more likely that Muʿadh was referring to the Qur'anic verse which states that combatants engaged in fighting Muslims could be executed.

Remission of 'blood money'   Other *hadith* are used by the proponents of the death penalty to support their views. One, included in Abu Da'ud's compendium of *hadith*, is relevant here. A blind Muslim killed his female slave for continuously slandering and reviling the Prophet despite the blind man's attempts to stop her. On hearing of what the man had done, the Prophet reportedly declared that there should be no retaliation or demand for blood money made on the man.[77] What is noticeable in this *hadith* is that there is no mention of whether the slave was Muslim or not. Unless she were a Muslim turned apostate, the question is irrelevant to the discussion on apostasy. More importantly, there are also doubts about the authenticity of the *hadith*.[78]

Other hadith   In another *hadith*, a woman called Umm Marwan reportedly became an apostate, and the Prophet ordered that she be put to death.[79] However, this *hadith* too remains of questionable authenticity. Even if this were authentic, the Hanafi jurist Sarakhsi argues that the woman was reportedly put to death because she was fighting against Muslims, not because she was an apostate who had reverted to her original faith. A similar event, not directly related to apostasy, is reported by Sarakhsi. According to him, a woman named Umm Furqah was executed on the orders of Abu Bakr, the first caliph, for inciting her sons to fight the Muslims.[80]

Reports Attributed to Companions as Evidence

Proponents of the death penalty also cite reports attributed to the Companions, on the grounds that if the Companions imposed a punishment for apostasy, this must have been based on the practice of the Prophet. In one tradition, the Companion Ibn Masʿud reportedly captured some people from Iraq who had rejected Islam and become apostates. He wrote to Uthman, the third caliph, seeking his opinion on the correct course of action. Uthman's instruction was that Ibn Mas'ud should remind them of the religion of truth, Islam, and of the confession they had made earlier that there is no god but Allah. If they acquiesced, he should let them free; if they did not, he should execute them. Ibn Mas'ud duly complied with this advice.[81]

'Wars of Apostasy' as Evidence

Among the most commonly used traditions in support of the death penalty for apostasy is one relating to the so-called 'wars of apostasy' (*hurub al-riddah*) in the time of Caliph Abu Bakr.[82] During this period, many Arabs who had accepted Islam or who had concluded peace treaties with the Prophet rebelled against the central authority of Medina. Some rejected Islam and reverted to their former religions, while others simply refused to pay *zakat* to the caliph, thus avoiding their tax obligations to the central authority based in Medina. For many of them, the Prophet's death meant the relationship they had had with the Prophet of Islam was ended.

Many Muslim historians and jurists have considered the events connected to the wars against these rebels as one phenomenon; that is, as a fight against apostates.[83] However, this appears to be unwarranted. There was no united rebellion against the central authority of Medina; different groups, clans or tribes had rather different aims and objectives.[84] Some of these tribes were not even Muslim, or at least a large part of the tribe was not. Tribal representatives visiting the Prophet in Medina in year 9/630 came when they realized that the Prophet's power had by then extended to large parts of Arabia, and that it was in their interests to side with him or make peace, at least nominally. While some accepted Islam others did not, or did so only nominally.

Several of the tribes whose members reportedly committed the crime of apostasy did not actually reject Islam.[85] They were Muslims but felt that the financial obligations they had accepted during the Prophet's time should not be borne under his successors.[86] These tribes believed that their relationship was with the Prophet and that when he died this could not be automatically transferred to the new central authority in Medina, as represented by Abu Bakr. They saw their position as reasonable, taking into consideration the tribal customs that existed at the time, and the way tribal relationships had been long established in pre-Islamic times. Because of the Prophet's stature and importance, the authority he enjoyed when he was alive could not, in the view of the tribes, be automatically transferred to his successor.

When the Prophet died, many of the tribal leaders felt that there was no need for them to maintain the relationship; some were even ready to fill any vacuum that followed by claiming prophethood for themselves. Signs of this were present in 9/630, an example being the leaders of tribes such as Banu Tamim and Banu Hanifah. It is in this context that the sudden emergence of false prophets, from Musaylamah, to Sajah, and to Tulayhah, can be understood. Since the Prophet's authority and power were based on his prophethood, this also represented to many the shortest way to elevate the status of one tribe above others, as well as to redirect to themselves the material benefits Muslims had achieved under the Prophet.

Abu Bakr's decision not to negotiate or to allow concessions to the rebels and later to fight, particularly against those who refused to pay *zakat* to the central authority in Medina, was met by strong objections from a number of senior Companions, most notably 'Umar b. al-Khattab (d.23/ 644)[87] who felt that the caliph did not have the authority to fight other Muslims. 'Umar argued that, because these people were indeed Muslims, as was indicated by the fact that they declared that there was no god but Allah and that Muhammad was the messenger of Allah, and performed the prayers, there were no legal grounds for Abu Bakr to take up arms against them.[88] For 'Umar, paying *zakat* to the central authority was not as important as it was for Abu Bakr. For the caliph, however, the matter was not so simple; in addition to being a religious obligation, the survival of the central authority of Medina depended in some respects on the payment of *zakat*. This was primarily a political and financial issue, rather than the religious issue which later jurists and historians made it out to be.

Had Abu Bakr not pursued his policy, it is conceivable that the nascent Muslim community would have disappeared and any expansion of Islam within or outside Arabia would have been blocked, and the mission of the Prophet might not have endured. It was Abu Bakr's political acumen as well as his strategic thinking that led him to fight for survival. The support he received from the generals of Mecca and Medina enabled him to raise several small armies, which he directed against rebelling tribes. Within two years he managed to bring most of the rebellious tribes under the control of Medina. The battles that Abu Bakr fought were not, strictly speaking, religious; they were largely political, waged to sustain the central authority of Medina and protect the community and institutions the Prophet had established. It would be difficult to argue, on the basis of such events alone, that there should be capital punishment for apostasy.

Context of Capital Punishment for Apostasy

In early Islam, several forms of punishment were practised for political or religious reasons, some of which were sanctioned by the religion while others were not. Capital punishment by the state for political offences began to occur soon after the time of the 'rightly guided caliphs' (*Rashi-dun*), that is, during the Umayyad period. Although the *Rashidun* caliphs were engaged in various battles, they themselves were not engaged in personal vendettas or political assassinations. They generally observed Qur'anic and prophetic guidelines with regard to capital punishment.

The caliphate of Mu'awiyah brought the beginning of politically motivated punishment. He faced substantial opposition in Iraq, to where a large number of Arab Muslims migrated from Arabia, settling in Kufa and Basra. Many of these settlers came from nomadic backgrounds and had strong tribal affiliations. The spirit of resisting what they considered to be the dubious central authority in Damascus led many in Iraq to challenge continually the caliph and his governors. In order to prevent insurrection in Iraq, the caliph gave the governor of Iraq, Ziyad b. Abihi (d.53/673), full authority to suppress dissent. This involved brutal force, executions, crucifixions and general control of all those suspected of political agitation. These same policies were followed later by al-Hajjaj b. Yusuf (d.96/714), governor of Iraq, during the reign of 'Abd al-Malik b. Marwan. For Hajjaj, the value of human life was even less than for Ziyad b. Abihi. The number of people killed or executed for political reasons by governors such as Ziyad b. Abihi and al-Hajjaj b. Yusuf ran into hundreds if not thousands. Even eminent and pious scholars were not spared.

A further example of the execution of Muslims for political ends was seen on a massive scale during the Abbasid revolution (126/743–132/750). It is reported that the number of people executed by Abu Muslim al-Khurasani, one of the leading figures of the revolution in the Eastern part of the caliphate, approached many thousands of men, women and children. Any boy taller than five 'spans' (*shibran*) was killed if Abu Muslim doubted his loyalty to the Abbasids. There were also mass killings of Umayyads in Syria by Abu al-'Abbas al-Saffah (d.136/754). These killings were certainly not religiously sanctioned. Such killing was aimed at using terror to force the population to submit to political authority. In this, the limitations placed by the Qur'an and the Prophet on taking a person's life were of no interest to these and many other political authorities. Simply opposing the caliph or the governor could lead to execution without recourse to any form of justice.

During that period, the first/seventh and second/eighth centuries, Muslim jurists were developing the scholarly discipline of Islamic law (*fiqh*). Given that in the post-*Rashidun* environment, capital punishment was imposed with such ease, particularly in relation to offences against the state, the climate must have influenced the scholarly field too, despite efforts by the jurists to limit the impact of this environment in the intellectual domain.

Those raised and schooled in such an environment would find it extremely difficult to divorce themselves from the cultural and sociopolitical realities of the day. Capital punishment was widely used and for a variety of reasons. Jurists of the first/seventh to the third/ninth centuries considered punishment and death for apostasy within the ethos of their time. How they read early Islamic history as well as Qur'anic and prophetic texts perceived to be in support of capital punishment can therefore be understood as natural, logical and relevant for their day. Had they lived in the late twentieth century, in which capital punishment became out of step with the ethos of the time, their responses to the punishment of apostasy may have been very different.

Conclusion: Sarakhsi's View of the Punishment

Sarakhsi (d.490/1096), the great Hanafi jurist, believed that the death penalty for apostasy weakened the 'enemy',[89] that is the unbelievers. In the early Islamic period, non-Muslims who did not have peace treaties with the Muslims and were in a state of war were considered 'enemies' of Islam and the Muslim community. The world was divided into the realm of Islam (*dar al-islam*) and the realm of unbelief (*dar al-kufr*). By becoming a non-Muslim the apostate thereby joined the enemy, thus contributing to the enemy's strength. Sarakhsi also argues that apostasy was of the utmost gravity; it would have been the modern equivalent of treason or sedition. He points out that the reason for the punishment (= death) was not to persuade someone to change their religion, whether from Islam or from any other. For him, 'the offender deserves execution because of his insistence on unbelief (*kufr*)'. He adds: 'Don't you see that if he becomes a Muslim [again] punishment no longer applies because of a lack of [this] insistence (*israr*).' According to Sarakhsi, if a punishment is to be imposed for a particular offence (as with a *hadd* punishment), it will not be annulled by repentance. He says that, although changing of religion or asserting unbelief are serious offences, they remain matters between the person and God.[90] For Sarakhsi, the punishment for such an offence is postponed until the Hereafter (*dar al-jaza'*). What is done in this world is what he calls 'legitimate policies which bring about benefits to the people' (*siyasatun mashru'ah li masalih ta'ud ila al-'ibad*).[91] Sarakhsi goes on to say in the same context:

> By insisting on unbelief (*kufr*), he [the apostate] becomes [like] one who is waging war against Muslims. Therefore, he should be executed [as a precaution against] this [potential] waging of war.[92]

We conclude that the evidence for the death penalty for apostasy lies largely in some isolated *hadith* (*ahad*) as well as with certain events that reportedly took place during the time of the Prophet and the Companions. Closer scrutiny of the textual evidence reveals no substantial evidence on this matter. Given the ambiguity of the evidence available for the punishment, Sarakhsi's reading appears to be appropriate as a basis for arriving at a view in keeping with the modern period.

Chapter 5

Evidence against Capital Punishment for Apostasy

There are many verses in the Qur'an that clearly state that no one should be forced to accept or follow a particular belief or religion. The duty of the Prophet and the other messengers before him was only to convey the message, not to compel anyone to accept it. The theme of non-imposition of a belief or religion was dominant throughout the Meccan and Medinan periods of the Qur'an. In particular, in Mecca, a message of tolerance was strongly projected. This does not mean that the Qur'anic message changed once the Prophet moved to Medina and founded a stronghold for Islam. Many verses from the Medinan period also indicate clearly that what was required of both the Prophet and the Muslims was to keep conveying the message of God to the people, not by force but by discussion and persuasion.

To make the Qur'anic position clear, and to help the reader locate the text in the timeframe of the Prophet's mission, the meaning of the actual verses, rather than later interpretations, is quoted below. Where it is known whether the Qur'anic text comes from the Meccan or Medinan period, this is indicated in brackets after the verse, in order to provide the reader with some sense of the timing of the text.

There is a strong thread of personal responsibility running throughout the Qur'an. It also says that each person is given the capacity to discern right from wrong.[1] It is a personal decision as to which, if any, belief system to follow:

> Whoever chooses to follow the right path, follows it but for his own good; and whoever goes astray, goes but astray to his own hurt; and no bearer of burdens shall be made to bear another's burden.[2] (Mecca)

> And say: 'The truth [has now come] from your Sustainer: let, then, him who wills, believe in it, and let him who wills, reject it.'[3] (Mecca)

> Means of insight have now come unto you from your Sustainer [through this divine writ]. Whoever, therefore, chooses to see, does so for his own good; and whoever chooses to remain blind, does so to his own hurt. And [say unto the blind of heart]: 'I am not your keeper.'[4] (Mecca)

According to the Qur'an, God's plan for humankind is not that all should follow the same path. People have the choice whether or not to follow

God's path. Since this is the basic principle, the Prophet's task was only to explain to people the difference between right and wrong, not to coerce them to become believers.[5] Had God willed He would have guided all to the right path:

> And [thus it is:] had your Sustainer so willed, all those who live on earth would surely have attained to faith, all of them: do you, then, think that you could compel people to believe?[6] (Mecca)

> Nay, but God alone has the power to decide what shall be. Have, then, they who have attained to faith not yet come to know that, had God so willed, He would indeed have guided all humankind aright?[7] (Medina)

> And [because He is your Creator,] it rests with God alone to show you the right path: yet there is [many a one] who swerves from it. However, had He so willed, He would have guided you all aright.[8] (Mecca)

> Say: '[Know,] then, that the final evidence [of all truth] rests with God alone; and had He so willed, He would have guided you all aright.[9] (Mecca)

> ... but [remember that] had God so willed, he would indeed have gathered them all unto [His] guidance. Do not, therefore, allow thyself to ignore [God's ways].[10] (Mecca)

The Prophet's duty was to deliver the message, not to determine who should or should not believe it:

> ... the Apostle is not bound to do more than clearly deliver the message [entrusted to him].[11] (Medina)

> No more is the Apostle bound to do than deliver the message [entrusted to him].[12] (Medina)

> Pay heed, then, unto God, and pay heed unto the Apostle; and if you turn away, [know that] Our Apostle's only duty is a clear delivery of this message.[13] (Medina)

> And if they surrender themselves unto Him, they are on the right path; but if they turn away – behold, your duty is no more than to deliver the message.[14] (Medina)

Nor is the Prophet responsible for what others do. Each person is responsible for their own decisions and the result of such decisions will also be borne by that person. In the area of belief, in particular, this personal responsibility is paramount. Since each person, on the Day of Judgement, will be asked about their actions (and not about what other people may or may not have done) it follows that the matter of belief and faith is also left to each individual to decide. The Qur'an kept reminding the Prophet and the Muslims of this, in both the Meccan and Medinan periods:

And [so, O Prophet,] if they give thee the lie, say: 'To me [shall be accounted] my doing, and to you, your doings: you are not accountable for what I am doing, and I am not accountable for whatever you do.'[15] (Mecca)

Say: 'O you who deny the truth! I do not worship that which you worship, and neither do you worship that which I worship. And I will not worship that which you have [ever] worshipped, and neither will you [ever] worship that which I worship. Unto you, your moral law, and unto me, mine!'[16] (Mecca)

Fully aware are We of what they [who deny resurrection] do say; and you can by no means force them [to believe in it].[17] (Mecca)

Say [O Prophet]: 'O humankind! The truth from your Sustainer has now come unto you. Whoever, therefore, chooses to follow the right path, follows it but for his own good; and whoever chooses to go astray, goes but astray to his own hurt. And I am not responsible for your conduct.'[18] (Mecca)

. . . and to convey this Qur'an [to the world]. Whoever, therefore, chooses to follow the right path, follows it but for his own good; and if any wills to go astray, say [unto him] 'I am only a warner!'[19] (Mecca)

. . . and yet, to all this your people have given the lie, although it is the truth. Say [then]: 'I am not responsible for your conduct.'[20] (Mecca)

Whoever pays heed unto the Apostle pays heed unto God thereby; and as for those who turn away – We have not sent thee to be their keeper.[21] (Medina)

And so, [O Prophet,] exhort them; your task is only to exhort: you cannot compel them [to believe].[22] (Mecca)

Even if the Prophet and all believers wished it, not all people would become believers:

Yet – however strongly you may desire it – most people will not believe [in this revelation].[23] (Mecca)

Truly, you cannot guide aright everyone whom you love: but it is God who guides him that wills [to be guided] . . .[24] (Mecca)

Those who refuse to become believers will receive their punishment on the Day of Judgement. There is no punishment specified in this world:

But as for him who, after guidance has been given to him, cuts himself off from the Apostle and follows a path other than that of the believers – him shall We leave unto that which he himself has chosen, and shall cause him to endure hell . . .[25] (Medina)

And We send [Our] message-bearers only as heralds of glad tidings and as
warners: hence, all who believe and live righteously – no fear need they have,
and neither shall they grieve; whereas those who give the lie to Our messages –
suffering will afflict them as a result of all their sinful doings.[26] (Mecca)

Now as for him who rebels against God and his Apostle – truly, the fire of the
hell awaits him.[27] (Mecca)

In confirming individual freedom of choice, the Qur'an assumes that a
person is capable of making that choice. This assumption is important, as it
gives meaning to the choice. Human beings are endowed with this capability, as well as with the ability to discern right from wrong. From the
Qur'anic point of view, this is unique to human beings within the creation
of God. God created angels to be obedient to Him. On the other hand, God
gave to many other species only certain natural instincts but no moral
discernment. Human beings from the very beginning were conceived as
creatures endowed with the capability of making moral choices and of
being answerable for these.

Having created human beings, God also gave power to what the Qur'an
refers to as 'Satan' (*Iblis*). According to the Qur'an, when Satan asked God
for permission to lead astray those human beings who would follow him,
God granted it. Satan then made the promise that he would capture as many
souls as possible in this way. If God had wanted all human beings to
remain obedient, like the angels, He could have made them so, and He
could have restricted Satan's actions as well. Instead, God gave a free hand
to Satan, and to human beings He gave the potential to follow His path or
the path of Satan.[28]

Recognition of the Diversity of Religions

The Qur'an not only gives people freedom of belief, but also recognizes
that different peoples follow different belief systems and religions, and that
these are dear to them.[29] The Qur'an refers to other religions, particularly
the 'revealed religions' like Judaism and Christianity, with respect. In many
instances, the Qur'an recommended sceptical Christians and Jews to go
back to their own scriptures to find the truth. It advised them to solve
certain problems they faced at the time by reference to what their scriptures
had to say on those issues, while recognizing their scriptures as sacred texts
from God.[30] Moreover, the Qur'an says that all those who believe in God
and do good deeds will be well rewarded by Him:[31]

... for, truly, those who have attained to faith [in this divine writ], as well as
those who follow the Jewish faith, and the Sabians, and the Christians – all who
believe in God and the Last Day and do righteous deeds – no fear need they
have and neither shall they grieve.[32] (Medina)

Recognition of diversity in religion is based on the concept of the single source of 'revealed' religions as well as the equality and fraternity of humankind:

> O people! Behold, We have created you all out of a male and a female, and have made you into nations and tribes, so that you might come to know one another. Truly, the noblest of you in the sight of God is the one who is most deeply conscious of Him.[33] (Medina)

Prohibition of Conversion by Force

The Qur'an, on the basis of the idea of freedom of belief and the broader concept of religious tolerance, teaches that there is no compulsion in religion, and that it is entirely up to the individual to choose which religion they should follow. The Qur'an commands Muslims not to force others to accept Islam:

> There shall be no coercion in matters of faith. Distinct has now become the right way from [the way of] error: hence, he who rejects the powers of evil and believes in God has indeed taken hold of a support most unfailing, which shall never give way: for God is all-hearing, all-knowing.[34] (Medina)

Given the importance of this verse for freedom of belief, it is essential to explore the views associated with the understanding of this verse in the *Tafsir*, in particular, in reports attributed to some of the early Muslim authorities. A number of early Muslim scholars believed that this verse was related only to the 'People of the Book', who were not to be forced to profess Islam if they paid *jizyah* tax, while others believed that this verse was abrogated by the verses commanding Muslims to engage in fighting (*qital*). According to the latter, all people of all religious traditions should be invited to profess Islam; if they refused to do so or to pay *jizyah*, they were to be fought against until they were killed.[35] This appears to be the general understanding of many jurists and interpreters of the Qur'an. One example of a verse that is believed to have abrogated Qur'an 2:256 is the following:

> O you who have attained to faith! Fight against those deniers of the truth who are near you, and let them find you adamant; and know that God is with those who are conscious of Him.[36] (Medina)

Jalal al-Din al-Suyuti (d.911/1505) is well known for compiling a variety of reports from the Prophet, Companions and Successors that are relevant to any given verse in his commentary on the Qur'an, *al-Durr*. He cites a report attributed to one Sulayman b. Musa, according to whom the verse 'There shall be no coercion in matters of faith' was abrogated by one that commands Muslims to go to war against unbelievers (*kuffar*) and hypocrites (*munafiqun*).[37] Another report says that the verse was abrogated by the command to fight the People of the Book in Qur'an 9:73.[38] Yet another, attributed to Qatadah, suggests that it was the pagan Arabs who did not have any revealed religion who were forced to accept Islam 'by the sword', while Jews, Christians and Zoroastrians were spared coercive conversion provided they paid the *jizyah* tax.[39] A similar report is attributed to al-Hasan, and confirms the freedom from coercion for the People of the Book (Jews and Christians).[40]

Suyuti also quotes several other sources[41] in relation to the occasion of the revelation of this verse. In one report, attributed to Ibn ʿAbbas, the verse is said to have been revealed in connection with an incident involving the Medinan Jewish tribe, Banu al-Nadir. When the Banu al-Nadir were forced out of Medina (4/626), they were accompanied by some children of the Muslims of Medina (*Ansar*), who had earlier converted to the Jewish faith. The Muslim parents intended to force these Jewish children to profess Islam, but this was prohibited in accordance with the above verse (2:256).[42] In another report, again attributed to Ibn ʿAbbas, the verse in question was revealed when a man who had two Christian sons but was himself a Muslim wanted to force the sons to become Muslims. The man reportedly said to the Prophet: 'Should not I force them [to accept Islam]? Both of them have refused to profess anything but Christianity.'

These reports seem to indicate that coercion could be used with pagan Arabs but not with the People of the Book. If this were true, then religious freedom is likely to have been a narrow concept and specifically applied. This interpretation is, however, problematic, as the Qur'an states in many other verses that coercion should not be used to bring others into the fold of Islam. A great number of verses of both the Meccan and the Medinan periods emphasize that no one should be forced to believe in God. In addition, this view seems to be confusing permission to fight unbelievers (for reasons spelt out in a number of verses in the Qur'an) with the use of force to compel people to believe. Fighting is permitted to defend one's religion, faith and one's territory against actual or potential aggression or to end persecution,[43] not to convert people. There is no verse in the Qur'an that says in clear terms that a person may be forced to believe in God or in the religion of Islam. In fact, there are many verses that directly or indirectly say that force should not be used for this purpose, and that belief is a voluntary choice. Discussing the meaning of this verse (2:256), another prominent exegete of the Qur'an, Razi (d.606/1209), notes:

This [verse] means that God did not rest the matter of faith on compulsion or coercion, but rather based it on free will and the ability to choose. . . . This is what is intended here when God made clear the proofs of the divine oneness [*tawhid*]. He said that there was no longer any excuse for a rejecter [*sic*] of faith to persist in his rejection. That he should be forced to accept faith is not lawful in this world, which is a world of trial. For in coercion and compulsion in the matter of faith is the annulment of the meaning of trial and test.[44]

In the modern period, Sayyid Qutb (d.1966), in his interpretation of the verse, emphasizes that non-coercion in religion is a fundamental principle in Islam:

> The issue of belief as brought about by this religion is a matter of conviction followed by explanation and comprehension. It is not a matter of coercion and force.[45]

For Sayyid Qutb, coercion is against the nature of Islam, which addresses the individual's own conviction. In the absence of such conviction, no force is effective. For Qutb, belief or religion is not simply a matter of outward appearances and physical activities, but signifies moral commitment, a clear sense of purpose, and a strong connection between the creation and the Creator. These give meaning to life. For Qutb there is more than one dimension to the individual. Religion, he says, addresses the mind, the conscience and the very nature of the person. A person accepts religion on the basis of knowledge, reason and conviction. These then lead a receptive individual to divine guidance.[46] Qutb continues:

> Freedom of belief is the first human right which gives the attribute of '*insan*' (humanity) to the human being. Whoever robs a human being of freedom of belief in fact robs him of his humanity.[47]

Qutb goes on to say that the Qur'an not only prohibits coercion but also absolutely negates the legitimacy of the very existence of it, which is a far more effective device.[48]

Emphasizing that coercion should not be used, Suyuti quotes a report according to which the second caliph, 'Umar, used to ask one of his slaves to become a Muslim citing the advantages he would have if he did. However, the slave was not interested and refused. On this, 'Umar withdrew, quoting the verse 'There is no coercion in religion'. There is also a similar report referring to 'Umar's inviting an old Christian woman to become a Muslim; she refused whereupon 'Umar recited the same verse.[49]

The majority of reports cited by Suyuti[50] appear to support the view that there should not be any coercion in the matter of belief or religion. If those reports are authentic, the verse would have been revealed in Medina, around the year 4/626, which (as mentioned earlier) is the year in which the Jewish tribe, Banu al-Nadir, was forced out of the town. At that time, the Prophet was in a relatively strong position to coerce Christians, Jews or others remaining in Medina to become Muslims if he had wanted to do so. This was after the famous battles of Badr and Uhud in the years 2/624 and

3/625 respectively. By this time the young Islamic state had demonstrated its ability to resist its opponents and to press ahead with its agenda, at least within Medina.

Suyuti's references to other verses that abrogate this verse (2:256) one do not appear to be very strong. First, as we saw earlier in this chapter, an overwhelming number of verses in the Qur'an strongly support the view that belief cannot be forced. Second, if early Muslims had followed the idea of abrogation, after the conquest of each town in the period of conquests the Muslim armies would have forced the inhabitants to convert, which was not the case. Even if an exception were made in the case of the People of the Book, others such as Zoroastrians, Hindus, Buddhists or idolaters would have been forced to convert, which again did not happen. The Qur'an does not allow the waging of war for the purpose of conversion, but allows it within the context of combating those unbelievers who were threatening the security of the nascent Islamic state of the Prophet. The Qur'an commands that Muslims should not fight those unbelievers with whom they are on peaceful terms or who do not oppress them and are not hostile.

It is true that there are a few verses in the Qur'an that command Muslims to 'kill polytheists' and imply that nothing but submission to the Prophet is acceptable. These verses on the whole were revealed towards the end of the Prophet's mission, and were related to the political situation of the Muslim community vis-à-vis some of the non-Muslims who were still actively engaged in efforts to harm it. Several reasons are given for the command to the Prophet to kill the polytheists 'wherever they are found'.[51] If these non-Muslims gained an advantage over Muslims they would (a) not respect the terms of any existing peace treaty; (b) violate their oaths despite a covenant; (c) attack the faith of Muslims; (d) plot to expel the Prophet from Medina; and (e) initiate aggression against Muslims. The combined effect of these fearsome prospects led the Qur'an to command Muslims to be well-prepared and ready for war in case it was necessary. Even then it commanded the Muslims to be fair and just:[52]

> And fight in God's cause against those who wage war against you, but do not commit aggression – for, truly, God does not love aggressors. And slay them wherever you may come upon them, and drive them away from wherever they drove you away – for oppression is even worse than killing. And fight not against them near the Inviolable House of Worship unless they fight against you there first; but if they fight against you, slay them: such shall be the recompense of those who deny the truth. But if they desist – behold, God is much-forgiving, a dispenser of grace. Hence, fight against them until there is no more oppression and all worship is devoted to God alone; but if they desist, then all hostility shall cease, save against those who [wilfully] do wrong.[53]

> Tell those who are bent on denying the truth that if they desist, all that is past shall be forgiven them; but if they revert [to their wrongdoing], let them

remember what happened to the like of them in times gone by. And fight against them until there is no more oppression and all worship is devoted to God alone . . . and if they turn away [from righteousness], know that God is your Lord Supreme . . .[54]

Given the critical stage of the mission after the Prophet's migration to Medina, and the need for political stability and a base for further expansion of the Community, it was important to face head-on any political or military opposition, be it from the idolaters (polytheists) or the People of the Book. This was particularly relevant towards the end of the Prophet's mission.

The same could be said about the People of the Book who continued their opposition to the Prophet in Medina. The Prophet had hoped that the Jews, who had knowledge of revelation and prophecy, would follow him, but this hope was dashed when the three main Jewish tribes in the town, each in its own way, began to act against the Prophet as well as the interests of the Muslim community. The clashes between the Jewish tribes and the Muslim community brought an end to their presence in Medina. Some of the Jews who were expelled from Medina reportedly regrouped and collaborated with the Meccan opponents of the Prophet to wage war against the Muslims, for instance in the battle of Khandaq (5/627). It is in such a context that the Qur'an says the following about the People of the Book:

> [And] fight against those who – despite having been given revelation [earlier] – do not [truly] believe either in God or the Last Day, and do not consider forbidden that which God and His Apostle have forbidden, and do not follow the religion of truth [which God has enjoined upon them], till they [agree to] pay the exemption tax with a willing hand, after having been humbled [in war].[55]

There is no evidence to suggest that the Prophet fought the People of the Book who remained in Medina or among neighbouring tribes and lived harmoniously with the Muslims.

Contrary to popular belief among many Muslims, the verses in the *Surah* of Repentance (*Surat al-Tawbah*) revealed in 9/630, which took a particularly hard line against a number of groups, were not aimed at non-Muslims who were at peace with the Prophet. They were clearly aimed at those Arab idolaters, hypocrites and People of the Book who were demonstrably in a constant struggle to eliminate Islam. Even in this context, the Qur'an exhorted that justice should be maintained in all aspects of Muslims' dealings with others. The Qur'an also insisted that Muslims maintain their peace agreements with various groups, as long as the groups kept their side of the bargain.[56] There is nothing in the Qur'an to suggest that the Muslim community was required to exploit its strength by crushing the non-Muslim population just because they were non-Muslim.

Verses that command Muslims to fight unbelievers refer to special cases, and should not be taken as a basis for saying that freedom of belief in Islam was given only in the early period when Islam was weak, or that this freedom was not intended to be for all times and circumstances. If these verses were a complete abrogation of earlier ones on religious freedom (which are themselves absolute), the result would be an abrogation of a large number of verses emphasizing not only freedom of belief but also the nature of the relationship between God and people, and the importance of sincerity in faith.

Careful reading of the relevant texts in the Qur'an and *sunnah* indicates that there is no reason to believe that freedom of belief as such was abrogated. There is no direction from the Prophet that the verses related to non-coercion in matters of belief were abrogated. Some *hadith* do exist (and even some Qur'anic texts, for instance in *Surah* 9) to indicate that towards the end of his mission, the Prophet was expected to use force against certain groups of both Arab idolaters and People of the Book. If this was to force them to accept Islam, the general principle that there should be no coercion in religion would have to be rethought. But there is no indication in the Qur'an to suggest that forced conversion was their objective. The verses appear rather to have been in response to political and security demands of the community.

Qur'anic References to Punishment for Apostasy in the Hereafter

Several verses in the Qur'an suggest that there is punishment for the serious sins of rejecting Islam and for committing apostasy. However, this punishment appears to be in the Hereafter, in the life after death. The Qur'an says:

> . . . [Your enemies] will not cease to fight against you till they have turned you away from your faith, if they can. But if any of you should turn away from his faith and die (*fayamut*) as a denier of the truth – these it is whose works will go for nought in this world and in the life to come; and these it is who are destined for the fire, therein to abide.[57]

In the interpretation of this verse, Shawkani (d.1250/1834), a well-known interpreter of the Qur'an, does not make any reference to the execution of the apostate. He appears to take the view that the apostate is expected to die a natural death (as indicated by the term *fa yamut* 'and die') while being in the state of unbelief.[58] The apostate is 'destined for the fire', in the Hereafter. It is significant that the term used in this verse for death is *yamut* (literally 'he dies'), not *yuqtalu* (literally 'he is slain'). In another verse, the Qur'an uses both terms to indicate that the two forms of death are distinct. With reference to the Prophet's death, the Qur'an says:

And Muhammad is only an apostle; all the [other] apostles have passed away before him: if, then, he dies (*mata*) or is slain (*qutila*), will you turn about on your heels?[59]

If the apostate were to be 'slain', the verse would have used that term. Elsewhere, the Qur'an says:

Truly, as for those who are bent on denying the truth after having attained to faith, and then grow [ever more stubborn] in their refusal to acknowledge the truth, their repentance [of other sins] shall not be accepted: for it is they who have truly gone astray.[60]

Truly, as for those who are bent on denying the truth and die as deniers of the truth – not all the gold on earth could ever be their ransom. It is they for whom grievous suffering is in store; and they shall have none to succour them. [61]

Several views exist in the *tafsir* literature about the identity of the people to whom these verses refer. They include Muslims who became apostates and then moved to Mecca and there 'grew ever more stubborn in their refusal to acknowledge the truth', or who joined the community of Muslims but remained as hypocrites, or Jews who believed in Moses but refused to believe in Jesus or Muhammad. These different views are based on a number of traditions related to the 'occasion of the revelation' of the verse. However, both verses appear to be referring to people who apostatized from Islam[62] on the basis that the first verse says 'denying the truth after having attained to faith' (*kafaru ba'da imanihim*).

While the phrase 'their repentance shall not be accepted' is used by some proponents of the death penalty today as Qur'anic evidence for the punishment, it is interpreted by many leading *tafsir* authorities[63] to mean that God will not accept their repentance *if they repent when death is imminent*. Before that, repentance of the apostate will be accepted.[64] It is clear that there is no mention of a temporal death penalty here; the verses imply that the apostate lives in a state of unbelief until death. Their 'grievous suffering is in store' and they will suffer this in the Hereafter. This interpretation is supported by the following two verses:

How would God bestow His guidance upon people who have resolved to deny the truth after having attained to faith, and having borne witness that this Apostle is true, and [after] all evidence of the truth has come unto them? For, God does not guide such evildoing folk. Their requital shall be rejection by God, and by the angels, and by all [righteous] people.[65]

Verse 3:86 uses the phrase 'who have resolved to deny the truth after having attained to faith' (*kafaru ba'da imanihim*), which is the same phrase used in verse 3:90 quoted above. Verse 3:87 then specifies that the punishment of these apostates will be 'rejection by God, and by the angels, and by all [righteous] people', but it does not mention 'execution' as a punishment. In another verse related to punishment in the Hereafter, the Qur'an says:

> On the Day [of Judgement] when some faces will shine with [happiness] and some faces will be dark [with grief]. And as for those with faces darkened, [they shall be told:] 'Did you deny the truth after having attained to faith? Taste, then, this suffering for having denied the truth!'[66]

Again, the verse is referring to those who 'deny the truth after having attained to faith', a clear reference to apostates but without any mention of a temporal punishment. More importantly, the Qur'an says:

> Behold, as for those who come to believe, and then deny the truth, and again come to believe, and again deny the truth, and thereafter grow stubborn in their denial of the truth – God will not forgive them, nor will He guide them in any way. Announce to such hypocrites that grievous suffering awaits them.[67]

This verse (4:137) is in the context of a series of issues related to hypocrites (*munafiqun*). The verses following (4:138–45) are all related to hypocrites and the way they relate to believers, unbelievers and Islam in general. This verse is perhaps the clearest Qur'anic text to indicate that although some early Muslims repeatedly apostatized, the Qur'an still did not impose a temporal punishment on them. Instead, it refers to the 'grievous suffering' that awaits them, which appears to be a clear reference to punishment in Hell.[68] If there were any instructions for temporal punishment for apostasy in the Qur'an, this is where we would most likely find them.

None of these verses dealt with here, although they are in the context of apostasy, refers to a temporal punishment for rejecting Islam. All speak of punishment *after death*. All without doubt consider apostasy a major sin for which the Qur'an promises severe punishment, but that is God's prerogative, not a state function.

There is a reference, however, in verse 9:74, to punishment *both* in this world and the next:

> [The hypocrites] swear by God that they have said nothing [wrong]; yet most certainly have they uttered a saying which amounts to a denial of the truth, and have [thus] denied the truth after [having professed] Islam: for they were aiming at something which was beyond their reach. And they could find no fault [with the Faith] save that God had enriched them and [caused] His Apostle [to enrich them] out of His bounty. Hence, if they repent, it will be for their own good; but if they turn away, *God will cause them to suffer grievous suffering in this world and in the life to come* [author's emphasis] . . .[69]

But the punishment 'in this world' is interpreted by Shawkani, for instance, as punishment 'by killing, enslaving, and plundering',[70] an obvious reference to war, not necessarily to execution.

What seems to be obvious is that in the Qur'an there is no clear and unambiguously stated temporal punishment (death) for rejecting Islam or apostatizing from it. If punishment for apostasy were to be at the behest of individuals or of the state, there would most likely be references to it, as there are references to offences such as adultery and theft and to their punishments.[71] More importantly, verse 4:137 (quoted above) clearly indicates that the Muslims in question committed a series of defections from Islam and yet were allowed to remain alive. They were free to continue their activities without the punishment of death. S.A. Rahman, having explored the meaning of this verse, says:

This is a striking pronouncement and almost conclusive against the thesis that an apostate must lose his head immediately after his defection from the faith. The verse visualizes repeated apostasies and reversions to the faith, without mention of any punishment for any of these defections on this earth. The act of apostasy must, therefore, be a sin and not a crime. If he [a person] had to be killed for his very first defection, he could not possibly have a history of conversions.[72]

On this point, one contemporary Muslim scholar, Awa, says:

We do not find in the texts of the noble Qur'an related to apostasy any temporal punishment [specified] for the apostate. However we find therein repeated threats and strong warnings of punishment in the Hereafter. There is no doubt that such threats do not come unless they are related to a major sin. It is sufficient that Allah (glory be to Him, the Most High) has promised the believers that He will forgive all of their sins, and has warned those who revert to unbelief after they become believers and then increase in their defiance in unbelief, that God will not forgive them and will not show them the true path. Apostasy in the view of the Qur'an is a major sin even though Qur'anic verses do not impose a temporal punishment.[73]

Lenient Approach by the Prophet

In his 13 years of preaching in Mecca, the Prophet attempted to convince the Meccans that his message was reasonable, beneficial and represented true guidance from Allah. His only method was to talk to people, put forward his claims, ask his opponents to think about what he was preaching, reflect on it and then, if convinced, to follow the religion. On several occasions he expressed the wish that the people of Mecca would follow God's religion. The Qur'an repeatedly says that the Prophet was sent not to force people into professing Islam but rather to warn them. The Prophet did not claim to be empowered to compel anyone to accept Islam. From the beginning, the Qur'an warned the Prophet that he should not be overly enthusiastic, or too concerned about people not following the new religion. The Prophet was to be patient, and to know that God guides whomever He will. The Qur'an also reminds Muslims that prophets before Muhammad had come to convey the message, not to compel people to follow it.

Apart from the Qur'anic instructions to the Prophet to be lenient, the main evidence for his leniency to apostates is his attitude towards the hypocrites (*munafiqun*) of Medina. These were Muslims who outwardly professed belief in God and the Prophet, but inwardly did not believe. Secretly, they used every opportunity to discredit the Prophet, while maintaining publicly that they were true to the faith. If the criteria of apostasy as developed in Islamic law are applied, these so-called hypocrites were the first apostates in Islam. The Qur'an recounts their beliefs and practices on several occasions. For the Prophet and the Qur'an, there was no legal difference between a hypocrite and an apostate; this distinction was made in Islamic law at a later period. Confirming the view that essentially there is no difference between a hypocrite and an apostate, the Hanafi jurist Sarakhsi says clearly that a hypocrite (*munafiq*) is like an apostate (*murtadd*). He equates apostasy and hypocrisy in the case of ʿAbd Allah b. Ubayy b. Salul, the leading hypocrite in Medina at the time of the Prophet, by saying, 'he was an apostate even though he was a hypocrite' (*wa huwa murtaddun wa in kana munafiqan*).[74] Referring to the hypocrites, the Qur'an says:

> And there are people who say, 'We do believe in God and the Last Day,' the while they do not [really] believe. They would deceive God and those who have attained to faith – the while they deceive none but themselves, and perceive it not.[75]

The Qur'an calls these people liars, mischief-makers, fools and unbelievers.[76] It is clear from the Qur'anic description that they were opportunists, living among the Muslims but spreading hatred, distrust and doubt about Islam, the Muslims in general, and about the Prophet:

> And when they [hypocrites] are told, 'Believe as other people believe,' they answer, 'Shall we believe as the weak-minded believe?' Oh, truly, it is they, they who are weak-minded – but they know it not!
> And when they meet those who have attained to faith, they assert, 'We believe [as you believe]'; but when they find themselves alone with their evil impulses, they say, 'Truly, we are with you; we were only mocking!'[77]

Despite this behaviour of the hypocrites, neither the Qur'an nor the Prophet ordered their execution. Even when some Companions asked the Prophet that certain 'hypocrites' should be executed, he refused.[78] In one incident, a man sought permission from the Prophet to execute a hypocrite.

The Prophet asked whether the hypocrite confessed that there was no god but Allah and whether he performed the obligatory prayer to which the man said, 'Yes'. The Prophet then said that such people should not be executed, and that he, the Prophet, was prohibited from engaging in such an act.[79] In effect, the Prophet treated such people well, to the extent that, when ʿAbd Allah b. Ubayy b. Salul, perhaps the most well known of the hypocrites, died, the Prophet prayed for him on the day of his death, despite apparent objections from a senior Companion like ʿUmar b. al-Khattab.[80]

That the Prophet tolerated those who repudiated Islam is more clearly evident in the Treaty of Hudaybiyyah (6/628), which the Prophet concluded with his Meccan opponents. One of the terms of that treaty allowed a Muslim to repudiate Islam, return to Mecca as an apostate and remain there:[81]

Whoever of Quraysh comes to Muhammad without permission of his protector (or guardian) [as a Muslim], Muhammad is to send back to them; whoever of those with Muhammad [as a Muslim] comes to Quraysh [as an apostate] is not to be sent back to him.[82]

If apostasy were a crime to be punished by death, the Prophet would not have permitted the inclusion of such a term. Instead, he behaved generously towards those who either repudiated Islam openly but did not rise against the community, or those who were nominal Muslims without strong conviction. He does not appear to have ordered their harassment, let alone their execution. There is also evidence that, on many occasions, the Prophet insisted that he did not know what was in people's minds and hearts in terms of belief, unbelief, sincerity or insincerity. In one *hadith* the Prophet is reported to have said that he had not been ordered to delve into people's hearts. In another report, when Usama b. Zayd killed someone in battle despite the victim pronouncing that there is no god but Allah, the Prophet was very angry and asked Usama, 'Did you open his heart and check if he was telling the truth?' From the Prophet's point of view, it was up to God to judge a person's sincerity.[83] The Prophet also prohibited Miqdad b. ʿAmr al-Kindi from killing another person who declared his faith only at the threat of imminent execution.[84]

There is an interesting tradition in both *Bukhari* and *Muslim* about a nomad who became a Muslim but later wanted to leave Medina and revert to his previous religion:

A Bedouin came to the Prophet, peace be upon him, and pledged his allegiance to him. The next day he came back, ill with fever and said repeatedly: 'Return my pledge to me,' but the Prophet refused three times. Then, the Prophet said, 'Medina is like a bellows which rejects what is dross and recognizes what is pure'.

This man several times sought permission from the Prophet to be released from Islam but the Prophet declined, before eventually allowing him to leave Medina and revert to idolatry. Had the Prophet wanted to impose capital punishment for apostasy, he could have done so. In this case, he could have refused to allow the man to leave Medina but did not.

Tolerance on the part of the Qur'an and the Prophet was neither opportunistic nor inconsistent. Some of the verses related to this tolerance were revealed early in the Prophet's time in Mecca. Some may argue that this tolerance was merely an illusion, that, in reality, the Prophet did not have the power to enforce adherence to Islam when he was in Mecca, and that tolerance was the best strategy at the time. It is true that, in the early period of his mission, the Prophet could not have imposed any kind of view on his followers or on anybody else in Mecca because he did not have the means or the power to do so. He had only a few followers in a position to come to the defence of Islam, and even then only in a small way. Moreover, many verses of the Meccan period reminded the Prophet that he was sent only to transmit the message from God.

The Prophet, having migrated to Medina, established the nucleus of an Islamic community and made serious efforts to establish a working relationship with the non-Muslim communities there on the basis of common interests in the security and safety of Medina, and of equality and freedom of religion. This indicates that he was willing to deal with people as individuals and communities, whether they chose to follow him or not. The 'constitution of Medina', which provided guidelines for the relationship between Muslims and non-Muslims in the town, indicates that non-Muslims were to enjoy inter alia freedom of religion. Non-Muslims, such as Jews for example, were clearly given the opportunity to remain committed to their religion and to practise their faith without restriction or interference. There is no evidence to suggest that this religious freedom was limited in any way up to the conquest of Mecca in the year 8/630 or even after that.

Lenient Attitude of the Early Authorities

There is some evidence to suggest that 'Umar b. al-Khattab, one of the Companions and the second caliph, also demonstrated the lenient attitude of the Prophet in his dealings with some of the apostates. According to one tradition, the Companion Abu Musa executed one Juhaynah and his colleagues for apparently becoming apostates. Anas b. Malik, reporting, said:

I came to see 'Umar b. al-Khattab, who said: 'What did Juhaynah and his companions do?' . . . I said: 'O Leader of the Believers. Is there anything but execution [as punishment for them]?' Then 'Umar said, 'Had you brought them [to me], I would have offered Islam to them. Had they repented, I would have accepted this; otherwise I would have put them in prison'.[85]

This perhaps indicates that they should have been spared death.

In another tradition, again attributed to 'Umar, he was reportedly informed that a certain Arab had become an apostate and had been executed. 'Umar indicated that he should have been imprisoned for three days, fed and given drink [that is, they should have treated him gently], and should have had Islam preached to him. On the third day, he might have accepted Islam. Then 'Umar said, 'O Allah, I did not attend that execution, and did not order it, and I did not know about it.'[86]

Perhaps following 'Umar's lenient approach, some leading authorities of the early Islamic period, such as Ibrahim al-Nakha'i and Sufyan al-Thawri, appear to have believed that an apostate should continue to be asked to repent indefinitely, and that the death penalty should not be imposed. Had there been a unanimous agreement among the early Muslims regarding the execution of apostates, these prominent authorities would not have expressed such a tolerant view of the punishment of apostasy. As previously noted, Sarakhsi, the famous Hanafi jurist, is among those who appear to reject the idea of the death penalty for change of religion. According to Sarakhsi, conversion from Islam to another religion is one of the greatest of offences, yet it is a matter between Man and his Creator, and its punishment is postponed to the Day of Judgement.[87]

Conclusion

There is ample evidence to suggest that capital punishment for apostasy, as understood in Islamic law, is problematic, if it is to be based on texts from the Qur'an and *sunnah*. This is not to deny that there have been many *ulama* who have sincerely believed that the punishment for apostasy should be death. Some *ulama* have been extremely harsh on apostates and have denied them even the chance to repent, while others have wanted to give apostates the chance to repent and revert to Islam, thereby regaining freedom and the right to live.

The law of apostasy was developed in Islam on the basis of a few isolated *hadith*, at a time and in circumstances that differ radically from today. Then, Islam was the dominant religion. It was also politically, militarily and economically powerful. People were organized according to their religious affiliations; inter-group relations were governed strictly by religious laws, and these laws were generally in the hands of religious authorities. Social mobility depended upon ancestry, religious affiliation, or both. Excommunication and branding someone as a heretic were easy means of depriving that person of basic rights. Unlike today, there was no independent authority concerned with individual human rights. Nor was there a concept of the nation-state as we know it. Religious minorities at that time were not usually considered equal to the dominant majority, and such minorities' loyalty to the host community was at times perceived to be questionable.

Crimes for which temporal punishment is set down in the Qur'an are primarily acts in which one person deprives another of the right to function harmoniously in society. Some Muslim scholars recognized this central function of religion long ago by dividing the rights of a Muslim into 'rights of God' and 'rights of Man'. To protect what was called 'rights of Man', appropriate laws as well as punishments were to be enforced. As for infringing the rights of God, punishment was not temporal; it was to be enforced only by God in the Hereafter. For example, the Qur'an sets clear punishments for stealing, even though the prohibition of theft is mentioned only once in the text. But the Qur'an specified no temporal punishment for failure to perform the prayers (*salat*) or pay the alms tax (*zakat*), despite the fact that the Qur'an mentioned the term *salat* and its derivatives more than 99 times, and *zakat* and its derivatives more than 32 times, while instructing Muslims to carry out those obligations. All this indicates that temporal punishment is, on the whole, only mandatory for acts that infringe the rights of other people, such as theft and murder. This suggests that temporal punishment has no place in the more subtle domain of belief.

The question of apostasy in early Islamic history was closely associated with the security of the Muslim community, defined in terms of combating treachery and aggression. People were divided into three major groups: believers and unbelievers who were at peace with Muslims, and unbelievers who were at war with Muslims. Believers, by definition, supported Islam and were actively engaged in it. The unbelievers (who were not at peace with the believers) were actively engaged against Islam. Anyone who became a Muslim joined the believers, and anyone who rejected Islam usually joined the side of the unbelievers who were not at peace with Muslims. Thus the issue of apostasy was closely related to both the identity and the survival of Muslims. Any tradition from the Prophet indicating that apostates should be killed needs to be understood within this broader political context. Nor was unbelief on its own a justification for killing anyone. There is nothing in the Qur'an or in the *hadith* to suggest that all unbelievers (*kuffar*) are to be killed or fought against. Similarly, apostasy on its own would not be a justification for killing people, unless they were actively threatening or fighting the Muslim community. Unbelievers were to be left alone with their conscience.

Islam is not a religion bent on persecuting all those who do not believe in it, or who leave it for one reason or another. Islam recognizes diversity of religion, even though it does not approve of religious forms that it perceives have been derived from non-divine sources. Islam regards life as a testing ground, one of the most important aspects of which is freedom to choose a belief system and a way of life. If this right is taken away, the testing becomes purposeless and meaningless. Measures should not be taken by any religious or political authority to curtail this fundamental freedom given by God to human beings, even in the name of preventing them from falling into error. Such curtailment of freedom is against this right given by the Qur'an to the individual. The Qur'an asserts that human beings will be held responsible by God on the Day of Judgement for the stewardship of this right and for their actions.

Chapter 6

Apostasy and the Position of Muslim Thinkers in the Modern Period

Unlike the case in the pre-modern period, there is a significant level of diversity among Muslim thinkers and scholars of the modern period on the issue of capital punishment for apostasy. In the pre-modern period, and right up to the modern period, death for apostasy was taken for granted in Islamic law. Today, three main positions seem to be emerging: (1) the pre-modern position with no change; (2) the pre-modern position with restrictions; and (3) total freedom to move to and from Islam. The latter position constitutes a direct challenge to the pre-modern position on apostasy. Given the sensitive nature of the issue, in the following an attempt will be made to quote the authors verbatim, where possible and relevant.

The Pre-Modern Position Restated

The vast majority of Muslim scholars writing on the issue of apostasy today follow the pre-modern position on apostasy (see Chapter 4). They rely on the *ijtihad* of pre-modern jurists on apostasy with all of its details, as if that *ijtihad* was immutable. Even the *ijtihad* regarding the apostasy of women and minors is followed to the letter in some modern writings.[1] Thus, the law on apostasy as it exists in pre-modern Islamic legal manuals is reproduced for modern consumption without giving due consideration to either the degree of authoritativeness of this pre-modern *ijtihad* or the changed conditions of the modern period.

For those who follow the pre-modern position, then, apostasy is prohibited and no Muslim is allowed to convert to another religion or commit any of the offences which would make them an apostate. Apostasy, for these scholars, is punishable by death. Consequently there is no obligation to recognize freedom of religion as understood in Article 18 of the Universal Declaration of Human Rights (1948). The line of reasoning of those who hold to the pre-modern position can be demonstrated through the following two *fatwas*.

In responding to a question about the punishment for apostasy, one *mufti* (someone qualified to issue religious edicts) argues that the punishment is instituted for the 'protection of the religion':

The person who knows the truth and believes in it, [but] then turns his back on it, does not deserve to live. The punishment for apostasy is prescribed for the protection of the religion and as a deterrent to anyone who is thinking of leaving Islam. There is no doubt that such a serious crime must be met with an equally weighty punishment. If the *kuffar* [unbelievers] do not give people the freedom to cross a red light, how can we give freedom to people to leave Islam and disbelieve in Allah when they want to?[2]

In response to a question relating to the death penalty for apostasy, another *fatwa* lists several reasons why this penalty is justified, following the pre-modern position:

- This is the ruling of Allah and His Messenger, as the Prophet – peace and blessings of Allah be upon him – said: 'Whoever changes his religion, kill him.'
- The one who has known the religion which Allah revealed, entered it and practised it, then rejected it, despised it and left it, is a person who does not deserve to live on the earth of Allah and eat from the provision of Allah.
- By leaving Islam, the apostate opens the way for everyone who wants to leave the faith, thus spreading apostasy and encouraging it.
- The apostate is not to be killed without warning. Even though his crime is so great, he is given a last chance, a respite of three days in which to repent. If he repents, he will be left alone; if he does not repent, then he will be killed.
- If the punishment for murder and espionage (also known as high treason) is death, then what should be the punishment for the one who disbelieves in the Lord of mankind and despises and rejects His religion? Is espionage or shedding blood worse than leaving the religion of the Lord of mankind and rejecting it?[3]

Muhammad Mutawalli al-Shaʿrawi, a contemporary preacher from Egypt, is more candid. He leaves no doubt about the pre-modern interpretation of freedom of religion. For him, there is no conversion once a person becomes a Muslim. When asked 'Why does Islam say that there is no coercion in faith, and yet it commands the killing of the apostate?', he answers by saying that a person is free to believe or not to believe, but once an individual embraces the faith (Islam) they are subject to all its requirements, including its stand on the punishment for apostasy.[4] This position is representative of the pro-punishment Muslims who follow the pre-modern argument.

The Pre-Modern Position Restricted

A number of Muslim scholars and thinkers contributing to the debate have felt that the pre-modern position on apostasy is unworkable in some respects and have therefore attempted to introduce some limitations. The most obvious limitation is their emphasis on the association of apostasy with 'treason', though what 'treason' is remains undefined in much of the literature.[5] Second, they equate Islam with a socio-political order or a 'state'. In their view, such an order based on Islam can only accommodate Muslims as its members. Apostates, by their rejection of this order, are effectively excluding themselves from its membership. Their action becomes equivalent to 'treason' which deserves the punishment of death. Third, the punishment must be enforced by the state alone and not by private individuals, thereby excluding vigilantism. A fourth limitation is the declaration that the punishment is not prescribed (*hadd*) by God or the Prophet but is a discretionary (*ta'zir*) punishment. This makes it susceptible to change over time. However, it seems that scholars who follow this line are more interested in justifying the punishment than anything else.

Among Muslim modernists, Rashid Rida seems to have given up the pre-modern view that the Muslim who abandoned Islam should be put to death. He makes a distinction between the apostate who revolts against Islam and is therefore a danger to the *ummah*, and those who abandon it quietly as individuals. The first should be put to death, if captured, the second category not.[6] Here Rida's view seems to be that the pre-modern *ijma'* (consensus) on the execution of the apostate is not really based on a clear text of the Qur'an and therefore can be abandoned.

Another Muslim of the modern period, the Pakistani scholar Abul A'la Maududi (d.1979), made a substantial contribution to what we might loosely call 'modern Islamic political thought'. He wrote numerous booklets and other works on various aspects of Islam. One of the issues he tackles is the question of human rights and, within this, the question of the right to freedom of religion. In his pamphlet *Human Rights in Islam* Maududi appears supportive of many of the rights bestowed on citizens in a secular democracy. However, in other works, particularly in his major work on the punishment of apostates,[7] Maududi justifies the punishment of death on the ground that the Qur'an, the *sunnah* and the rulings of early caliphs and *ulama* all regard apostasy as an act of 'high treason'. For Maududi, belief in Islam is not just a matter of personal faith. It suggests membership in a social order implemented by the state. A change of faith, therefore, is tantamount to treachery, making such a traitor a potential enemy of the state. Just as states such as Britain or the United States consider high treason a major crime, so, for Maududi, Islam prescribes capital punishment for apostates.[8]

Maududi seems to sense a moral problem in executing the apostate for merely rejecting the religion of Islam for another such as Christianity. After all, religion is supposed to be something which one should profess sincerely, as is abundantly clear from the Qur'an and *sunnah*. Maududi addresses this problem by expanding the definition of religion: he transforms the concept of religion by equating 'religion' with 'state' to some extent. For him, the organizing of society, the negotiating of the concerns of this world and the shape of government are all part of Islam; it is a complete ordering of life, in all its aspects. Maududi states:

> A faith and idea of this nature cannot be made into a game for the liberties of individuals. Nor can the society, which establishes the order of civilization and state on that faith, make way for any brainwave to enter, then to be displaced by another brainwave, to come and go at will ... An organized society which has chosen the form of a state can hardly provide a place within its sphere of activity for people who differ from it in fundamental matters. Differences of lesser significance can more or less be tolerated. But it is very difficult to give people a place in society and make them a part of the state if they completely oppose the foundations on which the order of society and the state are established.[9]

Maududi's view of Islam as a state makes it difficult to accommodate the apostate within it, once the apostate rejects Islam. The apostate, for him, is a constant danger to the community of believers and 'a permanent plague spreading among the people and a source of fear lest also the other whole and healthy members of society be permeated with his poison'. Maududi believes therefore that it is 'better to punish him by death and thereby at one and the same time to put an end to his own and society's misery'. At the same time Maududi appears to concede that when the state is not based on Islam (that is, when there is no Islamic state) then the apostate should not be punished.

Maududi makes a distinction between a state based on an Islamic socio-political order and a state which is not so based. He also makes a distinction between a religion that is merely concerned with the afterlife and metaphysical matters, and a religion whose concerns include both earthly matters and heavenly ones. He points out that eligibility for punishment is not merely based on change of religion but also on the notion of an Islamic socio-political order. For him, it is this rejection of a 'divine' socio-political order that amounts to high treason. Maududi's analysis, therefore, is sharper than those who follow the pre-modern position on apostasy without analysing the issue, and simply pronounce death as the punishment of apostasy.

It seems that Maududi and many other scholars like him are in the difficult position of dealing with the question of freedom of conscience and religion vis-à-vis the largely unanimous view of the punishment for apostasy. As indicated above, pre-modern Islamic law prescribes only coercion in the case of apostasy from Islam. This coercion can be exercised by forcing the person to repent and return to Islam or otherwise putting that person to death. Maududi, like many others, has wrestled with this problem. In *Human Rights in Islam*[10] Maududi does not mention punishment of death for apostasy, implying that Muslims should also be free to change their religion. Criticizing Maududi on this point, Ahmad says:

> Regarding the question of freedom of belief, Maududi, it seems, is quite dishonest. In his pamphlet *Human Rights in Islam* published by The Islamic Foundation, U.K., there is no mention of the doctrine of apostasy. Instead he cites the famous Qur'anic verse: 'There should be no coercion in the matter of faith' . . . The article is obviously directed towards the Westernized public with a view, it seems, to project a tolerant image of Islam. However in his main English book on political thought, The *Islamic Law and Constitution*, he adopts a dogmatic stance, though this is done apologetically.[11]

In fairness to Maududi, one could say that since there was unanimous agreement on the punishment of apostasy among pre-modern Muslim jurists, it would be very difficult for a modern scholar to oppose such a position in Islamic law. However, in the latter part of the twentieth century, Muslim scholars began to explore this issue in a more detached way. They also started looking at pre-modern Islamic law somewhat more critically. Contributors to this new approach include Muslim scholars deeply rooted in the Islamic tradition and law, as well as activists of the Islamic movement of the twentieth and early twenty-first centuries.

In line with Maududi, Ismail al-Faruqi (d.1986), the architect of the Islamization of Knowledge Movement, maintains capital punishment for apostasy, relating it to abandonment of an Islamic world order. However, he emphasizes that converts have the option of 'emigrating' from the Islamic state:

> . . . To convert out of Islam means clearly to abandon its world order which is the Islamic state. That is why Islamic law has treated people who have converted out of Islam as political traitors. No state can look upon political treason directed to it with indifference. It must deal with the traitors, when convicted after due process of law, either with banishment, life imprisonment, or capital punishment. The Islamic state is no exception to this. But Islamic political theory does allow converts from Islam to emigrate from the Islamic state provided they do so before proclaiming their conversion, for the state does not keep its citizens within its boundaries by force. But once their conversion is proclaimed, they must be dealt with as traitors to the state.[12]

In Faruqi's scheme, apostates do not seem to have many options but to leave the Islamic state or face the death penalty.

Awa, a contemporary jurist who has written on apostasy, makes the interesting point that punishment is to be inflicted in cases where the apostate becomes a cause of harm to the community:

The punishment is inflicted in cases in which the apostate is a cause of harm to the society, while in those cases in which an individual simply changes his religion the punishment is not to be applied. But it must be remembered that unthreatening apostasy is an exceptional case, and the common thing is that apostasy is accompanied by some harmful actions against the society or state. A comparison between the concept of punishing those who commit treason in modern systems of law and those who commit apostasy in Islamic law would be useful. Assuredly, the protection of society is the underlying principle in the punishment for apostasy in the legal system of Islam.[13]

Taking the question of treason as a justification for punishment one can argue that there are two types of apostates: one who maintains peace, and another who conspires against the Islamic state by acts of rebellion and crime. In line with this view, it is the latter form of apostasy which is likely to be considered treason. In this case, the apostate is no longer an apostate as much as he is a dangerous criminal who is a threat to the society.

Yusuf al-Qaradawi, one of the most prominent neo-revivalist scholars of the late twentieth century, supports the death penalty but argues that vigilantism should not be employed to implement punishment. It can only be imposed by the state:

Apostasy from Islam after willingly accepting it and subsequently declaring an open revolt against it in such a manner which threatens the solidarity of the Muslim community is a crime punishable by death. No one is compelled to accept Islam, but at the same time no one is permitted to play tricks with it, as some Jews did during the Prophet's time . . .

In any of these instances, the death penalty can be implemented only by the proper authority after due process of law prescribed by the *shari'ah*; individuals cannot take the law into their own hands, becoming judges and executioners, since this would result in absolute chaos and disorder.[14]

The Pre-Modern Position Challenged

A number of thinkers and scholars have argued that capital punishment for apostasy is not in line with the spirit of Islam and therefore the whole issue should be rethought. For them, times and circumstances have changed significantly and this should be taken into account when dealing with the matter. Those who hold these views range from the so-called secular Muslims to leaders of Islamist movements.

The founder of Pakistan, Muhammad Ali Jinnah (d.1948), represents the view of many 'secular' Muslims on the question of religious freedom. Jinnah at one time advocated the unity of Hindus and Muslims in India. However, he later changed his position, arguing for a separate Muslim state in which Muslims would rule and be the majority. Jinnah appears to have been a typical example of a secular Muslim. Religion does not seem to have played a prominent role in his personal life. He did not have dogmatic views on many of the issues Muslims were struggling with at that time. More importantly, Jinnah had a Shi'i background. Yet in his quest for a Muslim state, he apparently had no difficulty in gaining the support of both Shi'is and Sunnis, managing to bypass sectarian differences. Although Jinnah seems to have put some emphasis on the role of Islamic law in the new state of Pakistan, he declared several times that it would not be a theocratic state but a modern democracy. Stressing the importance of religious freedom in his address to the members of the Pakistani Constituent Assembly on 11 August 1947, Jinnah said:

> We should begin to work in that spirit and in course of time all these angularities of the majority and the minority communities, the Hindu and the Muslim community – because even as regards Muslims you have Pathans, Punjabis, Shias, Sunnis and so on and among the Hindus you have Brahmins, Vashnavas, Khatris, also Bengalees, Madrasis, and so on – will vanish . . . You are free to go to your temples, you are free to go to your mosques or to any other places of worship in this State of Pakistan. You may belong to any religion or caste or creed – that has got nothing to do with the business of the State . . . We are starting with this fundamental principle that we are all citizens and equal citizens of one State.[15]

A more direct challenge comes from figures like Al-Sadiq al-Nayhoum (d.1995), born in Libya, and a specialist in comparative religion, who argues that the 'Islam' inherited from the *salaf* (pious ancestors) is not the Islam of the Qur'an but a 'distorted' Islam. According to him, execution of the apostate has nothing to do with the Qur'an which clearly prohibits coercion in religion. Rather, the punishment comes directly from Jewish law, and therefore should be rejected.[16] Several who criticized Nayhoum's rather provocative 1993 article on this issue attempted to demonstrate that the punishment really was Islamic and therefore justified.[17]

Another critic of the death penalty, retired Chief Justice of Pakistan, S.A. Rahman, after an analysis of the relevant texts of the Qur'an on apostasy, concludes:

> The position that emerges, after a survey of the relevant verses of the Qur'an, may be summed up by saying that not only is there no punishment for apostasy provided in the Book but that the Word of God clearly envisages the natural death of the apostate. He will be punished only in the Hereafter.[18]

Similarly on the *hadith* evidence, after a thorough analysis of the texts available, he had this to say:

> It has been seen that even the strongest bulwark of the orthodox view, viz. the Sunnah, when subjected to critical examination in the light of history, does not fortify the stand of those who seek to establish that a Muslim who commits apostasy must be condemned to death for his change of belief alone. In instances

in which apparently such a punishment was inflicted, other factors have been found to co-exist, which would have justified action in the interest of collective security.[19]

Among Muslims who have argued that there is no temporal punishment for 'simple' apostasy is a leading Egyptian modernist scholar, the late Mahmud Shaltut, Shaykh al-Azhar (d.1963). For Shaltut, the death penalty in early Islamic history was really a punishment for crimes against the state. He further argues that the punishment for apostasy is really based on isolated *hadith* and that *hudud* (prescribed punishments) cannot be established on such a foundation. For him, unbelief alone is not a justification for the punishment.[20]

Several other Muslim scholars of the modern period have argued that the punishment of death does not apply to apostasy per se. Subhi Mahmassani, a legal scholar, is of the view that the death penalty is connected to high treason, not to a simple act of renunciation of faith.[21] Mohammad Hashim Kamali, another legal scholar, also argues:

It may be said by way of conclusion that apostasy was a punishable offence in the early years of the advent of Islam due to its subversive effects on the nascent Muslim community and state. Evidence in the Qur'an is, on the other hand, clearly supportive of the freedom of belief, which naturally includes freedom to convert. Moreover the Qur'an provides no punishment for apostasy despite the fact that it occurs in a large number of places in the text, and this remains to represent the normative position of the Shari'ah on non-subversive apostasy that is due purely to personal conviction and belief.[22]

Confirming this view, Kamali says: 'The Qur'an prescribes absolutely no temporal punishment for apostasy, nor has the Prophet, peace be upon him, sentenced anyone to death for it.'[23]

Muhammad Salim al-Awa, a contemporary thinker and a prominent contributor to the debate on the punishment of apostasy, introduces an element of flexibility by arguing that the punishment is not a prescribed punishment (*hadd*) but a discretionary punishment (*ta'zir*). The difference is that if the punishment is prescribed it cannot be changed, but if it is a discretionary punishment it can be changed from time to time, as recognized in Islamic law. Despite the common view among Muslim jurists as well as among Western orientalists that apostasy from Islam is a crime for which the death penalty is prescribed,[24] in Awa's view, it should be classified as a crime for which discretionary punishment may be applied.[25] He argues:

The Qur'anic verses concerned did not prescribe any punishment for apostasy but simply declared it to be a great sin. Secondly, the Prophet who said these words ['Whoever changes his religion kill him'] about apostates never himself had an apostate put to death.[26]

Jamal al-Banna, another recent contributor to the debate, says that in the modern period the state should not interfere with people's religion and belief under any circumstances. In arguing that belief should be based on freedom and conviction Banna makes four points. First, he specifies that the Qur'an mentions apostasy in many places but does not impose any temporal punishment. Second, as the Qur'an makes freedom of belief a basic right, this establishes a fundamental principle of Islam which corresponds with reason and logic. Third, there is nothing from the Prophet to suggest that he executed an apostate because of his apostasy. Fourth, Banna argues that in order to use the import of a *hadith* as a fundamental principle, one has to study the *hadith* very carefully, considering all aspects of it. One should also establish that that *hadith* had been narrated properly, that is, in the exact words of the Prophet, not just in their general meaning. For him, Muslims should not rely on a *hadith* whose text does not correspond to the actual words of the Prophet, in order to execute a person or to restrict their freedom. The meaning of such a text can change with time and one should be cautious in using such *hadith* to support the serious penalty under discussion. Banna is referring to *hadith*s such as 'Whoever changes his religion, kill him.' He also argues that the idea of apostasy during the time of the Prophet was linked with enmity and warfare against Islam. It was not merely change of religion that was at issue, as evidenced by several cases where Muslims reverted to their former religions but were not executed.[27]

For Shaykh Muhammad Sayyid Tantawi of Egypt, Muslims who renounce their faith or turn apostate should be left alone as long as they do not threaten or belittle Islam. If Muslims are forced to take action against an apostate, it should not be because they had given up the faith but because they had turned out to be an enemy or a threat to Islam.[28]

Shabbir Akhtar emphasizes the importance of sincerity in belief and argues that faith should not be based on hypocrisy and coercion:

> My own view ... is that the potential risks inherent in the offer of religious freedom are worth taking. Why? Well, if there is a God, I would argue, it can be expected a priori that he wants a voluntary response born of genuine gratitude and humility themselves rooted in reflection and morally responsible choice. Seen in this light, heresy and even apostasy are morally more acceptable than any hypocritical attachment to orthodox opinion out of the fear of public sanctions. Fortunately, for us, we have the evidence of the Koran itself in favour of this view: 'there should be no compulsion in religion' (2:256). Unfortunately, however, many learned authorities have sought to cancel this noble sentiment by finding verses within the sacred volume that favour the opposite opinion ... Suffice it to say here that even in terms of a pragmatic (as opposed to a moral or religious) outlook, there is much to be said in favour of religious freedom.[29]

Relying on the Qur'anic verse 2:256, the Sisters in Islam of Malaysia have argued strongly in favour of freedom of religion for all citizens, including

Muslims. This group is interested in furthering women's rights as well as human rights in general, but within an Islamic framework. Their basic proposition is that since there was no coercion to embrace Islam in the Prophet's time, this situation must continue in the modern period, regardless of the learned opinion of scholars or consensus. The Sisters in Islam believe that 'Islam itself means submission to the will of God; and the willing submission of the self to faith and belief must be attained through conviction and reason, not through coercion and duress.' Their view is that all citizens of the state must have total freedom of religion and that no punishment should be imposed for 'simple' change of faith. It is only when apostasy is accompanied by crimes such as brigandage such a punishment should be imposed.[30]

Hasan al-Turabi, leader of the Muslim Brotherhood in Sudan, expressed his views on apostasy in a 1996 interview.[31] He argues that an apostate should not be put to death. Turabi says that he believes in freedom of belief and that no one should be compelled to believe. He adds that the *hadith* which commands Muslims to execute the apostate is specific to its historical context. It is also specific to the earliest Muslim community, and refers to a Muslim 'who deserts his fellows and joins the enemies of Islam', not to one who apostatizes by writing a book criticizing Islam, a reference to the Salman Rushdie incident (1989). For Turabi, the Qur'anic verses that prohibit compulsion and coercion are numerous and so are the sayings and practices of the Prophet, and this non-compulsion or freedom of belief should override the case for coercion. From his point of view:

> Freedom of faith is one of the primary principles of religion. However, the main problem is that Muslims have ceased to deal directly with the main sources of their faith. They are content with memorizing quotations which, to them, represent the interpretations of previous generations who borrowed from their forefathers. As a result, over the generations, the main source has been forgotten.[32]

For Turabi, this issue needs to be investigated through studying the Qur'an and *sunnah* and by means of *ijtihad*, not by repeating what earlier scholars have said. However, Turabi has been criticized by a number of observers of the Sudanese Islamist movement for being inconsistent. On the one hand he argues that the punishment of death should not be imposed for apostasy, while on the other he apparently supported the death penalty for apostasy in the past, as in the case of Mahmud Taha, a critic of the Sudanese regime, executed in 1985.

Rashid al-Ghannushi, a leading thinker from Tunisia also possessing a Muslim Brotherhood background, expressed similar views to Turabi.[33] In a 1998 interview Ghannushi declared that the Muslim has the freedom to change religion.[34] When asked whether a Muslim has the right to apostasy, he stated that 'the available evidence concerning apostasy do not attain the level of certainty required for it to be included in the legal (*shar'i*) sanctions (*hudud*) that the Muslim ruler is obliged to effectuate [*sic*] in all cases'.[35] Drawing on the Hanafi view that female apostates should not be executed as they do not 'carry arms', Ghannushi adds that apostasy is really a 'political crime left for the [political] leader to judge the most appropriate method for its treatment'. He concludes by saying that he is inclined to accept the view mentioned here 'since it is more in harmony with Qur'anic evidence which all assert the principles of freedom of belief, and forbidding of compulsion ... whilst leaving the matter of judging what is hidden within hearts solely with Allah'.[36]

Conclusion

The debate on apostasy in the modern period has gained added importance as it relates to the debate on human rights. Whether Muslim scholars acknowledge it or not, the debate on human rights including the right to 'freedom of belief' has become central in discussion not only in the West but also among Muslims. In this debate some prefer to hide behind the pre-modern juristic line or restate that position, while others seek to find a way to harmonize this with a modern human rights stance on the matter. Others offer a fresh look at the issue and go straight to the foundation texts of the Qur'an and *sunnah*. One of the new positions emerging among many Muslims today is that the Qur'an supports the view that freedom of belief is an essential aspect of Islam.

Chapter 7

Apostasy Law and its Potential for Misuse

There is no centralized religious authority or institution in Islam, particularly in Sunni Islam, to determine which interpretation of scripture is valid. In Sunni Islam, each religious scholar is a potential interpreter of the Qur'an and of religion. Thus there are innumerable schools, sects and trends within Islam – legal, religio-political, theological or mystical – some of which are labelled un-Islamic and even 'heretical' by those who oppose their beliefs and practices. Despite this labelling, each considers itself to be the true representation of Islam. In its sphere of influence, each is considered 'orthodox', while those opposed to it and differing significantly are considered 'heterodox' or are found to be wanting.

In the pre-modern period, Muslims in a particular locality often functioned under the authority of a common system, sharing a legal as well as a theological school of thought. This is not generally the case today. The frequent movement of people through migration, the communications boom and consequent wide circulation of printed and electronic material on religion has altered this homogeneity even within the same locality. A breakdown of the traditional hold of legal or theological schools has led to a multiplicity of theological, legal and religio-political positions within the same locality. This is true even in the most conservative and relatively 'closed' communities (in religious terms), such as Saudi Arabia where the Hanbali legal school and Wahhabism prevail. This unprecedented diversity in religio-legal and theological views means that there is great potential for labelling one's theological, legal or religio-political opponents as apostates. As outlined in Chapter 3, the classical legal texts on apostasy and the understanding of such texts in the modern period are not very helpful in arriving at a precise idea of what constitutes apostasy; definitions often seem too broad in their scope, or too loose. Competing 'apostasy lists' are often contradictory; what one religious scholar sees as apostasy may not be apostasy at all for another.

Although there is no 'priesthood' or clerical class in Islam, in almost all Muslim communities a clerical class does function *de facto* as the 'official' religious establishment. This class is the 'official' *ulama* (as opposed to the non-official independent *ulama*), the legal/theological scholars who are considered among the prominent religious authorities in the locality and are often associated with the state bureaucracy. Governments in most Muslim

99

nations include a ministry or department that deals with religious affairs. The 'official' *ulama* are closely associated with the ministry, often employed by it and thus seen as officially incorporated into the state. These official *ulama* may issue religious edicts (*fatwa*) at the request of the government or the public. They play a significant role in determining what is theologically and legally acceptable within their jurisdiction. They become the guardians of religious 'orthodoxy' on behalf of the state at the local level. Nonconformity with the state-sanctioned 'orthodoxy' on the part of individuals can lead to charges of heresy, apostasy or unbelief. The trend in the Muslim world is for these official *ulama* to follow the broad direction the state sets for them, or to function within the parameters of state ideology or policy positions.

Given this situation, one could argue that in a Muslim society, accusation of apostasy is one of the most dangerous and powerful tools available to an individual or a group to eliminate an opponent or a competitor (political or religious). Similarly it can be highly effective in suppressing dissent and maintaining the status quo. In the following, we will explore two examples which demonstrate the potential for misuse of the law of apostasy.

Accusation of Apostasy as a Means for Encouraging Private Acts of Violence

Relying on early Islamic precedent in which private acts of vengeance against apostates in the name of Islam were tolerated to a degree, some Muslim extremist groups today feel it is their duty to punish those they consider apostates even before the courts have decided whether the alleged offender is guilty. Thus the mere accusation of apostasy or blasphemy is often sufficient in some Muslim communities for the alleged offender to be condemned to death, not by the law but by private individuals or mob violence, which is rationalized by the perpetrators as being in defence of Islam. When a Muslim sees another Muslim renouncing Islam, the belief is that they should cause the apostate as much harm as possible, even as far as killing them. It is also considered a matter of the 'honour' of one's community. The dishonour brought upon one's family and community by conversion to another religion demands redress. It can only be rectified by the apostate's reverting to Islam or by vengeance inflicted on the apostate. This is made easier as tradition suggests that private citizens who murder apostates and blasphemers are absolved of any wrongdoing. Thus, in some Muslim societies these acts go unpunished.

When a person, Muslim or non-Muslim, through speech, writing or any other act, is considered to have committed blasphemy (which is equivalent to apostasy in the case of a Muslim who commits the offence of blasphemy), for example by portraying the Prophet unfavourably or criticizing him, the community in which the act took place sometimes takes the law into its own hands. For instance, the late Ayatollah Khomeini of Iran issued a *fatwa* declaring the novelist Salman Rushdie an apostate for his depiction of the Prophet in his novel *Satanic Verses*. Similarly, when the Bangladeshi feminist writer Taslima Nasreen apparently criticized the Qur'an and Islamic law, several religious leaders in Bangladesh issued *fatwa*s declaring the writer to be an apostate and calling for her execution. In both cases, private acts of violence were encouraged by religious leaders.

Similar cases of private violence against alleged blasphemers and apostates have been documented by human rights organizations; for example in Pakistan, where a blasphemy law has been in place since 1986.[1] According to the US Department of State Human Rights Report (2000), the blasphemy provisions of the Pakistan Penal Code[2] have been used by rivals and local authorities to threaten, punish, or intimidate Ahmadis (Qadiyanis), Christians and even orthodox Muslims. According to the report, Pakistani government officials and police also arrest Muslims under blasphemy laws; in fact, government officials maintain that about two-thirds of the total blasphemy cases that have been brought to trial have affected Muslims.[3] The report goes on to say that, although no one has been executed by the state under any of these provisions, religious extremists have killed some persons accused under them.[4]

Abuse of laws similar to those on apostasy, such as blasphemy laws in Pakistan, attests to the ease with which people can accuse others of committing offences. The United States Commission on International Religious Freedom declared in 2001:

> There appears to be widespread agreement among government officials, legal advocates, and leaders of many religious communities in Pakistan that the criminal provisions against blasphemy are being abused.[5]

According to the report of the Commission, one of the main ways of abuse of the laws was as follows:

> To initiate a blasphemy case, any person can file a First Information Report (FIR) at the local police station. By doing so in a public way, a crowd of angry persons can be assembled and the police will take the accused into custody, ostensibly (and at times sensibly) for his or her own safety. Once local feelings have been aroused, local officials are reluctant to release the accused before trial. The instigators of such charges (alleged to be almost always false) are reported to fall into three categories: (a) those who have a personal dispute with the accused that is unrelated to religion (but the blasphemy law is a convenient way to attack them); (b) representatives of small but active organizations characterized as 'fundamentalists' and 'extremists' that operate throughout the country that target 'deviant' Muslims, Ahmadis, Christians, and other religious minorities for prosecution; and (c) local Muslim religious leaders who are either ideologically or organizationally aligned with or sympathetic to the aforementioned groups.[6]

Examples of such abuse are widely reported by human rights organizations and others interested in the welfare of marginalized groups. In Pakistan, in one case, Catherine Shaheen, a Christian headmistress of a government school, reportedly was falsely accused of blaspheming the Prophet Muhammad. Her accusers, some of her colleagues, were said to have been jealous of her recent promotion. To avoid being imprisoned or killed, she fled her home and had to live in hiding.[7] Similarly, a 22-year-old Christian named Rafiq was promoted within the insurance office where he worked. Jealous co-workers sought revenge against him by accusing him of importing Christian literature and distributing it in public. For their safety, his family had to move away.[8] In another case, as a result of international pressure, a Christian boy, Salamat Masih, was ultimately acquitted of blasphemy charges. However, a *fatwa* has since been issued against him by some religious extremists. He has fled Pakistan, leaving behind family and friends. While awaiting trial, his brother and co-defendant Manzoor Masih was killed by extremist gunmen.[9] Even judges and lawyers face intimidation. There have been reports that in blasphemy cases in Pakistan, for instance, some judges declare the accused guilty out of fear of the public or extremist religious leaders. Lawyers are intimidated and tend to avoid defending accused blasphemers for fear of their own lives.

Given the influence of the religious leaders, there is a strong belief in certain groups of Muslims that the *fatwa*s of these leaders can be relied upon (and should be followed), even where the state does not have a law against apostasy or blasphemy. Since many Muslims believe that Islamic law should be the law of Muslims even if it conflicts with existing 'secular' laws, such *fatwa*s assume more authority than the so-called 'man-made secular' laws of the country. In Egypt, in 1992, extremists murdered the anti-Islamist writer Farag Foda. It is reported that, at the killers' trial, the respected Muslim scholar Muhammad al-Ghazali testified that Foda deserved to die and that there is no punishment for the killers of apostates in Islamic law.[10]

Accusation of Apostasy as a Tool for Suppressing Dissent

In the modern period a number of Muslim extremists have labelled Muslim states and societies 'un-Islamic' (*jahili*). This move was popularized largely on the basis of the ideas and writings of figures such as Maududi and Qutb. The term *jahili* has been taken up by extremist offshoots of the Muslim Brotherhood in the Arab world and those with a similar ideological orientation elsewhere, who, in their struggle against the state, label their governments, political elites and societies in general *jahili*. Extremists see themselves as the 'true Muslims' and their Muslim opponents as apostates or unbelievers. It suits the extremists' revolutionary purposes to consider the majority of society, including political authorities, government officials, journalists and teachers, to be *jahili*. If a Muslim is outside Islam from the extremists' point of view, they see it as justifiable to eliminate that person. The accusation of apostasy can thus be used to terrorize opponents, especially high profile or influential figures, and silence opposition to a particular political or religious agenda.

Intellectuals

As in other religious traditions, in many Muslim communities clashes are common between intellectuals who challenge the status quo and the religious or political elite in whose interests it is to sustain it. Often such intellectuals are silenced through accusations of apostasy or heresy. To demonstrate this point, we will cite examples from Egypt, although similar examples are found elsewhere in the Muslim world.

An example of this was the issue of the Islamic caliphate (*khilafah*) in the early twentieth century. This institution of Islamic governance, the Ottoman caliphate, was finally abolished by Kemal Atatürk of Turkey in 1924. However, there was considerable debate in the aftermath of this, in Egypt as well as in other Muslim lands. The traditional view was that maintaining this institution was a religious obligation and that any attempt to abolish it would be tantamount to unbelief (*kufr*). The number of claimants to the title of caliph also increased and included King Faruq of Egypt. It is not surprising that when Egyptian intellectuals such as ʿAli Abd al-Raziq and ʿAbd al-Hamid al-Zahrawi al-Himsi minimized the importance of the institution of caliphate in their writings, the official religious establishment as well as the political elite became enraged. ʿAli ʿAbd al-Raziq was accused of heresy, as if by discussing the issue and questioning the Islamicity of the institution of the caliphate he had become a heretic. He was dismissed from his teaching post at al-Azhar University, Cairo, and deprived of a role in public affairs.

More recently, in 1993, Nasr Hamid Abu Zayd, a professor of Islamic studies at Cairo University and author of several works in the area of Qur'anic studies and Islamic philosophy, was accused of apostasy. A case was filed against him in the Giza Primary Court by one Youssef al-Badry, the chief plaintiff, under a rarely used Islamic principle of *hisbah*. ʿAbd al-Sabur Shahin, a fellow professor of Arabic at Cairo University, who had opposed Abu Zayd's promotion application for professorship earlier, was part of the group that brought the case against him. The defence argued that *hisbah* did not exist in Egyptian law and therefore they questioned the very basis of the case. In January 1994 the Court found for the defence but Badry and Shahin appealed on the basis of the constitutional amendment of 1980 that *shariʿah* was the principal source of Egyptian law. A second trial began. In June 1995 Judge ʿAbd al-ʿAlim and two others of the Cairo Court of Appeals:

neatly circumvented the fact that the court had no jurisdiction to declare anyone an apostate: they simply found, in an unprecedented ruling, that Abu Zayd's writings in and of themselves proved him to be an apostate. They declared, in effect, that he had convicted himself. Thereby, the court pronounced, he had lost the right to be married to a Muslim woman, and it ordered him to divorce [his wife] Ebtehal.[11]

Threats were made against Abu Zayd's life. Some scholars from al-Azhar University of Cairo called on the government to carry out the 'legal punishment for apostasy' in order to force him to repent. During Friday prayers *shaykhs* and *imams* made calls for Abu Zayd's death. He and his wife became virtual prisoners in their home, requiring security guards. In July 1995 Abu Zayd and Ebtehal fled to the Netherlands. A year later, in August 1996, the Court of Cassation, Egypt's equivalent of the Supreme Court, upheld the verdict of the Court of Appeals: a ruling unparalleled in the Islamic world.[12]

Again in Egypt in 2001, lawyer Nabih al-Wahsh brought a charge of apostasy against the prominent feminist writer Nawal al-Saadawi. Wahsh filed a separate lawsuit with the personal status court, demanding that Saadawi, 70, be divorced from her husband, Sherif Hattata, 78, on the grounds of apostasy. Wahsh claimed that Saadawi's views 'ousted her from the Muslim community'[13] and therefore she could not remain married to a Muslim. This was based on the idea that Islamic law prohibits Muslims from marrying apostates. Moreover, in his view, the Muslim community is allegedly empowered by Islamic law to defend its tenets against any transgressions through the exercise of so-called *hisbah*.[14] The Grand Mufti, Sheikh Nasr Farid Wassel, reacted by urging Saadawi to retract her statements or face apostasy charges. Wahsh considered the Mufti's comments to be a *fatwa* corroborating his complaint.[15] According to Khaled Dawoud of the *Al-Ahram* newspaper, whether Saadawi wins or loses, the case sends a stark warning to other writers:

> Within this atmosphere any intellectual, any novelist, will have to take into consideration these kinds of pressures and the presence of these groups and the presence of these kinds of lawyers who are ready to sue you just because of your ideas.[16]

Similarly, Saʿid al-ʿAshmawy, an Egyptian Islamic scholar and retired judge, was accused of apostasy for his opposition to the implementation of Islamic law, which he considers to be man-made.[17] More recently, Hasan Hanafi, a professor of philosophy at Cairo University, was also accused of denying Qur'anic texts on miracles,[18] an act tantamount to apostasy according to his opponents.

Books and Works of Art

Related to the silencing of intellectuals is the banning of books that do not meet the standards of 'orthodoxy' set by the religious establishment; this is becoming increasingly frequent in Egypt and in a number of other Muslim nations. The final say in matters related to books that have some relevance to religion in Egypt lies with al-Azhar, the guardian of orthodoxy there, which occupies the position of religious censor. Islamists outside al-Azhar also play a major role in censorship by calling for the banning of books they consider to be against Islam. Al-Azhar first became formally involved in censorship in 1985, when Law 102 of 1985 gave it the authority to regulate publications of the Qur'an and the *hadith*. Its powers soon began to grow and today it is involved in the banning of not only books directly related to the Qur'an and *hadith* but also a number of other books which may be incidentally related to 'religion'.[19]

Banning books has a long history in Egypt. In 1925 ʿAli ʿAbd al-Raziq's book *al-Islam wa Usul al-Hukm* (Islam and the Principles of Government) was banned. In 1926 Taha Hussein was attacked by al-Azhar for his *Fi al-Shiʿr al-Jahili* (Pre-Islamic Poetry). Although Hussein 'repented' and rewrote his book, he was dismissed from his university post by Prime Minister Ismail Sidki in 1931. In 1981 Fikri al-Aqad's *Fi Fiqh al-Lughah al-ʿArabiyyah* (Arabic Linguistics) was banned because it suggested that certain words in the Qur'an had ancient Egyptian origins.[20]

Recently, an Egyptian state security court sentenced Salaheddin Mohsen, a minor author who had said he did not believe in Islam, to three years in prison with hard labour for writings deemed offensive to Islam. The court also ordered that all of Mohsen's books and publications be confiscated for containing what it described as 'extremist' ideas.[21] In another case, Ala'a Hamad's *A Distance in a Man's Mind* and *The Bed* were banned because they were judged blasphemous by a committee of Islamic scholars from al-Azhar.[22]

In a review of Syrian writer Haidar Haidar's novel, *A Banquet for Seaweed*, in the 28 April 2000 issue of a Cairo tabloid, *Al-Shaʿb*, a columnist named Muhammad Abbas asserted that the book was nothing less than a viciously anti-Islamic tract.[23] Since this novel had just been reissued in the modern Arabic classics series sponsored by Egypt's Ministry of Culture, Abbas argued that the government of a Muslim country was itself promoting atheism and blasphemy. The columnist concluded by urging his government, and the Islamic world as a whole, to rise up in defence of Islam or forfeit their right to be called Muslims. According to one commentator, Rodenbeck:

Abbas's piece soon had dramatic results. Mosque sermons took up the cry against this insult to the faith, and soon after, the biggest riot Egypt had seen in a decade erupted at al-Azhar, Cairo's one-thousand-year-old Islamic university. Crowds of Koran-waving students surged out of the university's dusty suburban dormitories, demanding that the blasphemous author be punished and that the Minister of Culture resign. The police responded with tear gas, baton charges, and rubber bullets, injuring and arresting scores of protesters.[24]

In another case, pursuant to a 1983 *fatwa* issued by Cairo's al-Azhar University outlawing the representation of prophets in any artistic work, the Egyptian courts listened to the plaintiff, 'a God-fearing Egyptian Muslim citizen', and in December 1994 ordered the security services to seize all copies of the film *The Emigrant* by Youssef Chahine and banned its export.[25]

Accusations of apostasy in Egypt – which until recently was a haven for intellectuals, cultural activities and Islamic scholars – appear to have created a climate of fear for its intellectuals, literary figures and liberal Islamic scholars. Censorship of books, films, plays and television programmes by the official religious establishment is on the rise, leading to a gradual stagnation of creative, intellectual and cultural work.[26] Many blame the decline of the production of books and other cultural artefacts such as films and plays on the emergence and strengthening of the official religious establishment and on its expanding role in censorship.[27] It is reported that after the Court of Cassation of Egypt upheld in 1996 the verdict of the Court of Appeals that Abu Zayd's writings proved him to be an apostate, some eighty lawsuits were filed in the next two years against intellectuals, artists, academics and journalists, which many Islamists won. This led inter alia to the banning of a series of films and books.[28]

Journalists

The targeting of journalists and intellectuals in Algeria by extremists in the 1990s is another example of the use of laws on apostasy to remove opposition. Because of their influence through their writings and speeches against the Islamist movement, these journalists and intellectuals have been depicted as apostates who should be eliminated. Lazhari Labter cites the following *fatwa* issued by the AIS (*L'Armee Islamique Du Salut* or the Islamic Salvation Front Army), the military wing of the Islamic Salvation Front (known as FIS) in October 1994. That *fatwa* decreed the death penalty for 22 Algerian journalists and writers. Of the 22 condemned as apostates, two journalists, Said Mekbel, editor-in-chief of the daily *Le Matin*, and Zine-Eddine Aliou-Salah, from the daily paper *Liberte*, had already been killed when Labter's book *Journalistes Algeriens*[29] was published in 1995. The text of the *fatwa* reads:

> God has said: 'The wrongdoers will soon find out which [horrible] end awaits them.'

The squadrons of the Islamic Salvation Front Army have on many occasions warned against the manoeuvres of this tyrant apostate and his depraved collaborationist press. They have given them more than one opportunity to repent but this proved useless with a people who do not understand and are bent on continuing their war against the religion of God and the *mujahidin* (the fighters for the faith) who chose to uphold the emblem of *jihad* for the sake of God in this blessed land.

What proves the hate of this apostate and collaborationist press vis-à-vis the Muslims is that which has been written recently by the Communist oriented newspaper *Liberte* regarding the factional divisions between the *mujahidin* and the leaders of the Islamic Salvation Front, with the intent of causing discord and confrontation between the Muslims.

As the apostate and collaborationist press has not ceased its war against Muslims, the *mujahidin* (the fighters for the faith) have established a list of journalists condemned to death in order to purify this country from their relentless venom. Below, are the names of the twenty two journalists and writers.[30]

A *fatwa* like this serves as a stern warning to journalists not to engage in a media war against extremists.

Political Authorities

Accusations of apostasy can also be used against powerful political opponents; a number of Muslim rulers have been accused of apostasy in the modern period. These include Mustafa Kemal Atatürk, who abolished the caliphate (*khilafah*), secularized Turkey, abolished the *shari'ah* law and established equality for men and women in Turkish law; Habib Bourgiba (d.2000), the first President of Tunisia, for his alleged views on the Qur'an and other religious institutions; Muammar al-Gaddafi of Libya for his views expressed in the *Green Book*; Anwar al-Sadat (d.1981), the late Egyptian President, assassinated for concluding a peace treaty with Israel; and Benazir Bhutto, the former Prime Minister of Pakistan, for apparently criticizing her country's blasphemy law.[31]

Many extremists consider a number of rulers in the Muslim world today to be apostates because, in their view, these rulers do not implement Islamic law and do not observe the Islamic commandments and prohibitions in their personal lives. Accusations of apostasy are therefore used to delegitimize rulers and their rule in the eyes of the community and can be a real threat to a ruler's life, a case-in-point being the assassination of Sadat of Egypt.

Conclusion

As indicated in this chapter through these examples, accusations of apostasy can be used by anyone – religious leaders, theologians, politicians, extremists and even ordinary citizens – to get at one's opponents. Mere accusation can lead to the endangering of a person's life. The accused is often subject to harassment, intimidation and violence and even banishment from their community, without any redress. Given the potential for injustice and wrongful accusation and destruction of life, it is important for Muslim scholars today to take a close look at the notion of apostasy and think through ways and means of limiting its potential for such misuse.

Chapter 8

Reasons for Apostasy and Understanding its Fear among Muslims

The debate on apostasy and its punishment is also linked today to a wider debate on the activities of Christian missionaries in the Muslim world and the challenge this poses to Muslims. Both Islam and Christianity are missionary religions; of all the major religious traditions, they are the most 'evangelical'. Consequently, they compete with each other for adherents.

The historical relationship between Islam and Christianity in the seventh and eighth centuries CE was one of outright competition. Islam spread with extraordinary rapidity, reaching Alexandria in Egypt by 22/642, spreading across to Europe as far as France by 114/732 and, on the eastern flank, occupying Persia in 23/643 and Sind (now in Pakistan) by 94/712. Islamic power continued virtually unabated until the sixteenth century. However, from the eighteenth century onwards, European Christian powers systematically brought much of the Islamic world under their control and colonized it. Since then, Muslims have been on the defensive. Christianity gained access to Muslim lands, converting many Muslims, particularly in Southeast Asia and parts of Africa. Much of the Muslim propagation of Islam (*da'wah*) in the twentieth century, in places such as Indonesia, was in response to the continuing fear of Christianization of hitherto Muslim lands. In the heartland of Islam in the Middle East, North Africa and South Asia Christianity had not had spectacular success in converting Muslims. However, the success of Westernization leading to secularization among many Muslims there is seen by many Muslims as an indirect 'Christianization' of their societies. To arrest this trend, a number of Muslims today argue that Muslims need to revive the punishment for apostasy as a deterrent for would-be converts. While the laws of apostasy can apply to any conversion from Islam, the debate seems to be fiercer with regard to conversion to Christianity, perhaps because conversions from Islam have been largely to Christianity rather than to other religions such as Judaism, Hinduism or Buddhism. More importantly, Christianity is seen to be in direct competition with Islam at a global level and it alone evokes images of defeat for Muslims from the crusades, Spain, colonialism and the abolition of Caliphate. Thus the ghost of Christianity lurks behind the Muslim debates on Islam and the West, Westernization, secularization and even the debate on apostasy.

Reasons for Apostasy

Despite the dearth of research on the issue of conversion from Islam to other religions, it appears that Muslims are converting. The success of missionary activities in Indonesia is a good example, where Muslims in significant numbers have converted to Christianity. Similarly, there are reports of Muslim conversion to Christianity in parts of Africa, the Indian subcontinent and the Middle East, as well as among Muslim minorities in countries with a Christian majority. Nonetheless, it seems that conversion from Islam is a taboo subject for many Muslims, even among those who live in Western countries. The reasons why a Muslim might convert to another religion such as Christianity are not a matter generally discussed; many Muslims seem to find this topic a difficult one. For Muslims, Islam is the self-evidently true and ultimate religion and they assume that it would be highly improbable for a Muslim to turn away from this self-evidently true religion to another such as Christianity which, for many Muslims, is a 'corrupted' and 'distorted' religion based largely on myths and legends. If a person converts from Islam, the argument goes, they must be insane. To the average Muslim, the truth and validity of Islam and the falsity of all other religions must be apparent to anyone (Muslim or non-Muslim). Frithjof Schuon, a Western convert to a mystical variety of Islam, explains the average Muslim's mindset:

> The intellectual – and thereby the rational – foundation of Islam results in the average Muslim having a curious tendency to believe that non-Muslims either know that Islam is the truth and reject it out of pure obstinacy, or else are simply ignorant of it and can be converted by elementary explanations; that anyone should be able to oppose Islam with a good conscience quite exceeds the Muslims' power of imagination, precisely because Islam coincides in his mind with the irresistible logic of things.[1]

Missionary Activities

Muslims generally view conversion to other religions as a matter of inducement or of subtle pressure by well-resourced missionaries who come to poor communities and induce Muslims to abandon Islam. The linking of missionary outreach with provision of the basic necessities of life such as food, clothing, health care and education, impacts profoundly on a poverty-stricken Muslim. Humanitarianism can become confused with religious truth and thus conversion becomes a relatively easy matter. Missionary activity is not only limited to Muslim-majority lands; it also occurs in countries where Muslims are a minority, as in Western countries. There too, significant numbers of Muslims may find themselves at the bottom of the socio-economic ladder and therefore vulnerable.

Material support given by missionaries can be sufficient inducement for some such people to change religion. It is these material benefits, many Muslims argue, that force nominal Muslims to convert to Christianity from a need to survive, not from a conviction that Christianity is superior to Islam.

Westernization

It is generally acknowledged that many Muslims are impressed by the superior strength of the West and what it represents in terms of scientific achievements, military and economic might, and consumerism. Many Muslims have come under the influence of what is referred to as 'Westoxication',[2] a phrase used to indicate a general neglect of Islam as a guiding force in one's life, the adoption of Western ways of doing things, from clothing to eating, and the attraction of a materialistic lifestyle. The Iranian thinker, ʿAbdolkarim Soroush comments on the reception of Western culture in Islamic nations such as Iran:

> In this encounter [between Islam and the West], we had nothing left in the storehouse of our religious and native cultures save a few dried up formalities, habits, and conventions. Inattentiveness, poverty, hunger, ignorance, and tyranny reigned. If we had a few thinkers among us, they were too few and insignificant to swell a countertide. Thus, when the current of well-groomed ideas of the French Revolution, outfitted with the weapons of science and technology, entered this country [Iran], they found no hindrance or resistance and proceeded to enchant and mesmerize us all.[3]

In the process, Islam is relegated to a low priority, and has hardly any influence on such a person's lifestyle. This Westernization, so it is believed, explicitly or implicitly facilitates conversion and thus apostasy.

Marriage or Change of Personal Status

Conversion from Islam also occurs as a result of a relationship with someone of the opposite sex and to facilitate marriage, in both Muslim majority and Muslim minority contexts. In nations that implement Islamic law in the area of personal law, one reason for conversion is to change one's personal legal status.[4] Conversion enables parties to accomplish objectives impossible to achieve under their original legal status. For example, a Roman Catholic woman married to a Roman Catholic man would be barred from divorcing, but if she wanted a divorce she could sever her marital tie by converting to Islam.[5] Similarly, a Muslim wife in an intolerable marriage may convert to move out of that relationship if her husband refuses to divorce her.[6] Cases of such conversions exist in India, for example, where apostasy is not punished and, at the same time, Muslim personal law exists for Muslims. Indian courts have had to deal with several such cases, and it is not always clear which personal law applies if a spouse converts to or from Islam. In some cases the court has held the view that, where one spouse converts, say to Islam, and the other remains in their original religion, for example Hinduism, the case has to be decided according to 'justice, equity and good conscience'.[7] In order to close this loophole, several Muslim states such as Kuwait have ruled that conversion from Islam by a wife is not a basis for annulment of the marriage,[8] while in other states conversion from Islam by either spouse can be the basis for annulment.

Limitations on the Scope of Choices

One of the reasons for rejecting Islam, particularly in the West, it is believed, is the lack of appropriate religious guidance to youth. For many young people, particularly those living in the West or in societies heavily influenced by the West, Islam as it is presented by ultra-conservative religious leaders may appear to belong to a different era, unrelated to the modern world, and irrelevant to their needs. These religious leaders sometimes alienate the younger generation also by rejecting certain aspects of modern life as un-Islamic, immoral and akin to unbelief (*kufr*).

Reinforcing this alienation of youth is the increasing tendency on the part of *some* religious leaders to increase the scope of what is considered prohibited, by declaring *haram* what they consider to be 'unsuitable' for a Muslim. This is despite the fact that many of the activities or customs they consider to be forbidden may not have clearly formulated Qur'anic or *sunnah* prohibitions against them. Music is a good example. The wholesale ban on music by some ultra-conservative Muslims has no clear basis either in the Qur'an or *sunnah*.

The scope of *haram* has become so wide that even many practising Muslims find it almost impossible to function today while remaining faithful to the religion as defined by some ultra-conservative religious leaders. The problem has been exacerbated by the increasing power of these leaders across the globe in the last decades of the twentieth century. At times, these leaders prohibit what the *shariʿah* in fact leaves open and limit the freedom that the Qur'an and *sunnah* give to Muslims. Similarly they endeavour to prevent the rethinking of outmoded customs, ideas and institutions that appear to be largely cultural. Declarations that such attempts are tantamount to apostasy or heresy serve to diminish respect for religion as a vital force, and may lead some to conclude that what the traditional religious establishment represents as Islam does not have much relevance in the modern period. Some Muslims therefore opt out of Islam altogether and join other religions which may appear to meet their needs, while others remain nominal Muslims only. This phenomenon of growing numbers of 'cultural Muslims' or 'nominal Muslims' is today widespread among all Muslim communities.

State Misuse of Religion

In addition to the attitudes of the ultra-conservative religious leaders, the misuse of Islam by political authorities in the Muslim world to suit their own political agendas plays a significant role in driving some Muslims away from Islam. In states where Islam is the official religion, the state often supports a particular brand of Islam, stripping it of all that the state considers to be inconsistent with its ideological orientation and attempting to project its brand of Islam through channels such as religious education, mosque appointments and the mass media. For example, the state in most Muslim societies, from Turkey to Malaysia, controls religious education. It also appoints *imams* in mosques, often regulates what the *imams* can or cannot say in their sermons, and generally controls religious activity so that it conforms to the state ideology and its religious orientation. The Islam that is presented can often be devoid of spirit, with a sole focus on particular rituals that are unrelated to the spiritual needs and life of the individual or of the community. Religion then becomes a matter of state-sanctioned symbolism, rituals and ideology, resulting in the silencing of many religious leaders and activists. Other forces, such as atheism, materialism or hedonism fill the space left by religion.

Increasing Contact with Other Traditions

Another reason for conversion is that people are increasingly coming into contact with others from around the world and with other religions, traditions and modes of thought. In the twentieth century, Marxism, socialism and nationalism made great inroads into the Islamic body politic. Muslims came to be attracted to these competing ideologies and were often guided by them at the expense of a religious commitment to Islam. At the same time, religions other than Islam, such as Christianity, made inroads into Muslim communities. More importantly, atheism represented an option for Muslims uncomfortable with Islam as a religion. The competitors in the marketplace of ideas, including religious ideas, benefited significantly from the lack of in-depth awareness of Islam on the part of many nominal Muslims.

Influence of the Discourse on Human Rights

One issue that is often ignored in this context is the development of a powerful discourse on human rights during the modern period. Attempts are being made by human rights organizations and activists throughout the world to accord the average person a basic form of dignity previously available only in a limited fashion. When it emerged in the early seventh century, Islam recognized a number of basic human rights, representing a significant improvement on the existing norms in Arabia at the time. By the twenty-first century, various new rights have come to be recognized; yet some Muslims (including some *ulama*) from a more conservative background, have not yet come to terms with this reality. They are still arguing on the basis of the rights Islam recognized in the seventh century, assuming that nothing much has changed in this area over the past fourteen hundred years. Often when the issue of human rights is raised with such Muslims, the response is 'Islam gave these rights fourteen hundred years ago. Muslims do not need "Western" human rights schemes'.

Such a position does not take into account the extent to which human rights concerns have penetrated the Muslim world. Human rights discourse has become the discourse of both Muslims and non-Muslims; it is not merely a Western phenomenon. The human rights that Muslims are arguing for are, generally speaking, consistent with those specified in the Universal Declaration of Human Rights and other major human rights conventions, including those relating to women, children and religious minorities. Furthermore, arguments by Muslims against human rights often lead those who strongly believe in such rights but have little knowledge of their religion to question the relevance of Islam in a period when human dignity has become an important concern for many, including Muslims. This is particularly true in the debate among Muslims on women's rights, which more conservative Muslims find difficult to accept. Such rejection of the contemporary debate on women's rights is unlikely to deter many Muslim women from arguing for such rights. The stronger the rejection the more determined these women are likely to become.

Conversion Confessions: Examples

On the basis of conversion 'confessions' by Muslims, it is possible to cite a number of other personal reasons for conversion. Because of the problematic nature of apostasy and its possible punishment, converts from Islam are highly cautious, particularly if they are living in Muslim communities. In order to explore possible reasons for conversion, it is therefore essential to find sources where converts can discuss their case freely without revealing their identity. For this reason, a number of Internet sites were chosen for discussion in this chapter, and a number of letters, comments and views on the subject were found. The website of the Institute for the Secularization of Islamic Society (ISIS) contains an extensive range of comments, some of which appear to be genuine. However, it must be said that the anonymous nature of the comments may attract anti-Muslim propaganda and therefore should be viewed with some caution. The following observations are based largely on 'conversion confessions' on this website.

In this context, even issues such as the 'head cover' (*hijab*), polygamy, and the relationships between the sexes can provoke some Muslims to rebel against Islam. For one Samia, apparently a convert from Islam to Christianity, the 'proof' of the difference between Islam and Christianity was 'the mixing and relationship between the sexes, the former [Islam] forbidding it, and the latter [Christianity] allowing it'.[9] Another convert comments:

> And why is it that a woman is lower than a man? Is my mother lower than me? Why is it that a Muslim can have 4 wives? Can a woman not have 4 husbands then?[10]

A third convert says:

> I never understood how covering added anything positive to prayer. I still don't (the 'out of respect for God' explanation just doesn't cut it) and that is one of the many reasons, big and small, for my gradual disbelief in Islam.[11]

One reason for conversion given by some is the alleged 'violent' nature of Islamic teachings in the Qur'an, *hadith* and Muslim history. One convert alleges that the Qur'an encourages violence against non-Muslims, calling for death for those who do not come to the fold of Islam:

> I could no more accept the brutal treatment of those who chose not to accept Islam. Faith is a personal matter. I could no more accept that the punishment of someone who criticizes any religion must be death.[12]

Another reason given in these 'confessions' is increasing familiarity with Western humanistic values and reading of the foundation texts of Islam in the light of those values. One convert says:

> I suppose it was my acquaintance with the western humanistic values that made me more sensitive and wet [*sic*] my appetite for democracy, free thinking, human rights, equality, etc. It was then that when I read again the Qur'an I came across injunctions that were not at par with my newfound humanistic values.[13]

The oft-repeated view among a number of Muslims that all people except Muslims are unbelievers and therefore will end up in Hell appears to be one justification given by some converts for their conversion:

After living many years in the West and being received kindly by people of other religions or of no religion, who loved me and accepted me as their friend; who let me into their lives and their heart I could no [longer] accept the following mandates of [the] Qur'an [58:22; 3:118–120; 5:51].[14]

One Bilal Khan, born into a Muslim family in the United States, gives the reason why he became a non-Muslim as follows:

What was the cause of my disbelief, you may ask? Mainly, this: the idea that inhumane people can go to heaven merely by saying *'La ilaha illa Allah'* while kind-hearted peace-loving individuals are eternally condemned just because they believe what makes sense to them.[15]

Some converts criticize the Qur'an or the character of the Prophet and justify their conversion by what they consider to be 'faults' in both. One convert refers to his or her conversion as follows:

My reason for leaving Islam is very simple. I simply read the Qur'an. For me it was as easy as just reading the Qur'an and using a little reason, logic, and thinking.[16]

The reasons given by these converts would, from a committed Muslim's point of view, be the result of a lack of understanding of the true nature of Islam, its foundation texts and its history. Nonetheless, however superficial or misguided these reasons may seem, they represent a challenge to Muslim religious leaders in their efforts at conveying to these sceptical Muslims what Islam truly is and what it represents to people today.

Understanding the Fear of Apostasy

The Muslim experience of modern history is closely connected to Western colonization of Muslim lands in the nineteenth and twentieth centuries. For many Muslims a close relationship exists between colonialism, Christian missionary activities among Muslims, conversion and apostasy. Colonial administrations, where they existed, were seen to be often hostile to Islam, and intent on eliminating Islam's influence in society, and their perceived support of Christian missionary activity in largely Muslim lands was considered an affront to Islam. With the success of the missionaries in places such as Indonesia and parts of Africa, Muslims were leaving their religion and embracing Christianity, the religion of the colonial power. The fear was, and still is, that increasingly aggressive Christian missionaries, supported by a once-colonizing West, want nothing less than Christianization of large parts of the Muslim world. Where direct Christianization failed, Westernization and secularization (linked again indirectly to Christianity and the West) are believed to be intent on achieving it. The fear of conversion (explicit or implicit) and apostasy is thus related largely to this set of issues.

One of the key strategies adopted by many Muslims in the modern period has been to prevent Muslims from being absorbed into the sphere of influence of the West, the former colonial powers, as well as Christian missionaries. Much of the *da'wah* by Muslims in the twentieth century, be it in Indonesia or parts of Africa, is often driven by such concerns. A number of Muslim thinkers like Maududi and Qutb attempted to address the issue by focusing on the negative aspects of Western civilization, portraying it as a morally bankrupt civilization on the verge of collapse, and therefore Muslims should not be too impressed by its superficial attractions.

An example that illustrates how Muslims during the colonial period attempted to keep this distance between the colonial power and themselves is the debate on the status of Muslims who sought the citizenship of the colonial power. In the nineteenth and early twentieth centuries, several Muslims, in search of a better life and overwhelmed by the economic, political and intellectual dominance of the colonists, sought French citizenship, for example. This was the case in North Africa where the French, who were keen to integrate their colonial holdings, encouraged the idea of French citizenship, especially among the elite. If a Muslim married a non-Muslim French citizen and wanted to move to France, French citizenship was particularly attractive. However, there were other reasons, including the prospect of affluence, a good education and employment in France or in the indigenous land.

A number of Muslim intellectuals, particularly those who were active in the struggle for independence, argued that taking up citizenship of the colonial power was equivalent to apostasy. Since the issue of citizenship was perceived as linked to religious identity, any attempt to move away from the Muslim community by taking up foreign citizenship was tantamount to 'leaving' Islam. In this context, Algeria provides an interesting case.[17] Ali Merad has shown that the Islamic reformists (of *Islahi* or *Salafi* orientation) tended to interpret change of citizenship, popular amongst the French-educated class, in two significant ways. They saw it as either the abandonment of one's personal status (Islamic), making one no longer accountable to *shari'ah* law, or as an act of desertion of one's nation. Two Muslim reformist newspapers in North Africa famously denounced the taking of French citizenship. In 1930, T.A. Madani, in the *Shihab* paper said:

> We are now at a very critical point in our history. Today, two ways are open before us . . . one of these two ways is that of 'naturalization'. That is to say, the way leading to abandonment of one's nationality and language, the rejection of one's history and [Islamic] tradition . . .[18]

In another case, also in 1930, after a majority vote, the Muslim Student Union of North Africa in Paris rejected admission of all naturalized students as members. According to Merad this decision was based on a *fatwa*, which had appeared in the *Shihab*. The *fatwa* says:

> ... we understand that those who renounce the Islamic law could not be considered Muslim, given that Islam is not only a faith but also a religion and personal status at the same time. Hence, although the naturalized person [claims to] maintain his faith, he nonetheless, rejects our personal status when he takes the initiative [of taking that citizenship].[19]

Merad states that, in their campaign against naturalization, 'the reformist leaders had explicitly ex-communicated their coreligionists who had taken up French citizenship'.[20] He then quotes the Algerian Islamic leader, Shaykh Abdelhamid b. Badis (d.1940), according to whom 'those who renounce the Islamic law are necessarily (*daruriyyan*) apostates'.[21] Finally Merad refers to the *fatwa* of Shaykh Tahir b. 'Ashur of Tunisia, who affirmed that 'the naturalized [citizens] are apostates who can come back to Islam after they repent. The naturalized person may be considered a Muslim only after they repent and pronounce the Islamic confession of faith ("There is no god but Allah and Muhammad is the messenger of Allah") before a Muslim judge (*qadi*)'.[22] The debate here centred on an equation between citizenship and religion, doubtless facilitated by classical binary notions of *dar al-islam* (abode of Islam) and *dar al-kufr* (abode of unbelief). This position was an effective deterrent to those who wanted to 'leave' their community. What is to be noted here is that these Muslims who took up French citizenship did not necessarily give up their faith (Islam), nor did they openly reject Islamic law. Despite this, the *fatwas* equated them with apostates.

Fighting Apostasy as a Matter of Honour

Given the emphasis the Qur'an places on the salvation of the individual, it would be reasonable to expect that concern with apostasy in Islamic law should have been mainly, if not exclusively, a concern for the individual's fate in relation to salvation. From a Muslim point of view, by converting to a religion other than Islam, the individual is believed to be practically leaving the path of salvation for the path of eternal damnation, and therefore all attempts should be made to bring that person back to the fold of Islam. However, this concern for the individual's salvation does not seem to be a key focus of the debate on apostasy in Islamic law, in either its classical or modern context. If faith is, strictly speaking, a matter between the individual and God, why does apostasy cause such anxiety among Muslims and why is it seen as the ultimate betrayal of the Muslim community? The answer, in part, lies in the fear of desertion of one's 'tribe', so to speak. Being a Muslim means being part of the 'tribe' which confers certain rights. One's life depends on this affiliation to the tribe; outside this tribe there is no real existence as such. By converting, a Muslim is not only deserting a religion but also their tribe. Such a conversion is seen as bringing dishonour upon the community of Muslims, including one's immediate and extended family.[23] Like the 'honour killings' related to cases of rape or of women involved in sexual relationships outside marriage, seen in communities such as Lebanon[24] or Pakistan,[25] apostasy-related killing is also considered by some as a form of 'honour killing'.

In the minds of many Muslims, there is competition between Islam and other religions, in particular Christianity, for numbers. Christianity is seen to be the religion supported by the Western (read: Christian) powers. It is also seen by many Muslims as a religion that is inferior to Islam. For them, Christianity for a long time was on the defensive politically but is now not only challenging but also dominating the market for religion through its substantial financial, organizational and political power backed by the richest countries of the world such as the United States. Leaving Islam, particularly for Christianity, the main competitor, brings back melancholy memories of the golden era of dominant Islam, which was followed by the horrors of the Crusades; the expulsion of Muslims from the Iberian Peninsula; the defeat of the Muslims at the hands of European colonial powers; the colonial period; the collaboration of Muslims with the colonizers; the massive proselytizing efforts of the missionaries; the secularization and Westernization of Muslim societies; and finally orientalism, with its perceived attacks on Islamic culture and heritage. Desertion of Islam therefore means dishonour and disgrace to the community. If salvation of the individual is an issue, it is in practice seen to be a secondary issue.

PART II

PART II

Chapter 9

Religious Freedom in Malaysia: Overview and Restrictions

Malaysia is a federation with a constitutional monarchy. In 1957 the Federation of Malaya, as it was then called, obtained independence from the United Kingdom. Initial parties to the federation were Perlis, Kedah, Penang, Perak, Selangor, Malacca, Johor, Negeri Sembilan, Pahang, Trengganu and Kelantan. In 1963 the Federation of Malaysia replaced the Federation of Malaya with the inclusion of three additional states – Sabah, Sarawak and Singapore. Singapore left the federation in 1965 to become an independent state. In addition to the thirteen remaining states, the federation includes the Federal Territories of Kuala Lumpur, Putrajaya and Lebuan.

Nine of the thirteen states have hereditary rulers, while the remaining four – Penang, Malacca, Sabah and Sarawak – have governors.[1] The nine rulers and the four governors constitute the Conference of Rulers[2] which inter alia elects the king as the head of the federation for a five-year term[3] and may agree or disagree to the extension of any religious acts, observances or ceremonies to the federation as a whole.[4] The king acts as the head of the religion of Islam in the Federal Territories as well as in the four states without any hereditary ruler, while state rulers act as the head of Islam in their respective states.

The Federal Constitution is the supreme law of the nation.[5] It divides legislative powers of the federation between Parliament and state legislatures. Islam and Islamic law fall under state jurisdiction.[6] Prior to British intervention in the region, Islamic law (as modified by Malay custom) was applied as the law of the land.[7] However, through a series of treaties beginning with the Pangkor Treaty in 1874 and exertion of direct and indirect influence, the British were able to reduce Islamic law to Muslim Personal Law applying to Muslims only.[8] It was in this limited sense that the framers of the Constitution and the fathers of independence understood the role of Islam. It is in this context that Article 3(1) of the Constitution declares Islam the 'official religion' of the federation. Islam as the official religion does not mean that Malaysia is an Islamic state. It also does not mean that the courts, by relying on Article 3, can declare laws that are contrary to Islam or Islamic tenets to be unconstitutional.[9] Professor Lionel Astor Sheridan, an expert on constitutional law in Malaysia, believes that the notion 'Islam as the religion of the federation' means that official ceremonies at federal level are to be regulated in accordance with the religion of Islam.[10]

Initially there was strong opposition to the adoption of Islam as the state religion even in the limited sense of Muslim Personal Law applying to Muslims only. The primary objection came from rulers who were afraid that it could require them to give up their position as the head of the religion of Islam in their respective states. The Constitutional Commission summed up their objection in the following words:

> [I]t is Their Highnesses' considered view that it would not be desirable to insert some declaration such as has been suggested that the Muslim Faith or Islamic Faith be the established religion of the federation. Their Highnesses are not in favour of such a declaration being inserted.[11]

Opposition also came from the large non-Malay and non-Muslim migrant worker populations mainly from China, India and Sri Lanka. On the eve of independence these people formed nearly half the population in Malaya and controlled a significant percentage of the national economy. For their part, ethnic Malays strenuously objected attempts by the colonial government to grant citizenship rights to these migrants.

Despite this opposition, Islam was adopted in the 1957 Federal Constitution as the official religion of the federation. The rulers were assured that their status as the head of Islam in their respective states would continue. As further assurance, no head of the religion for the entire federation was appointed, although the Constitution allows the king to represent various rulers at the federal level in respect of matters to which the Conference of Rulers had agreed.[12] As a compromise with the non-Muslim 'migrants', Malays agreed to grant them citizenship, as well as religious freedom. In return, the migrants agreed to give up their opposition to Islam as the official religion of the federation.

Islam and Malay Identity

Malays were converted to Islam around the thirteenth century through propagation by *sufi* missionaries, interaction with Arab and Persian traders and en masse, following the conversion of one of their kings.[13] Since then Malays have shown great reluctance to change their religion, despite attempts by Christian missionaries during the colonial period. Islam has become so much a part of the Malay identity that Article 160(2) of the Constitution defines 'Malay' as one who habitually speaks the Malay language, practises Malay custom and professes the religion of Islam. Some of these essential distinctions are fast disappearing. For instance, observance of traditional 'custom' is not only difficult to determine among the general populace, but is probably not adhered to by many Western-educated Malay elites. Linguistic barriers between various races have been dismantled with the introduction of Malay as the sole official language.[14] This leaves Islam as 'the last remaining bastion of Malayness'.[15] Commenting on the constitutional definition of Malay, Mohamed Suffian, the former Lord President (then the highest judicial officer in the country) noted that even a genuine Malay is not a Malay for the purpose of the Constitution if, for instance, he does not profess the Muslim religion.[16] Defining 'Malay' in terms of Islam would mean that Malays who renounce Islam could not be regarded as Malays. On the other hand non-Malay citizens who habitually speak the Malay language, practise Malay custom and profess the religion of Islam satisfy the constitutional definition of Malay. In this sense the constitutional definition of Malay considerably relaxes ethnic boundaries within Malaysia by allowing non-Malay Muslim citizens to identify themselves as Malays.

A more comprehensive attempt to identify Malays and Malay culture with Islam was made in 1971 when the National Cultural Congress was convened by the federal government and held at the University of Malaya, Kuala Lumpur. The Congress sought to establish a common national culture within the multicultural and multiracial Malaysian society. The policy that emerged, known as the National Cultural Policy (NCP) was based on three principles, namely that national culture must be based on the culture indigenous to the region; the features of other cultures must be suited to the national culture before they can become part of the national culture; and that Islam should be an important feature of the national culture. There was strong opposition from the non-Malay and non-Muslim population, including objections by the Malaysian Chinese Association (MCA) and the Malaysian Indian Congress (MIC), partner with United Malay National Organization (UMNO) in the ruling coalition. Nonetheless the UMNO-led federal government endorsed the policy.[17] As a result of the NCP, Islam is now more closely identified with Malays and Malay culture.

Religious Freedom in Malaysia: Overview

Article 3 of the Constitution, although declaring Islam the religion of the federation, allows the peaceful and harmonious practice of other religions in any part of it. Religious freedom is further strengthened by Article 11, which gives every person the right to profess and practise their religion. It also protects individuals from paying any tax that is imposed, in whole or in part, for the purposes of a religion other than their own. It guarantees every religious group the right to manage its own religious affairs. It also allows groups to establish and maintain institutions for religious or charitable purposes, and to acquire, hold and administer property.

Article 12 consolidates religious freedom further by prohibiting discrimination, on the grounds of religion, race, descent or place of birth, in education or in financial aid.[18] It also gives every religious group the right to establish and maintain institutions for the education of children in its own religion without discrimination on the grounds of religion.[19] It further prohibits mandatory religious instruction or compulsory participation in any religious ceremony or act of worship other than that of a person's own religion.[20] The Article also empowers parents or guardians of a person under the age of 18 to decide that child's religion.[21] Article 8(2) protects citizens against discrimination on the basis of religion.

The framers of the Constitution and the fathers of independence regarded religious freedom as so fundamental as to warrant protection even during a state of emergency, when the legislative powers of the federation are transferred to the executive and legislation contrary to the Constitution can be enacted.[22] Thus if emergency laws violated constitutional provisions on religious freedom then such laws would be invalid.[23]

Further, religious freedom extends to *every person*. This means that, unlike other fundamental rights such as protection against banishment,[24] freedom of speech, assembly and association,[25] and rights in respect of education,[26] religious freedom is not limited to citizens only. The phrase 'every person' is broad enough to include Muslims and non-Muslims, citizens or residents: indeed anyone found within the borders of the country.

Restrictions on Religious Freedom

Despite these constitutional guarantees, freedom of religion in Malaysia is, in fact, subject to a host of restrictions. These include standard restrictions emanating from general laws relating to public order, public health and morality.[27] Even a casual glance at the Constitution reveals that, in Malaysia, it is the restrictions and not the rights that predominate. Religious freedom is no exception.

Restrictions on non-Muslims

The most significant restrictions from a non-Muslim point of view are those directed at the propagation and dissemination of other religions among Muslims. The Constitution allows state legislatures and, in respect of the Federal Territories, the Parliament to restrict the propagation of any religious doctrine or belief among persons professing the religion of Islam within that particular jurisdiction.[28] Pursuant to this provision, all the state governments as well as the federal government have enacted laws prohibiting the propagation of non-Muslim doctrines among Muslims.[29] These laws make it an offence to persuade, influence or incite a Muslim to be a follower or a member of another religion,[30] to subject a Muslim under the age of 18 to the influence of a non-Islamic religion,[31] and to send or deliver publications concerning non-Islamic religions to a Muslim,[32] especially in a public place.[33]

State laws also forbid non-Muslims to use certain Arabic or Islamic words and phrases in any publication or in a speech addressed to organized gatherings and which at the time of its making the person knew or should have known that it would be published or broadcast.[34] The 1981 Kelantan Enactment on Control and Restriction of the Propagation of Non-Islamic Religions bans the following:

Banned words are:
Allah; firman Allah; ulama; hadith; 'ibadah; ka'bah; kadi; ilahi; wahyu; mubaligh; syariah; qiblah; hajj; mufti; rasul; iman; da'wah; salat; khalifah; wali; fatwa; imam; nabi; sheikh

Banned phrases are:
subhanallah; alhamdulillah; lailahaillahllah; walillahilhamd; allahu akbar; insyaallah; astaghfirullahal azim; tabarak Allah; masyaallah; lahaula wala-quata illabillahi

Identical restrictions are found in several other state laws.[35]

Most of these words and phrases have specific meanings in Islam. The authorities probably fear that the use of these and other similar words and phrases in association with other religions could lead to confusion among Muslims. It was for this reason the Malaysian government banned the Indonesian translation of the Bible, called *Al-Kitab*. *Al-Kitab* itself is one of the names of the Qur'an. In addition to that, the translation also contained words such as *Allah* and *iman*, which authorities believed, could confuse Muslims. The ban was eventually lifted when the government allowed distribution through specially approved locations such as churches and bookshops that dealt exclusively with Christians.[36] However not all the banned words and phrases are uniquely Islamic. For instance, it is arguable whether the term *sheikh* listed in the Kelantan Enactment has any significant religious origin that should prohibit its use.

Banning these words and phrases has constitutional ramifications too. For instance, although most of these words are of Arabic origin and have specific religious meanings in Islam, they are now part of the Malay language itself. Under Article 152 of the Constitution, Malay is the national language. Therefore it could be argued that by banning these words the government is preventing citizens from using certain words that are part of the lexicon of the national language.

Restrictions on Muslims

It is not only non-Muslims in the country whose religious freedom is curtailed. Muslims too are subjected to a host of restrictions. In fact, Muslims are prosecuted and persecuted more often than their non-Muslim counterparts because of particular beliefs they hold or decline to hold. Some of the laws prohibiting propagation of false doctrines among Muslims are applicable to both Muslims and non-Muslims.[37] State laws not only prohibit the propagation of non-Islamic religions among Muslims but also prohibit the propagation of Islam among Muslims without permission.[38] Violation of these laws could result in a prison sentence or a fine.

The objectives of these restrictions appear to be threefold: first, to prevent the spread of religions other than Islam; second, to ensure the government's hegemony over religion and religious institutions; and third, to maintain the purity of the government-sanctioned version of Islam, which is a version of Sunni Islam. In 1997, the federal government proposed to amend the Constitution to make Sunni Islam the country's official branch of Islam. The proposal has since been dropped. However there are some state laws that reinforce Sunni Islam. For instance, Section 163(1) of the Kedah Administration of Muslim Law Enactment, 1962 makes it an offence to be in possession of any book or document or to give any instruction or ruling on Islamic law that is contrary to the belief of *Ahl al-Sunnah wa al-Jama'ah* (mainstream Sunni Muslims who unite around certain principles) or to the tenets of the Shafi'i, Hanafi, Maliki or Hanbali schools. Contravention of this law can lead to imprisonment for a term not exceeding six months or a fine not exceeding 1000 ringgit (RM) or both.[39] Various state laws also require *mufti*s and legal committees to consider Shafi'i tenets when issuing *fatwa*s. If such views are opposed to the public interest then reference could be made to the other three Sunni schools of law.[40]

Emphasis on Sunni Islam means non-Sunnis are a natural target for attention. In this respect Shi'is fare the worst. Followers of Shi'i teachings (who are extremely few in number and are generally Malays) are at times subjected to extra-judicial punishments in the form of arrests under the Internal Security Act, 1960 (ISA), which allows indefinite detention without trial. For instance, between October 2000 and January 2001 the federal government detained six followers of Shi'i teachings under the ISA. None of them was ever charged in a court of law. The police released one of the detainees, two were sent to restricted residence and the rest were detained for a two-year period,[41] which can be renewed indefinitely.[42] Interestingly, Shi'i teachings or views have never been declared 'deviant' by either the federal government or any of the state governments. Muslims who engage in non-Sunni teachings or practices are often labelled 'deviants', a term widely used by UMNO-led federal and state governments as well as by the Islamic Development Department (Jakim – a federal body under the Prime Minister's Department) in place of 'apostasy', *riddah* or *irtidad*.[43]

The government periodically tries to stamp out 'deviant' teachings by gazetting certain teachings as amounting to deviation and rehabilitating their followers.[44] Between 1971 and 1990 the government found that 44 groups contravened the Islamic faith in their teachings and practices. The

National Fatwa Council declared some of them to be *haram*.[45] In March 1995 the Islamic Centre in Kuala Lumpur, which was later upgraded into the Islamic Development Department (Jakim), identified 46 'deviant' Muslim groups including mystical *sufi* groups and *silat* (a form of Malay self-defence) associations,[46] and in November 1999 the Parliamentary Secretary to the Prime Minister's Department, Mohamed Abdullah, revealed that there were 51 groups active in preaching deviant teaching with more than 16 000 followers. This figure did not include over 13 000 who have been 'rehabilitated'.[47]

Occasionally state religious affairs departments ask mosque supervisors (*nazir*) to submit lists of suspected 'deviant' preachers. Their accreditation is then invalidated and they are barred from giving religious talks at mosques within that particular state. In July 1998, the Selangor Islamic Affairs Department invalidated accreditation of 20 preachers. This crackdown followed criticism of state religious officials for not acting quickly to ban the assistant *imam* of the state mosque in Selangor, Kamal Ashaari, from telling audiences that he saw a woman who renounced Islam transformed into a pig. He was later banned from giving religious talks.[48]

The distinction between deviant and non-deviant activities in Malaysia is not always clear. There are no guidelines as to what constitutes deviation and what does not. The government (often acting on the advice of various state religious councils) periodically gazettes certain activities or teachings as deviant. Its decisions on such matters, as in most other cases, are final. Aggrieved parties have no recourse to appeal, nor are they able to force the government to review its decisions or to give reasons for its decision. Most importantly, because various federal and state religious councils are under the control of their respective governments, it is relatively easy for the government of the day to obtain a declaration that a particular activity is or is not deviant. This provides the government with an opportunity to label religio-political opponents as deviants.

One such example is the *Arqam* case. In 1968 Ashaari Muhammad, a former school teacher and member of the then Pan-Malayan Islamic Party (PAS) (renamed *Parti Islam Se-Malaysia* in 1973), established *Arqam*. It was part of the *da'wah* phenomenon in Malaysia.[49] *Arqam* called for the rejection of a secular way of life in favour of an Islamic way of life. Its members believed in self-sufficiency and adherence to Islamic teachings. By the time of its ban in 1994, *Arqam* ran 48 small residential communities throughout peninsular Malaysia, in which a large number of its full-time members settled. These settlements were complete with their own schools and clinics. Its estimated 100 000 members were middle-class Malay professionals. Male members dressed in turbans and long robes while female members used loose clothes to cover their entire body. By 1994 *Arqam* had an estimated $115 million in worldwide assets.[50] As early as 1986, Ashaari, the movement's founder, announced in a book his belief in the imminent appearance of the *Mahdi*, who according to widely held Muslim belief would one day rule the world and restore religion and justice. The government immediately banned the book but took no punitive action against Ashaari or his followers.

As the movement grew stronger it began to challenge the government, in particular UMNO's right to represent Malays. It was this confrontational attitude, combined with some questionable religious beliefs and its growing popularity among Malays, that led to the arrest of its leaders and the banning of the movement.[51] Meanwhile Malaysia's then Defence Minister, Najib Tun Razak, claimed that *Arqam* leaders had a secret agenda to gain political power.[52] In 1991 the government set up a committee to investigate and take action against the movement. On 5 August 1994 the National Fatwa Council declared it unlawful and its members were told to disband. Twenty days later the Ministry of Home Affairs declared *Arqam* unlawful under the Societies Act (1966). Ashaari, who was living in Thailand at that time, was taken into custody by Thai police and handed over to their Malaysian counterparts. Following this, Ashaari and several aides were detained under the Internal Security Act. On 28 October 1994, Ashaari and six others confessed on Malaysian national television that they and their followers had deviated from Islamic teachings. They were then released without charge or trial. However their movements were restricted under the Restricted Residence Act, 1933.

A more interesting case is that of the *Nasrul Haq*, a group engaged in Malay martial arts. This was founded in 1977, under the auspices of the then Minister for Youth, Culture and Sports. Senior government officials, including the then Prime Minister Tun Abdul Razak and members of some royal families were patrons of the group. By 1978 *Nasrul Haq* had at least 300 000 members, of whom 114 000 were from Kelantan. It has been suggested that initially UMNO thought the group could be exploited to counter the growing popularity of PAS among Malay Muslims. However when it became clear that the group could not be firmly controlled, charges and harassment followed. Initially *Nasrul Haq* was accused of invoking Islam and Allah inappropriately, introducing the *sufi*-style of chanting (*dhikr*) into the self-defence sessions and of holding some sessions in mosques. Leaders were accused of using the title caliph and implying that anyone who died in the course of the practice was a religious martyr. It was condemned as sinful and deviant and banned in various states despite protest by its leaders that several other *silat* groups were engaged in similar practices.[53]

Despite such crackdowns, government and religious authorities avoid using the term 'apostasy' or similar terms to describe such people and their activities. The authorities probably feel that the use of such terms implies that the people so described are no longer Muslims. On the other hand, assumption of deviation or deviant teachings categorizes them as straying Muslims, which leaves open the possibility of rehabilitation. There is also the issue of jurisdiction (see Chapter 11). Islamic law is applicable only to

Muslims professing the religion of Islam. Therefore, once the government has declared a particular individual apostate or a particular activity equivalent to apostasy, it may no longer be able to take action against them, as they are no longer Muslims.

However, in extreme cases, government agencies are prepared to label a person an apostate. For instance, in August 1995, *mufti*s throughout the country made a joint statement that expressing an anti-*hadith* view was equivalent to becoming *murtadd* or committing an act of apostasy. This was in response to the anti-*hadith* movement of the 1980s and 1990s led by Kassim Ahmad, the former secretary general of the Malaysian Socialist Party. Ahmed wrote a book in 1986 entitled *Hadith: A Re-evaluation (Hadis Satu Penilaian Semula)* where he argued that *hadith* was not necessary because the Qur'an is complete, authoritative and transmitted directly from Allah. Further, he argued that *hadith*, being a human product, lacked revelational validity. He also claimed that *hadith* contributed to the disunity of the Muslim *ummah*, arguing that during the Umayyad rule political parties had invented *hadith* to justify their own position.[54]

Chapter 10

Apostasy Laws in Malaysia: Approaches of the Two Major Political Parties

Two major political parties – the United Malay National Organization (UMNO) and the *Parti Islam Se-Malaysia* (PAS) – represent Muslims in Malaysian politics. The two parties have different approaches towards the issue of apostasy. The largely secular UMNO-led federal and state governments propose rehabilitation and short-term detention for those who renounce Islam, while PAS, in line with its literal interpretation of Islamic law, calls for the death penalty for apostasy. Because of the dominance of the two parties in Malaysian politics it is necessary to examine apostasy laws in the light of their approaches.

PAS's Approach to Apostasy

PAS was formed in 1951 by a group of Malay religious scholars and entitled *Persatuan Islam Se-Tanah Melayu* (Pan-Malayan Islamic Party). It was later renamed *Parti Islam Se-Malaysia* (PAS) in 1973, and has presented itself as an alternative to the secularist UMNO. Until the 1999 general election PAS's electoral success was largely limited to the Malay-dominated East Coast states of Kelantan and Trengganu and, to some extent, Kedah. At various times the Party controlled the state governments in Trengganu and Kelantan. The Party's electoral success changed dramatically in the 1999 general election when it not only retained the control of Kelantan but also wrested control of Trengganu from UMNO. It won a total of 27 (out of 193) seats in the federal Parliament and 98 (out of 394) state assembly seats throughout the country. As a result it became the official Opposition in the country.

PAS's declared objective is that of establishing an Islamic state in Malaysia. An important aspect of this, it believes, is the implementation of *hudud* laws which are said to include the death penalty for apostasy. PAS believes that *hudud* laws will serve for the betterment of humankind. Being God's laws, they lack the deficiencies of man-made law. The Party also believes that the implementation of *hudud* laws will address growing crime rates and overcrowded prisons in Malaysia. Most importantly, the Party holds that those who reject *hudud* laws are apostates in that they refuse to accept the teachings of the Qur'an and the *sunnah*.[1] Interestingly, PAS

President and Chief Minister of the state of Kelantan, Nik Abdul Aziz Mat, based this ruling on a book (*Mastika Hadis*) published by the Prime Minister's Department.[2] PAS Deputy President, Abdul Hadi Awang, justified the death penalty for apostasy by equating apostasy with high treason. According to him, apostates betray Islam and their fellow Muslims by their actions. He argues that treason may carry the death penalty even in countries such as the USA and Japan.[3] PAS also believes that the death penalty for apostasy may deter Muslims and converts from renouncing Islam.

PAS has made two serious attempts to date to make apostasy punishable by death. The first was when the PAS-led government passed the Syariah Criminal Code (II) (Kelantan) Enactment, 1993, shortly after it wrested control of the state from UMNO in the 1990 general election. The second was in 1999 when the PAS Deputy President, Abdul Hadi Awang, attempted to introduce a private member's Bill in the Parliament to make apostasy punishable by death in the Federal Territories.[4] This second attempt, however, failed when the UMNO-led government used its overwhelming majority in Parliament to prevent the introduction of the Bill. Therefore discussion here will concentrate on the Kelantan Code.

Syariah Criminal Code (II) (Kelantan) Enactment, 1993

The Code is generally referred to as Kelantan *hudud* laws or simply as *hudud* laws because it incorporates *hudud* offences. It consists of six parts: *hudud*; just retaliation (*qisas*); evidence; methods of carrying out the punishments; general provision and court procedures. *Hudud* offences encompass theft; brigandage; adultery or fornication; slander; drinking liquor or intoxicating drinks; and apostasy. The punishment for these offences varies, and includes the death penalty; stoning to death; amputation of limbs; whipping; imprisonment from one year to life; fines; retribution; compensation and forfeiture of property.[5] As for apostasy, the Code prescribes the death penalty and confiscation of property if the apostate refuses to repent.

Apostasy under the Syariah Criminal Code

Section 23 of the Code deals with apostasy or *irtidad*. It defines apostasy as:

> . . . any act done or any word uttered by a Muslim who is *mukallaf*, being an act or word which according to Syariah [*shari'ah*] law, affects or which is against the *aqidah* (belief) in Islamic religion, provided that such act is done or such word is uttered intentionally, voluntarily and knowingly without any compulsion by anyone or by circumstance.[6]

Acts or words which affect the ʿ*aqidah* (belief) are those which deal with the fundamental aspects of the Islamic religion which are deemed to have been known and believed by every Muslim as part of their general knowledge about being a Muslim, such as matters pertaining to the pillars of Islam (*rukn islam*), pillars of belief (*rukn iman*) and matters of *halal* and *haram*.[7]

Anyone found guilty of apostasy is required to repent within a period of three days.[8] If the offender is reluctant to repent and remains intransigent, the Court has to pronounce the death sentence on him. Property, whether acquired before or after the commission of the offence, is forfeited to the public purse. But if the offender repents at any time before the sentence is carried out, he is freed and his property is returned. However he would still be required to serve a jail term not exceeding five years regardless of whether the repentance occurred before or after the death sentence was pronounced.[9]

Several objections have been raised against this Code in general and regarding apostasy in particular. Among the main concerns is the vague and broad nature of the definition of apostasy. Mohammad Hashim Kamali, an expert on Islamic law, believes the definition is so vague and general that it is likely to conflict with both the Qur'an and the provisions of the Constitution of Malaysia on the basic freedom of religion.[10] He argues that the Code fails to distinguish apostasy that does not involve any hostile and contemptuous attack on the fundamentals of Islam from blasphemy, which does involve such hostile and contemptuous attack. Kamali feels that the definition is so broad that it could include blasphemy, apostasy, unbelief and heresy.[11] Kamali also found expressions such as *rukn iman*, *rukn islam*, *halal* and *haram* too general and too broad.[12]

Terms like *halal* and *haram* are not always clear. For instance many Muslims consider marriage with a Christian or Jewish woman (*kitabiyyah*) – from 'People of the Book' (*ahl al-kitab*) – to be *halal* for a Muslim man. Similarly, many Muslims believe that it is *halal* for Muslims to consume animals slaughtered by someone from *ahl al-kitab*. Other Muslims, however, do not accept these actions as *halal* arguing that the real 'people of the Book' do not exist today. It could be argued, in the light of Section 23(2) of the Syariah Criminal Code, that to advocate the view that an animal slaughtered by someone from the *ahl al-kitab* of today is *halal* for Muslims, or that a Muslim man can lawfully marry a Jewish or Christian woman amounts to apostasy and, therefore, anyone found to have advocated such views should be sentenced to death. This would be contrary to specific injunctions of the Qur'an and the *sunnah* as well as inconsistent with the practices of the Prophet's Companions and prominent jurists of Islamic law throughout history. It would also mean that many Muslims, including some very eminent jurists, have committed and continue to commit apostasy by advocating these views.

As indicated, Section 23(1) of the Code defines apostasy as a word or an action by a *mukallaf*. Section 2(1) defines a *mukallaf* as a person who has attained the age of 18 and is of sound mind. This appears to be consistent with the Supreme Court decision in *Teoh Eng Huat v. Kadhi, Pasir Mas & Anor*[13] where the court held that a person below the age of 18 could not convert to another religion without the consent of a parent or guardian. If PAS genuinely believes that apostasy laws should be applied in the way they were applied in early Islam and in subsequent generations, then the age requirement appears to be at odds with the classical interpretation of the law, which adopts the age of puberty in defining a *mukallaf*. Although this is a minor point, it does show that some modern interpretations have crept into the Code.

Forfeiture of the offender's property as proposed by the code could, in some cases, lead to hardship for the offender's dependants. Confiscation of the property may have devastating consequences on these people and it could be argued that it is against the spirit of Islam. The problem would be complicated further if the offender left behind not only property but also liabilities in the form of debts, promises, commercial undertakings and so on. It is not clear whether such liabilities would be deducted before property confiscation or whether dependants or relatives would have to meet the liabilities while the property went to the public purse.

It is also not clear why a person should be imprisoned for up to five years after repentance. What is the basis for this? It appears to be too harsh a sentence. We might also ask why such punishment was not left to the discretion of the Syariah court as prescribed in Section 35 of the Code, relating to punishment for causing bodily injuries.

Even before the passage of this legislation in November 1993, the PAS leadership gave assurances that laws relating to apostasy would not be implemented until the public had been educated about them.[14] The rationale for this is unclear, given the straightforward punishment of death for apostasy,[15] particularly given that other aspects of the Code prescribe even harsher punishments such as stoning to death.[16]

One important question is: did the Kelantan legislature have the jurisdiction to prescribe the death penalty for apostasy? Interestingly, even the PAS leadership believed that the legislature did not have such jurisdiction and, without necessary amendments to the Constitution, the Code would violate the Constitution and federal laws. The reason for this was that under the Constitution the Parliament has exclusive jurisdiction in respect 'of criminal law . . . including the creation of offences in respect of any of the matters included in the Federal List or dealt with by federal law'.[17] A number of the offences under the Code such as theft, armed robbery, murder and criminal defamation were obviously offences within federal jurisdiction and dealt with by federal laws such as the Penal Code [revised 1997]. By enacting laws on federal matters, the state legislature exceeded its jurisdiction. Therefore to that extent the Code is unconstitutional.

Further, the federal Syariah Courts (Criminal Jurisdiction) Act, 1965 also limits the jurisdiction of the Syariah court to pass sentences of up to three years or a fine not exceeding RM5000 or six strokes of the whip or any combination thereof. Obviously punishments prescribed by the Code exceeded these limits.[18]

The Code also appears to be unconstitutional in so far as its application to non-Muslims is concerned. This is because Islamic law applies only to Muslims and the Syariah court has jurisdiction only over persons professing the religion of Islam.[19] The Code is unlikely to be saved by the fact that under the Code, non-Muslims have a choice whether or not to be governed by it.[20]

Because of these reasons the PAS-led Kelantan government refrained from implementing the Code. Instead it sought co-operation from UMNO to amend the Constitution. UMNO, however, refused to co-operate.

UMNO's Approach to *Hudud* Laws

The other major political party, UMNO, has been dominant in the public arena in Malaysia ever since independence. In partnership with other non-Muslim and non-Malay political parties, UMNO has dominated Malaysian politics both at federal and state levels. The UMNO leadership has never advocated an Islamic state in Malaysia. The country's first Prime Minister and the father of independence, Tungku Abdul Rahman, was sceptical about the very idea. He reportedly said that non-Muslims would be drowned if Malaysia were to become an Islamic state.[21] He made it clear that Malaysia is not an Islamic state as the concept is generally understood: 'We merely provide that Islam shall be the official religion of the State.'[22] There has been no change in this official position of the Party and its leaders ever since, despite the acceleration of Islamization by the UMNO-led government, particularly since the advent of Prime Minister Mahathir's leadership.

However, in September 2001, Mahathir took everyone by surprise when he stated that Malaysia was already an Islamic state even if it had not implemented *hudud*.[23] The government proposed inviting scholars from al-Azhar University in Egypt to prove its claim. This lateral shift in UMNO's leadership probably reflects the absence of a coherent methodology to counter PAS's onslaught in the name of religion.

UMNO's strategic response to PAS-sponsored *hudud* laws remains unclear. Initially the then Deputy President of UMNO and Deputy Prime Minister of Malaysia, Ghafar Baba, agreed to support the *hudud* laws in principle.[24] Prime Minister Mahathir gave various reasons, at times conflicting ones, for not supporting the laws. Occasionally he accused PAS of making the *hudud* laws a political issue in order to blame the federal government in the general election for preventing PAS introducing *hudud* laws in the state.[25] At other times he expressed the view that it was the 'PAS *hudud*' law and not really Islamic laws.[26] Then during the height of an important by-election in Trengganu in April 1992, the Prime Minister reversed his long-standing opposition to *hudud* laws and said that UMNO was prepared to help PAS remove the legislative obstacles in the Constitution so that PAS could implement *hudud* laws in Kelantan.[27] UMNO won the election but there was no support for *hudud* laws. UMNO and its leaders appear to lack a systematic approach to counter the PAS campaign to introduce *hudud* laws.

Five Categories of UMNO's Views on Hudud *Laws*

The first category of UMNO members comprises those who believe that *hudud* laws – and by implication the establishment of an Islamic state – are not appropriate in a multiracial and more importantly multi-religious society like Malaysia. This group does not question the appropriateness of *hudud* laws proposed by PAS; they would, at least in theory, agree to implement *hudud* laws if the social, religious and economic composition of the country were different. UMNO's then information chief, Datuk Mohd Yusof Nor, appeared to share this view when he asked PAS to take into account the multiracial composition of society before making apostasy a capital offence. To introduce such a provision, he thought, could undermine various measures taken by the UMNO-led government to enhance the dignity of Islam and develop Islamic laws in a gradual and orderly fashion.[28]

UMNO's second category comprises those who are more concerned about the timing of *hudud* laws, again without questioning their appropriateness. Abdul Hamid Othman, the Minister responsible for Islamic affairs from 1991 until his resignation in 2001, appeared to share such views. Commenting on the PAS-proposed federal Apostasy Bill, the Minister noted: 'It was not the government's intention to implement harsh penalties for offences such as apostasy but *it must be done at the right time*' (emphasis added).[29] Then in July 1999, the Minister said it was not practical to implement the Apostasy Bill in the country *under the present situation*. The Bill, he thought, would actually create fear among non-Muslims and distance them from Islam.[30] The advocates of this view have so far failed to explain why the present time is not conducive to implementing *hudud* laws, when and how the situation will change and what sort of framework would be needed for their implementation.

The third category comprises those who claim that the PAS version of *hudud* laws is not really Islamic. By implication it could be argued that this group supports, or at least leaves open, the option of *hudud* laws based on true Islamic teachings. Prime Minister Mahathir, who described PAS-sponsored *hudud* laws as un-Islamic[31] and a 'political gimmick with no sincerity',[32] shares this perspective. Rafidah Aziz, a Minister in the UMNO-led government, agreed in 1994. She suggested that the *hudud* laws proposed by the Kelantan government should be distinguished from, and were not the same as, the laws propagated by Islam.[33] Of all the arguments this last appears to be the weakest and least persuasive. If PAS-sponsored *hudud* laws are not based on true Islamic law, it is likely that UMNO would identify areas that are not in accordance with Islamic principles. They could co-operate with PAS to come up with a draft that would reflect the true principles of Islamic law. PAS has made such overtures to UMNO,[34] but the government has made it clear that it has no plans to hold a meeting with PAS to discuss issues such as apostasy.[35] From the reasons given by UMNO leaders in rejecting *hudud* laws it would appear that UMNO's reluctance to co-operate with PAS is mainly because it is not keen to see the introduction of *hudud* laws in the country, at least for the time being. It is not because it views the PAS-sponsored *hudud* laws as significantly different from the classical exposition of the Syariah law. But UMNO remains fearful that outright rejection of *hudud* laws could upset many Muslims and could further strengthen PAS.

The fourth category groups together those within and outside the government who believe that *hudud* laws are bad for foreign investment in the country. In March 1994 the International Trade and Industry Minister, Rafidah Aziz, suggested that the proposed *hudud* laws were scaring away some potential foreign investors.[36] Lim Kit Siang, then Opposition leader, expressed similar views when he attributed the country's deteriorating investment climate to irresponsible politicking on *hudud* laws.[37]

Finally there are those who either support the *hudud* laws or refrain from objecting to them. For instance, in 1993, when the PAS-led government introduced the *hudud* Bill in Kelantan all 36 members present, including two from UMNO, voted in favour of the Bill. The six MPs from the *Spirit of '46* Party also supported the Bill. This was led by Tengku Razaleigh Hamzah, one-time arch-enemy of Mahathir but who has since rejoined UMNO along with many other Party members. Razaleigh, in an apparent attempt to appease his Party allies, PAS and the Democratic Action Party (DAP), had earlier said that the *Spirit of '46* MPs would support the Bill, provided the religious rights of non-Muslims were not affected.[38] He also did not oppose the proposed federal Apostasy Bill, saying that it was up to the Parliament to debate it. This group is in a dilemma because opposition to *hudud* laws could be interpreted as opposing the introduction of Islamic law. This could alienate many Malays, especially the more religious Malays from Kelantan and Trengganu. Such opposition could also be interpreted as un-Islamic or at least sinful and could have serious electoral repercussions. The dilemma was reflected by one UMNO parliamentarian when he said, 'Even if we disagree, we can't oppose [it] because *hudud* provisions are prescribed in the Qur'an'.[39] Because of the fear of a possible backlash, very few, if any, Muslim politicians dare to reject the *hudud* laws altogether. Instead they point to alleged 'defects' in the drafting of the laws. However, these defects could be remedied with minor amendments and by judicial interpretation.

UMNO's fragmented approach towards *hudud* laws is yet to convince the general public that the PAS version of *hudud* laws is radically different from the classical position. Further, UMNO's arguments against the application of *hudud* laws are unlikely to alter the general Muslim belief that *hudud* laws have their origin in the Qur'an and the *sunnah* and therefore must be implemented.

After refusing to support attempts by PAS to impose the death penalty for apostasy, UMNO has proposed a rehabilitative approach involving short-term detention for apostates. This is not new. The UMNO-led federal and state governments have already adopted a similar approach in cases involving what they consider to be 'deviant' teachings. However, once again UMNO leaders failed to present a uniform approach towards the issue of apostasy. For instance, in August 1998 the then Minister responsible for Islamic affairs, Abdul Hamid Othman, said that Muslims need not fear persecution if they wish to renounce Islam, as actions would only be taken against Muslim apostates who abused or belittled the religion, or resorted to actions tarnishing the image of Islam. The Minister added that this was consistent with the provisions of the Constitution guaranteeing freedom of religion.[40] A day earlier, the Minister was quoted as saying that 'no action would be taken against those who committed apostasy if they did not "harm" the religion and other Muslims'.[41] It is not clear what the words 'belittle' or 'harm' the religion mean. Some state laws regard attempts to renounce Islam as amounting to contempt for the religion. It could be argued that this amounts to harming or belittling Islam. Moreover the Minister's remarks represent a total departure from his earlier views. In March 1995 he was quoted as saying that 'specific procedures [to govern cases of apostasy] were necessary as apostasy was a serious offence warranting the death penalty under Islamic law'.[42] The Minister's changed views in 1998 followed an official visit by the Grand Shaykh of al-Azhar University, Dr Muhammad Sayyid Tantawi. The Shaykh reportedly denied that apostasy is a punishable offence under Islamic law.[43] This appears to have given the Minister a pretext to modify his earlier views since al-Azhar University is held in high esteem by Malays, especially in the East Coast states of Kelantan and Trengganu.

UMNO-Backed Apostasy Laws: Examples

Several UMNO-led state governments have enacted laws prohibiting Muslims from renouncing Islam before obtaining a declaration from the Syariah court allowing such a renunciation.[44] Until the court grants a declaration the person is presumed to be a Muslim. In fact, labelling a Muslim an apostate, an infidel and so on, is in itself an offence.[45] The general approach of the existing laws on apostasy is indicated by the Syariah Offences (Malacca) Enactment, 1991. Under the Enactment, if a Muslim admits that he has left the religion of Islam or declares himself a non-Muslim, and the court is satisfied that he has indeed done something that can be interpreted as an attempt to change his religion, the court should order him to be detained in the Islamic Faith Rehabilitation Centre for a period not exceeding six months. He will be required to undergo a course of education and asked to repent.[46] During the detention the officer in charge is required to send a weekly progress report to the court.[47] If the detainee repents and the court is satisfied about the repentance, he will be released.[48] Identical provisions are found in several other state laws including the Council of the Religion of Islam and Malay Custom (Kelantan) Enactment, 1994 and the Syariah Criminal Offences (Sabah) Enactment, 1995. These two enactments allow detention for up to 36 months.[49]

Various state laws on the administration of Islamic laws also criminalize actions that could be construed as amounting to apostasy. For example, it is an offence to worship any beach, tree, open space, grave, forest, hill or any other thing or any person in any manner or for any purpose contrary to Syariah law;[50] to declare oneself or any other person a prophet, *imam mahdi* (who is believed to rule the world as the restorer of faith and justice), or *wali* (pious individual who is a 'friend' of God); to claim that one knows of supernatural things or events that are false and contrary to the teachings of Islam.[51] It is not permissible to bring into contempt the religion of Islam either by words or by action; to ridicule the practices or ceremonies relating to the religion of Islam;[52] to bring into contempt any law in force in the state relating to the religion of Islam;[53] to publish, distribute or print materials that are contrary to Syariah law;[54] to destroy or deface places of worship with the intention of insulting or degrading the religion of Islam;[55] or to insult, mock or criticize any sacred verse of the Qur'an or *hadith* or any saying considered sacred by Muslims.[56]

The Administration of Islamic Law (Negeri Sembilan) Enactment, 1991 as amended in 1995, adopts a totally different approach to the issue. Not only does it not prescribe any penalty for apostasy, it actually provides a comprehensive procedure for renouncing Islam. Under the law, application has to be made *ex parte* to a judge of the Syariah High Court in open court by the person who wishes to renounce Islam.[57] The application has to be supported by an affidavit stating all the facts including the grounds for renunciation. Upon receiving the application the judge may defer hearing for a period of 30 days and refer the applicant to the *mufti*.[58] But if the judge is satisfied that it is in the interest of the applicant and Islam generally to proceed immediately, he may hear the application and make an order as he thinks fit.[59] Once a person has obtained an order declaring that he has renounced Islam as his religion, he then registers the order with the Registrar of New Converts (*Saudara Baru*).[60] Until the order is registered the person is treated as a Muslim and continues to be subject to Islamic law and the Syariah court.

Proposed Laws

There have been reports since 1995 that the federal government is in the process of drafting a law to curb apostasy. The proposed federal law, known as the Faith Reform Bill, was drafted by the Islamic Development Department (Jakim), studied by the Attorney General's Office and approved by the Cabinet. According to reports it prescribes three years' imprisonment for those who renounce Islam or a maximum fine of RM5000 or both. Once passed, the law is expected to serve as the model for other state laws. It also proposed setting up a Federal *Aqidah* Rehabilitation Centre (*Pusat Pemulihan Aqidah*) where Muslims who tried to become apostates and those who spread 'deviationist' teachings would undergo education and mental rehabilitation. In March 1995 Abdul Hamid Othman, minister in the Prime Minister's Department, likened the centre to halfway houses used by the government to treat drug addicts. The minister felt that strong measures were needed because experience had shown that advice and persuasion by the government was ineffective to check the growing number of apostasy cases.[61]

Being a federal centre, it requires state approval for individuals from various states to be included in the programme since Islam and Islamic law fall under state jurisdiction.[62] Generally this would not be a problem because the UMNO-led coalition controls federal and all but two state governments. The government felt that a federal centre was necessary because not all states provided for the rehabilitation of such offenders. However, as the federal government has yet to table the Bill, its details remain sketchy. However this did not prevent the state of Perlis from passing the Islamic *Aqidah* Protection (Perlis) Bill, 2000 based on the federal model. According to Harun Hashim, the former Supreme Court Judge, the Perlis law was modelled on the federal Faith Reform Bill that he himself helped to draft. [63]

The *Aqidah* Protection Bill is the latest in a series of laws introduced by various states preventing Muslims from renouncing Islam. The objective of this particular Bill is to protect, rehabilitate and determine the ʿaqidah of Muslims in the state. The Bill treats attempts to change ʿaqidah as a serious problem warranting detention for up to one year. It confers wide discretionary powers on state appointed religious enforcement officers to investigate cases where a Muslim attempts to change ʿaqidah.[64] Attempts to change ʿaqidah may result not only from actions or deeds of a *mukallaf*, but also by 'any other means' that may be interpreted as constituting an attempt to change ʿaqidah and belief towards Islam.[65] The Bill does not define the phrase 'other means'. It is therefore up to the investigating officers to decide what constitutes 'other means'. As a result, officers may not only investigate attempts to change ʿaqidah resulting from words or deeds but also from their own understanding and interpretation of 'any other means'.

Investigation may commence upon receiving information (presumably from the general public) or where the officers have 'reason to suspect' that an attempt to change *ʿaqidah* is being made.[66] There is no legal requirement that the investigation be based on credible, sensible or reasonable information. Hence fanciful and baseless allegations and information may also be the basis for investigation. It is also immaterial whether the information came from political, religious or business rivals or even from disgruntled neighbours. Further, the officers are not required to disclose the source of their information to the person being investigated. For these reasons there is great danger that the provisions of the Bill could be abused both by the officers and the general public. The Bill does not address these problems. It does not prescribe any penalty for making baseless allegations questioning the *ʿaqidah* of innocent Muslims.

The officers may also undertake an investigation where they have 'reason to suspect' that an attempt to change one's religion is being made.[67] The phrase 'reason to suspect' means the investigation can be based on mere suspicion without even any remotely connected evidence. Further, because this aspect of the law is framed in subjective terms, it also means so long as the officer is satisfied that there is a 'reason to suspect' it is a sufficient ground for investigation. It is irrelevant if what the officer 'suspected' was grossly unreasonable or that no reasonable person would have suspected that there was an attempt to change *ʿaqidah*. One can think of numerous examples where the officers may have 'reason to suspect': Muslim students undertaking Bible studies as part of the syllabus; Muslim scholars taking part in a religious discourse with non-Muslims; a Muslim wandering around a church compound and so on. In these cases, or indeed in even more absurd ones, the officers may have 'reason to suspect' that an attempt to change *ʿaqidah* was made.

Not only does the officer have the power to investigate on arbitrary and fanciful grounds but also to conduct the investigation as if it were a criminal investigation.[68] In the course of investigation if the officer finds 'sufficient evidence or reasonable ground of suspicion' that an attempt to change *ʿaqidah* is being made, he or she seeks a summons requiring the appearance of the person[69] (provided the person is not below the age of 18 in which case whether Muslim or non-Muslim, the person could not change religion without the consent of a parent or guardian). If the person refuses to appear as directed then the officer may seek a warrant of arrest.[70]

In addition to the wide discretion conferred on enforcement officers, there are also serious procedural flaws in the Bill. For instance, once the person is brought before the Syariah court the judge asks them to repent.[71] The Bill is silent on whether the officer has to prove the allegations and, if so, whether the person should be given the opportunity to refute those allegations and whether the person can seek legal representation. The absence of these procedural safeguards makes a mockery of constitutional and statutory safeguards such as the right to be represented by a legal practitioner of choice, the right to know the charges and evidence against oneself, the right to rebut those charges and evidences, and, most importantly, presumption of innocence until proven guilty, which is not only a Western legal concept but also the very basis of Islamic criminal law.

Once the person repents their repentance is recorded and they are released. If the person refuses to repent then they are detained in an *Aqidah* Rehabilitation Centre for up to one year where they undergo rehabilitation and education.[72] The Bill is also silent on the nature of the rehabilitation and education the detainee is required to undergo. All it does is to empower the state Majlis Agama Islam dan Adat Isti'adat Melayu (Council of Muslim Religion and Malay Custom) to determine, by way of notification in the Gazette, any place or institution as an *Aqidah* Rehabilitation Centre.[73] The Bill also allows the state ruler to make rules in relation to the procedure of admission to or discharge from an *Aqidah* Rehabilitation Centre. Such rules are to be made following the advice of the Majlis and may prescribe a fine of up to RM1000 or imprisonment for up to six months.[74]

If the person repents while in detention the court records their repentance and orders their release. But if they refuse to repent, they are brought before the court just before the expiry of their detention period (if they have obligations under Islamic family law, then at least 30 days before the expiry of the detention period). Once again they are asked to repent. If they refuse, the judge proceeds to hear reasons for their refusal before recording the refusal to repent and making a declaration that the person is no longer a Muslim. If the person has obligations under Islamic family law, then the judge hears the case as if a divorce has occurred under the Enactment.[75] The judge covers claims of all parties. When he has decided on the liabilities and obligations of the parties he makes an order to the effect that (a) the person is no longer a Muslim and their marriage is dissolved, (b) determines the person's liabilities or obligations and (c) releases the person if they have not already been released upon the expiry of their detention.[76]

The net result of the Bill is that it takes away the prerogative of Muslims to determine their faith, giving it instead to the state. As a result of the law, the state has become the ultimate arbiter of Muslim faith and belief. It could be said that there are inherent dangers when the state becomes the ultimate adjudicator of personal faith. This is especially the case in countries like Malaysia where religious institutions and religious officials are subordinated to political authority. In such an environment there could be genuine fear that political authorities might use their office and authority to persuade religious officials to question the faith of their political opponents. In the past, PAS has labelled some UMNO officials as infidels. The proposed apostasy laws could lead to more such claims not only by PAS but also by UMNO, or at least these apostasy laws could be used against Muslims who do not adhere to the government-sanctioned version of Islam.

However, due to strong opposition, not only from non-Muslims but also from Muslims, the federal and state governments appear to have delayed the introduction and enforcement of these new laws.[77] The federal government is worried that these laws, which are aimed at protecting Muslims and Islam, could actually divide them. It would also appear that, because of strong opposition and criticism, the draft federal Faith Reform Bill will be far less severe than originally proposed. According to reports, the initial draft prescribed imprisonment for up to three years or a fine of up to RM5000 or both for renouncing Islam. However, the proposed law in Perlis, which is based on the federal model, prescribes detention for one year. As the state is ruled by the UMNO-led coalition, it is unlikely the final draft of the proposed federal law would be significantly different from the Perlis law.

Implications of Apostasy

The Federal Constitution defines a 'Malay' as a person who habitually speaks the Malay language, practises Malay custom and professes the religion of Islam. Therefore Malays who renounce Islam would stand to loose the preferential treatments conferred on Malays in the form of quotas for educational institutes, scholarships for local and overseas universities, easier loans to set up businesses, discounts on housing and so on.

There are far more serious consequences in renouncing Islam than losing material benefits. An apostate would almost certainly be regarded as a social outcast. Even other Malay Muslims would be likely to shun them. This is a far more effective deterrent because of the general closeness of families and the value placed on family in Malay society.

In the case of conversion there is no guarantee that the convert would be wholeheartedly embraced by other members of the new faith, who may be from a different race. Members of the 'new' religious clergy or missionaries, for example, or (where the conversion was for marriage purposes) in-laws may accept the convert, but outside that circle assimilation may remain a serious problem. Even Muslims from other races and new converts to Islam face similar problems, despite the fact that state governments have set up special agencies and funds to help new converts. As a result there are often separate mosques for Indian Muslims (generally referred to as *mamak*). In 1992 the government proposed building a special mosque for Chinese converts in Kuala Lumpur where Mandarin was to be the medium of communication.[78] If newly converted Muslims find it hard to adjust, the situation of a Muslim who renounces Islam in favour of another religion must be much more difficult given the entrenched racial divisions within society.

There is also the issue of identification and changing of names that follows the renunciation of religion, particularly Islam, because Muslims are subject to Islamic law. Generally it is easy to identify Muslims in

Malaysia by their names. Therefore when a person renounces or converts to Islam, they will probably need a change of name. To make such a change, officials at the Registration Department may rely simply on a statutory declaration pursuant to the Statutory Declarations Act, 1960. However, occasionally, the registration official demands a declaration from the Syariah court before making the change.[79] This may cause some hardship for a convert from Islam. Further, it could be argued that approaching the Department of National Registration to change one's name amounts to an attempt to renounce Islam prior to a Syariah court declaration that recognizes the renunciation, which is an offence under some state laws.[80]

Renunciation of Islam on the part of one's partner can also have serious consequences for a marriage. Under various state laws conversion from Islam itself does not automatically dissolve a marriage. The dissolution must be confirmed by the Syariah court,[81] a mere formality as continued cohabitation following renunciation of Islam may be regarded as adulterous under traditional Islamic law. However, these provisions could easily be abused by either spouse. Apostasy may be used as a device to annul a marriage. The Islamic Family Law (Federal Territories) Act, 1984, tries to prevent such abuse by making this an offence punishable by up to six months' imprisonment; and the Negeri Sembilan Islamic Family Law Enactment as amended on 2 September 1991 increased punishment for attempted dissolution of marriage through apostasy from six months' imprisonment to one year's imprisonment.[82]

Under Section 11 of the Islamic *Aqidah* Protection (Perlis) Bill, 2000, if the apostate persists in renunciation after the detention period expires, the judge must proceed to hear the liabilities and obligations the apostate has under Islamic family law. In addition to declaring that the person is no longer a Muslim, the judge then dissolves the marriage. State Islamic family laws prohibit awarding custody to a woman who renounces Islam.[83] Interestingly, these laws do not provide for situations where a father might renounce Islam. This is probably because various Islamic Family Law Enactments in Malaysia consider the mother to be the best entitled to custody of her infant children. If the mother were disqualified from having custody the right would pass to the maternal grandmother or maternal great-grandmother. Only in the absence of a maternal grandmother or great-grandmother would the father be considered for the purpose of custody.[84]

The effect of apostasy may continue even after the death of the apostate. In cases where the authorities believe that the deceased died as a Muslim and the family contests this, there may be a legal battle for custody of the body. This is to ensure the deceased gets a burial in accordance with their religious rites. In *Dalip Kaur v. Pegawai Polis Daerah, Balai Polis Daerah, Bukit Mertajam & Anor*[85] the appellant had applied for a declaration that her deceased son at the time of his death on 3 October 1991 was not a Muslim (having renounced Islam) and claimed that she was entitled to his body. The deceased was born and brought up in the Sikh faith but converted to Islam on 1 June 1991. His conversion was duly registered with the Majlis Agama Islam Kedah, in accordance with Section 139 of the Administration of Muslim Law Enactment, 1962 of Kedah. The mother appellant contended that, after conversion, her son had renounced Islam by a deed poll executed on 9 September 1991 and had resumed the practice of his old faith. It was also alleged that the deceased had been rebaptized by a Sikh priest and had regularly attended the congregation at the Sikh temple. He also continued to eat pork and had not been circumcised.

At the trial before the High Court, the learned Judicial Commissioner found that the signature on the deed poll was not that of the deceased. He also rejected the evidence relating to the rebaptism and the congregation at the Sikh temple. The Judicial Commissioner held that the deceased was a Muslim at the time of his death. The appellant appealed. At the hearing of the appeal, the Supreme Court remitted the case to the High Court for the Judicial Commissioner to refer certain questions of Islamic law to the Fatwa Committee of Kedah. The Committee was of the view that the deceased was a Muslim at the time of his death. The Judicial Commissioner then confirmed his earlier findings. Later the Supreme Court upheld the decision.

Reasons for the Introduction of Apostasy Laws

UMNO's interest in apostasy laws coincided with two events. It surfaced just six months after the crackdown on *Arqam*. It also followed the recapture of Kelantan by PAS and the subsequent passing of *hudud* laws. The urgency on the part of UMNO to introduce apostasy laws also followed attempts by PAS to introduce an Apostasy Bill in the federal Parliament. It is therefore not surprising that PAS claimed that the UMNO proposals were in response to its pressure, a political move rather than a real effort to come up with an Islamic solution to the issue.[86] However, a closer look would reveal that UMNO's efforts were not entirely driven by PAS; rather the latter may simply have hastened the inevitable. Even without PAS these laws would have been introduced at some stage, for the following reasons.

The federal government appears to be of the view that non-Muslims, especially Christians, are taking a more active role in spreading their religion among Muslims. In June 1998 the Youth wing of UMNO called on the federal government to take stern action against those who attempt to use the Constitution to entice Muslims to leave their faith.[87] According to Roslan Kassim, the then head of the UMNO Youth Movement, between 1991 and 1998, 689 Malays – 425 women and 264 men – had applied to change their religion at the National Registration Department. He was alarmed about the number of Muslims renouncing their faith. He felt that some Muslims were changing their religion 'as fast as changing cars, houses and even wives'.[88] However, the number of Muslims renouncing Islam is only a fraction of the number of people converting to Islam. For instance, between 1994 and 1997, 519 Muslims in the country applied to change their religion, while over 11 000 people in Malaysia converted to Islam.[89]

Furthermore, increasing numbers of government- and self-sponsored Malay students in Western educational institutions overseas are coming into contact with other faiths. These students are more vulnerable to the teachings of other religions, especially Christianity, which is active in spreading its message. Even though Malaysia is a multi-religious society, Malay students are shielded at home by various state and federal laws and government instruments, so they are often quite vulnerable when abroad. It was therefore not surprising when news surfaced from time to time that government-sponsored students in overseas universities were renouncing Islam in favour of other religions. In July 1992 the *mufti* of Perak was quoted as saying that 41 Malay women studying abroad had converted to other religions after marrying non-Muslim men in the United Kingdom. Authorities felt that boarding with non-Muslim families could have been one factor influencing their decision.[90]

The Malaysian government has also had to address the issue of Muslims renouncing or trying to renounce their religion in order to avoid certain legal consequences. These include having to submit to the jurisdiction of a Syariah court when they believed they could obtain better remedies in the civil courts. For example, in *Mohamed Habibullah Bin Mahmood v. Faridah Bte Dato Talib*,[91] the plaintiff (wife) petitioned for divorce in the Syariah court of Kuala Lumpur. She subsequently filed a suit in the High Court in Kuala Lumpur against her husband, claiming damages and an injunction to restrain the defendant from assaulting, harassing or molesting her and members of her family. Apparently she believed that the Syariah court would not grant such remedies to a Muslim wife. In an apparent attempt to avoid Syariah court jurisdiction, she allegedly renounced her faith.

Some states have tried to address this issue. Section 12 of the Crimes (Syariah) (Perak) Enactment, 1992 provides that: 'Any Muslim who declares himself to be a non-Muslim so as to avoid any action being taken against him under this Enactment or any other law in force is guilty of an offence and shall, on conviction, be liable to a fine not exceeding one thousand ringgit or to imprisonment for a term not exceeding three years or to both.'[92]

Another event that influenced the introduction of apostasy laws was the Nor Aisha story. This forced the government to adopt a harsher approach towards apostasy following widespread publicity. Aisha was a 25-year-old Muslim Malay who converted to Catholicism in October 1997 to marry her Christian boyfriend. In a complaint filed with the High Court she alleged that her family had kept her captive for 41 days to try to prevent her from marrying Joseph Lee, a 28-year-old ethnic Chinese. She reportedly said that she converted to Catholicism of her own free will. She later went into hiding with her boyfriend. Abdul Hamid Othman, Minister responsible for Islamic affairs at the time, suggested that the *Pusat Islam* (Islamic Centre, a federal body responsible for co-ordinating and overseeing Islamic activities) would advise the two families to allow the couple to marry. According to him 'such a marriage was not unusual in the country'.[93] The Minister's comments are interesting because under various state laws Muslim women cannot marry non-Muslims. For instance, Section 10 of the Islamic Family (Federal Territories) Law, 1984 states that: 'No man shall marry a non-Muslim except a *kitabiyyah*' and: 'No woman shall marry a non-Muslim'. Even more interesting is the fact that under the proposed laws on apostasy, if a person renounces Islam and refuses to repent, then the court must effect a divorce between the parties.[94] Aisha's story generated enormous interest throughout the country and led to calls to introduce tougher measures to curb apostasy.

Chapter 11

Apostasy Laws in Malaysia: Jurisdiction and Constitutionality

As noted earlier, the Parliament and the state legislatures have separate jurisdictions in Malaysia. Details of their respective jurisdictions are found in three lists attached to the Ninth Schedule of the Constitution. The three lists are Federal List, State List and Concurrent List. The Parliament can legislate only on matters enumerated in the Federal List or in the Concurrent List.[1] Similarly, state legislatures can only legislate on matters spelled out in the State List or in the Concurrent List.[2] In the event of any conflict between federal and state law enacted over a subject on which both the federal and the state legislatures have jurisdiction, then the federal law would prevail and the state law, to the extent of the inconsistency, would be void.[3]

Federal powers include, among other things, civil and criminal law and procedure and the administration of justice, including the constitution and organization of all courts, other than Syariah courts and jurisdiction and powers of all such courts.[4] State legislative powers include Islamic law, Islamic personal and family law, and the creation and punishment of offences by Muslims against precepts of Islam, except in regard to matters included in the Federal List. States can also legislate on the constitution, organization and procedure of Syariah courts; the control of propagating doctrines and beliefs among Muslims; the determination of matters of Islamic law and doctrine and Malay custom. Pursuant to these powers every state (and, in respect of the Federal Territories, the Parliament) has enacted its own set of Islamic laws. All the states also have established Syariah courts.

Islamic law applies to Muslims only and the Syariah courts have jurisdiction only over Muslims.[5] The Syariah courts generally consist of a Syariah Appeal Court, a Syariah High Court and a Syariah Subordinate Court.

Syariah court judges are appointed by the respective state rulers (for the Federal Territories the appointments are made by the king) and have jurisdiction only over Muslims. Although the Syariah courts are creatures of state laws they are not subordinated to the civil courts. Article 121 of the Constitution demarcates the jurisdiction of the two court systems. This Article was amended in 1988 to ensure that the civil courts would not have jurisdiction over matters within Syariah court jurisdiction. Prior to the

149

amendment, the judicial powers of the federation were vested entirely in the two high courts of equal jurisdiction[6] and the civil courts had the power to review decisions of the Syariah court by way of *certiorari*.[7] This caused concern among those entrusted with the task of administering Islamic law in the country. The objective of this new clause, therefore, was to prevent the High Court from exercising its power of judicial review over decisions of the Syariah court.[8]

However, Syariah courts do not derive their jurisdiction from Article 121(1A). It merely tries to ensure the civil courts do not assume jurisdiction on matters that come under the Syariah court jurisdiction. The Syariah court, being a creature of state law, must derive its jurisdiction from state laws enacted pursuant to Article 74 of the Constitution and read with the State List set out in the Ninth Schedule of the Constitution.

All states have enacted specific laws to regulate the conduct of Muslims in a wide range of areas such as marriage, divorce, custody, guardianship, consumption of alcohol, gambling, non-payment of *zakat*, non-observance of fasting, prayers and so on. State laws also confer exclusive jurisdiction in these matters to the Syariah court. However, the jurisdiction of the Syariah court to pass sentences is regulated by federal law. The federal Syariah Courts (Criminal Jurisdiction) Act, 1965 restricts the jurisdiction of the Syariah court to passing sentences of up to three years' imprisonment or a fine up to RM5000 or six strokes of the whip or any combination thereof.[9]

Jurisdiction in Apostasy Cases

Despite the apparent demarcation between civil courts and the Syariah courts, conflicts between the two court systems do arise. One particular area of conflict in recent years has been the issue of jurisdiction in apostasy cases. The reason for this type of conflict is that a number of state legislatures, despite having the power to legislate, have failed in the past to enact laws conferring explicit jurisdiction on the Syariah court to deal with apostasy cases. The question therefore is, does the Syariah court have jurisdiction over those matters stated in paragraph 1 of the State List even in the absence of an express state law conferring jurisdiction on the Syariah court? There are two lines of judicial decisions dealing with this issue. The first line of decisions affirms that, without express jurisdiction from state law, the Syariah court has no jurisdiction. This view was affirmed in *Lim Chan Seng v. Pengarah Jabatan Agama Islam Pulau Pinang & Anor.*[10] Justice Abdul Hamid of the High Court held that the Syariah court is not a creature of Syariah law. It owes its existence to the written laws of Parliament and state legislatures. In order to ascertain the question of jurisdiction of the Syariah court, reference needs to be made to these laws to establish whether jurisdiction over a particular matter is given to the Syariah court or the civil court. In this case His Lordship observed that to enable the Syariah courts in Penang to have jurisdiction over apostasy cases, the state legislature must first amend its 1993 Enactment and incorporate provisions to that effect.

In *Shaik Zolkaffily bin Shaik Natar & Ors v. Majlis Agama Islam Pulau Penang*[11] the High Court of Penang, in dealing with the question of jurisdiction, echoed similar views. The judge held:

> When there is a challenge to the jurisdiction of the High Court, the key is not whether the High Court had jurisdiction, but whether jurisdiction of the matter at hand is with the Syariah court . . . Jurisdiction to the Syariah court is given by state laws but if state law did not confer on the Syariah court any jurisdiction to deal with any matter in the State List, the Syariah court is precluded from dealing with the matter and the jurisdiction cannot be derived by implication.[12]

The High Court found that, because no jurisdiction was conferred on the Syariah court, jurisdiction rested in the civil courts.

In the final example, *Mohamed Habibullah bin Mahmood v. Faridah bte Dato Talib*,[13] Harun Hashim of the Supreme Court expressed his opinion 'that when there is a challenge to jurisdiction, as here, the correct approach is firstly to see whether the Syariah Court has jurisdiction and not whether the state legislature has power to enact the law conferring jurisdiction on the Syariah Court'.

This approach was not followed in the second line of cases where the High Court expressed willingness to affirm Syariah court jurisdiction even without any state law expressly conferring jurisdiction on it. In *Md Hakim Lee v. Majlis Agama Islam Wilayah Persekutuan, Kuala Lumpur*,[14] the plaintiff was a Buddhist who had embraced Islam under the name Md Hakim Lee. Subsequently, a deed poll and a statutory declaration, he renounced Islam and showed an intention to use the name Lee Leong Kim. He further claimed that his action was guaranteed by Article 11 of the Constitution (which guarantees religious freedom) and that no authority or body could limit or hinder that freedom. The defendant raised a preliminary issue of the jurisdiction of the High Court. Dismissing the application the High Court of Kuala Lumpur held:

> [H]is purported renunciation of the Islamic faith by the deed poll and the statutory declaration is outside the jurisdiction of this court to determine, on account of the ouster of the jurisdiction by art [Article] 121(1A) of the Federal Constitution. By virtue of para 1 in List II of the Ninth Schedule to the Federal Constitution [i.e. the State List], the jurisdiction lies with the Syariah court on its wider jurisdiction over a person professing the religion of Islam, even if no express provisions are provided in the Act [Administration of Islamic Law (Federal Territories) Act 1993] because under art 74 of the Constitution, it is within the competency of the legislature to legislate on the matter. Its absence from the express provision in the Act would not confer the jurisdiction in the civil court. The fact that the plaintiff may not have his remedy in the Syariah court would not make the jurisdiction exercisable by the civil court.[15]

The Federal Court expressly agreed with this view in *Soon Singh a/l Bikar Singh v. Pertubuhan Kebajkan Islam Malaysia (PERKIM) Kedah & Anor.*[16] The appellant in this case, brought up as a Sikh, converted to Islam without the knowledge and consent of his widowed mother while he was still a minor. Upon reaching 21 years of age, he went through a baptism ceremony into the Sikh faith, thereby renouncing Islam. He then executed a deed poll in which he declared unequivocally that he was a Sikh. Subsequently he sought a declaration from the Kuala Lumpur High Court that he was no longer a Muslim. Counsel for the respondent argued that the High Court did not have jurisdiction to grant such a declaration as the matter came under the jurisdiction of the Syariah court.

The Federal Court found that the validity of the appellant's conversion to Islam while a minor was no longer relevant as the appellant did not repudiate his conversion after he reached 18 years of age. On the question of jurisdiction the Court held:

> [T]he Jurisdiction of the Syariah courts to deal with conversion out of Islam, although not expressly provided for in some state Enactments, can be read into those enactments by implication derived from the provisions concerning conversion into Islam. It is inevitable that since matters on conversion to Islam come under the jurisdiction of the Syariah courts, by implication, conversion out of Islam, should also fall under the jurisdiction of the same courts. Thus the appellant's application for a declaration that he was no longer a Muslim came within the jurisdiction of the Syariah court and not that of the High Court.[17]

Thus it is now the settled law that the Syariah court and not the civil court has jurisdiction to determine whether a person has or has not renounced Islam. One of the reasons for confirming Syariah court jurisdiction over apostasy cases is that conversion out of Islam requires that certain requirements be complied with under the Syariah, which only the Syariah courts are sufficiently expert about and are thus the appropriate adjudicators in the case.

The difficulty of determining whether the Syariah court or the High Court had jurisdiction in apostasy cases was largely due to the absence of specific provisions in various state enactments. Because of this difficulty the Supreme Court in *Dalip Kaur v. Pegawai Polis Daerah, Balai Polis Daerah, Bukit Mertajam & Anor*[18] expressed the view that:

> [C]lear provisions should be incorporated in all the state Enactments to avoid difficulties of interpretation by the civil courts. This is particularly important in view of the amendment to art 121 of the Federal Constitution made by Act A704 of 1988. The new cl [clause] 1A of art 121 of the Constitution effective from 10 June 1988 has taken away the jurisdiction of the civil courts in respect of matters within the jurisdiction of the Syariah courts.

Heeding such advice, some state legislatures have provided specific provisions relating to the renunciation of Islam.[19] The Council of the Religion of

Islam and Malay Custom (Kelantan) Enactment, 1994 provides that 'Any matter which is stated to be *murtadd* (apostate) shall be decided by the court',[20] that is, the Syariah court. Until the court has declared that a person is no longer a Muslim that person is presumed to be a Muslim and will be subjected to Islamic law and the Syariah court jurisdiction.[21] Section 3 of the Islamic *Aqidah* Protection (Perlis) Bill, 2000 also gives jurisdiction to the Syariah court to (a) declare that a person is no longer a Muslim; (b) declare the religious status of a Muslim who has died; and (c) make any other order as it deems fit [in relation to the matters stated under paragraphs (a) and (b)].

This is a total departure from the earlier legislative approach in this area. Previously, state laws did not deal with conversion from Islam. They only dealt with conversion to Islam because generally more people convert to Islam than renounce it. The authorities perhaps also feared that by providing express provisions for renouncing Islam, the law would be recognizing the right to renounce Islam. The authorities may have felt that express provisions could actually encourage people to renounce Islam, especially if they believed or were led to believe that they could get better remedies in the civil court.[22] It was probably for such reasons that Section 146(2) of the Administration of Muslim Law (Perak) Enactment, 1976 was amended. The unamended Section reads: 'If any Muslim converts himself to another religion he shall inform the Court of his decision and the Court shall publicise such conversion'.[23] However, because of the increased number of apostasy cases brought before the civil courts, state legislatures have been forced to deal with the issue. By providing explicit provisions, the jurisdiction of the Syariah court in apostasy cases is also established beyond any shadow of doubt. In fact, even without such explicit provisions, the Federal Court has shown willingness to confer jurisdiction on the Syariah court in apostasy-related cases.[24]

Constitutionality of Apostasy Laws

The Constitution does not impose any restriction on a person's right or capacity to accept or reject any religion, including the religion of Islam. Religious freedom enshrined under Article 11(1) of the Constitution is available to Muslims and non-Muslims alike. There is nothing in the Article to suggest that this right is unavailable to Muslims who wish to renounce their religion in favour of another religion. The only restriction is that persons below the age of 18 may not change their religion without the consent of a parent or guardian. This was affirmed by the Supreme Court in 1986.[25]

The Constitution also confers wide discretionary powers on state assemblies and, in respect of Federal Territories, the federal Parliament, to deal with matters of Islam. However, no law, whether federal or state, can violate the Constitution, which is the supreme law of the country.[26] Therefore any law curtailing the right of an individual to change their religion, including Islam, would, if it violates religious freedom guaranteed under Article 11(1) of the Constitution, be unconstitutional. Therefore it is important to see whether Article 11(1) incorporates the right to leave a religion.

This issue arose in *Daud Mamat & Ors v. Majlis Agama Islam/Adat & Anor*.[27] The plaintiffs in this case were born Muslims of Malay parentage. They were initially charged under the Council of the Religion of Islam and Malay Custom (Kelantan) Enactment, 1994 with the offence of heresy and sentenced to 20 months' imprisonment by the Kelantan Syariah High Court. On appeal the Kelantan Syariah Court of Appeal revised the sentences and released them on a RM5000 good behaviour bond. They were also required to appear before the Syariah court judge every month for three years, whereupon they were to repent. When they failed to comply with the order, fresh charges (first charges) were brought. But before the conviction and sentencing of the plaintiffs under the first charges, the plaintiffs confessed in the open court that with effect from 16 August 1998 they had already apostatized. The presiding judge nevertheless proceeded to hear the case and found them guilty. Following the confession they were charged (second charges) under Section 103(3) of Council of the Religion of Islam and Malay Custom (Kelantan) Enactment, 1994, which allows the detention of Muslims who renounce Islam without Syariah court declaration for up to 36 months. The plaintiffs sought eight declarations from the High Court. They were:

1 They had the constitutional right to profess and practise the religion of their choice under Article 11(1) of the Constitution;
2 Article 11(1) prevails over any federal or state laws as regards the choice and practice of the religion;
3 The plaintiffs' right to profess and practise their religion of choice under Article 11(1) is to be decided by themselves alone and not subject to the declaration or confirmation of anybody else;
4 Any provision in the law, be it Federal or State, that does provide for the definition of a Muslim but does not recognize Article 11(1) of the Federal Constitution is void;
5 Any law, be it Federal or State pertaining to the religion of Islam will be inapplicable to the plaintiffs, as they had declared their apostasy and hence [were] protected by Article 11(1);
6 Any law that empowers the Syariah court to decide whether they had left the religion of Islam or not, or requires a declaration from such court as a precondition before they are considered as having left the religion of Islam, contravenes Article 11(1) of the Federal Constitution;
7 Any provision in the law, be it Federal or State that restricts or prevents the right of the plaintiffs to declare themselves not wanting to profess and practise the religion of Islam contravenes the said Article and hence [is] void; and

8   Pursuant to the above anticipated declaratory orders, the defendants or their agents are not entitled to demand or impose any conditions before they are considered as having left the religion of Islam.

The Court came to a number of interesting conclusions. First it concluded that the plaintiffs lacked actual 'grievances' because they failed to appeal against the conviction and imprisonment in relation to the first charges, while the second charges could not have been the basis for any grievances as they were still pending. The Court also rejected claims that the plaintiffs' constitutional rights to profess and practise their religion of choice had been compromised because they had stated in the open court that they had voluntarily renounced Islam. Interestingly the Court failed to consider the fact that the plaintiffs' alleged renunciation of Islam was not only invalid but in fact a criminal offence under the Enactment because it was done without obtaining a Syariah court declaration to that effect. As such, legally, the plaintiffs did not and could not have renounced Islam. Therefore the Court's suggestion that the plaintiffs somehow had a 'choice' and they exercised this choice by renouncing Islam does not appear to be the correct interpretation of the law. That interpretation would be correct if the plaintiffs had the power or liberty to choose or not to choose any religion without attracting any legal punishment. Clearly the plaintiffs had none under the Enactment.

The most interesting aspect of the Court's finding was that exiting from a religion is not a religion and hence could not be equated with the plaintiffs' right 'to profess and practise' their religion within Article 11(1) of the Constitution. The Court noted that if Article 11(1) were to read that 'every one has the right to renounce or profess and practice his religion' then a different interpretation of the Article would have been warranted. But because the Article does not include the right to renounce one's religion, the plaintiffs could not rely on that Article to argue that their right to religious freedom had been denied.

This approach unduly restricts the scope of religious freedom under Article 11(1) which, unlike other Articles on fundamental rights, is framed in considerably broad terms. For instance, religious freedom under the Article is not limited to citizens only but also extends to non-citizens in the country. In fact, even emergency laws could not touch on religious freedom. This shows the level of protection the framers of the Constitution intended to accord to religious freedom in the country. Therefore the High Court, too, should have adopted a more liberal approach in interpreting Article 11(1). Such a liberal approach would also be in line with the Australian High Court decision in *Adelaide Company of Jehovah's Witnesses Inc v. Commonwealth*,[28] where Chief Justice Latham, in dealing with Section 116 of the Australian Constitution, which bars the Commonwealth from establishing any religion, imposing any religious observance, prohibiting the free exercise of any religion or requiring any test as a qualification for any office or public trust under the Commonwealth, held that: 'The prohibition in s 116 operates not only to protect the freedom of religion, but also to protect the right of a man to have no religion.'[29] It being a common law country, decisions of Australian superior courts have persuasive authority in Malaysia.

Existing and proposed apostasy laws also violate religious freedom in so far as they restrict and even punish Muslims who attempt to renounce their religion by requiring them to repent or by detaining them for the purpose of rehabilitation and education. This is in violation of Article 11(1) of the Constitution, which is unambiguous in its stipulation of religious freedom. Further, Islamic law applies only to persons professing the religion of Islam and the Syariah court has jurisdiction only over Muslims. Non-Muslims cannot be subjected to Islamic law or to the Syariah court jurisdiction. All the Syariah court can do is determine whether a person has or has not renounced their religion. Beyond that, the power and jurisdiction of the court over non-Muslims ceases to be in effect. It is therefore important to find out at what point a person ceases to be a Muslim.

Various state laws provide that unless the court declares otherwise a person is presumed to be a Muslim and is subject to Islamic law and the Syariah court. There are, however, strong grounds to believe that when the Syariah court requires a person to repent or undergo rehabilitation and education in a rehabilitation centre, that person is no longer a Muslim or has come perilously close to renouncing Islam. Otherwise such measures would be meaningless. A Muslim who has done nothing to jeopardize their belief cannot be required to repent or to undergo education or rehabilitation. Only those who have or are about to renounce their religion can be required to undergo such a process. This means that when the Syariah court asks a person to repent or to undergo rehabilitation or education, the court has already 'determined' the person has renounced their religion or is very close to doing so. At the very least, demands for repentance or a detention order would give rise to a strong presumption that the person has, is about to or is likely to commit apostasy. And the court order is directed at eliminating such a possibility or, in the worst case, to reverse the situation completely by forcing or persuading that person to come back to the fold of Islam. Therefore once the court has 'determined' the religious status of the person by requiring them to repent or undergo rehabilitation or education, from that moment onwards the Syariah court has no jurisdiction over that person and any subsequent order would be null and void.

Once the court has 'determined' that a particular individual has committed apostasy, any subsequent order to undergo education would violate their rights under Article 12(3) of the Constitution which provides that 'No person shall be required to receive instruction in or to take part in any ceremony or act of worship of a religion other than his own'.

The High Court and Supreme Court decisions that confirm Syariah court jurisdiction in apostasy-related cases cannot and should not be interpreted as allowing state laws or the Syariah court to punish apostates or as upholding the constitutionality of any state law that prescribes such punishments. Syariah court jurisdiction in apostasy cases confirmed for specific reasons. First, because conversion to Islam is specifically given to the Syariah court and therefore, as a logical conclusion, conversion out of Islam should also vest in the Syariah court. Second, apostasy is a technical area and involves critical questions of religious law, for which only the Syariah court has expertise. Third, there are specific provisions in some state laws, especially in the more recent ones, that confer exclusive jurisdiction to the Syariah court to hear apostasy cases.

Section 90A of the Administration of Islamic Law (Negeri Sembilan) Enactment, 1991 adopts a somewhat different but legally more sound approach. Under this enactment, the Syariah court judge who hears the application for renouncing Islam, before making any order on the application, may defer the hearing for a period of 30 days and refer the applicant to the *mufti* for counselling with a view to advising the applicant to reconsider their wish to renounce Islam. This process involves no detention or compulsory education or rehabilitation. The applicant is at liberty to accept or reject the *mufti*'s view. This approach gives the accused time and opportunity to reconsider. It also allows the authorities to take necessary remedial measures, especially if the alleged apostasy results from misinformation and misunderstanding of Islam. In extreme cases the enactment allows the judge to proceed with the case immediately without referring the matter to the *mufti* if he is satisfied that it is in the interests of the applicant and Islam generally.

However, this approach has not been adopted in other existing or proposed laws. The common feature in most of the state laws on apostasy, as previously noted, is to detain actual and potential apostates and require them to repent. If they refuse to do so they are detained for a limited period of time for the purpose of rehabilitation and education. At the end of that period a declaration is made to the effect that the person has renounced Islam.

Despite doubts over the legitimacy of the existing and proposed apostasy laws, non-Muslims have shown reluctance to challenge them. The primary reason is perhaps due to the general deference accorded to other religions and belief systems by Malaysians of all religions and races which discourages questioning of anything associated with religion. Equally important is the fact that these laws have been introduced by UMNO-led state governments (except in Kelantan and Trengganu where the opposition PAS has been in control since 1991 and 1999 respectively). Therefore if the Court were to declare these laws unconstitutional then the UMNO-led coalition with its two-thirds majority in the Parliament could amend the Constitution to revalidate these laws.

Non-Malays (hence non-Muslims generally) are also reluctant to challenge these laws for historical reasons. Under the ethnic compromise

formula reached between Malays and non-Malays on the eve of independence, non-Malays recognized preferential treatment for Malays and the
supremacy of Islam in the country in exchange for citizenship rights. Since
then, religion has been considered a sensitive issue in Malaysia. The ever-
decreasing number of non-Malay and non-Muslim populations in the
country has also reduced the ability of non-Muslims to challenge such laws.
Since 1990 the percentage of Muslims has increased from 58.6 to 60.4 per
cent of the total population.[30] Also non-Muslims may be of the view that
opposition against apostasy laws within the Muslim community is likely to
force both federal and state governments to change their views on the issue.
Non-Muslims may also consider that their involvement in the apostasy
debate could ignite anger among some Muslims. It was for this reason that
the Chief Minister of Negeri Sembilan, Mohamed Isa Abdul Samad, warned
the opposition Democratic Action Party (DAP) in August 1992 not to
discuss matters concerning Islam.[31]

Closely related to the problem of jurisdiction and constitutionality is the
issue of *habeas corpus*.[32] The question is, can a person detained pursuant
to a Syariah court order for alleged apostasy apply to the High Court for
habeas corpus on the ground that their detention is illegal? Under Article
5(2) of the Constitution, the High Court is duty bound to inquire into
complainants of unlawful detention and, unless satisfied that the detention
is lawful, order them to be produced before the court to order their release.
In *Nor Kursiah bte Baharuddin v. Shahril bin Lamin & Anor*[33] the High
Court of Kuala Lumpur held that not only does the High Court have
jurisdiction to entertain *habeas corpus* applications by individuals detained
pursuant to Syariah court orders, but also that it has a duty to determine
whether or not the detention is illegal. The High Court dealt with the issue
more comprehensively in *Mad Yaacob Ismail v. Kerajaan Negeri Kelantan
& Anor and Other Applications*.[34] The applicants applied, among other
things, for *habeas corpus* on the ground that the detention orders issued by
the Syariah court were unlawful because once they renounced Islam the
Syariah court did not have jurisdiction over them. The High Court,
however, rejected the application on the grounds that the applicants had
failed to prove that the detention was unlawful. The Court held that under
Sections 8(1) and 9(1) of the Administration of Syariah Court (Kelantan)
Enactment, 1982 (which provide for the establishment of Syariah courts
and the Syariah court jurisdictions respectively) the Syariah court was a
court of competent jurisdiction and the sentence it passed was within the
relevant law, i.e. Section 102 of the Council of the Religion of Islam and
Malay Custom (Kelantan) Enactment, 1994 which allows the Syariah court
to detain Muslims who apostatize without a Syariah court order for up to
36 months.[35] The Court further observed that under Section 102(2) of the
same enactment, a Muslim who is confirmed to be a Muslim may not admit
that they are a non-Muslim unless this is confirmed by the Syariah court.
Until the Syariah court declaration, that person is presumed to be a Muslim.

As such the declaration of apostasy per se was insufficient legal grounds to accept them as a non-Muslim.

The effect of this decision is that, although the High Court has the jurisdiction to entertain *habeas corpus* applications involving apostate detainees, in practice it is very hard for an applicant to succeed. This is because in order to succeed the applicant must prove that the detention order by the Syariah court was invalid on the grounds that the Syariah court did not have jurisdiction to make that order. This is often difficult to prove as various apostasy laws, particularly more recent ones, confer explicit jurisdiction to the Syariah court to issue detention orders. As long as the Syariah court acted within its jurisdiction, the High Court could not and would not intervene.[36] Further, when dealing with detention orders issued by the Syariah court, the High Court proceeds on the assumption that the Syariah court is a court of competent jurisdiction with its orders subsisting until set aside under relevant laws and procedures.[37] Therefore if the Syariah court order was within its powers then there is nothing the High Court can or will do because *habeas corpus* cannot be issued for a person serving a sentence passed by a court of competent jurisdiction.[38] This would mean that, in practical terms, individuals detained pursuant to a Syariah court order for alleged apostasy have no remedies outside the Syariah court.

Chapter 12

Apostasy Laws in Malaysia:
The Future

In order to predict future trends in the treatment of apostasy one has to analyse the approach of the two major Muslim parties – the UMNO and the PAS – towards the issue.

PAS and its Modernization

In addition to apostasy laws, PAS has introduced several other measures such as a ban on gambling, restrictions on alcohol, the introduction of dress codes for female civil servants and separate checkouts for men and women at supermarkets, and has made attempts to introduce a land tax (*kharaj*) on non-Muslims. These and other reforms are part of a strategy to establish an Islamic state, in part an attempt to appease conservatives within the Party keen on a speedier implementation of Islamic law.

Despite these tactics, the Party has reformed and modernized many of its earlier policies and views. For instance, it has opened its membership to non-Muslims, although some members from the ruling coalition described this as contradictory to the Party's declared objective of establishing an Islamic state.[1] During the 1999 general election the Party's spiritual leader and the Chief Minister in the state of Kelantan, Nik Abdul Aziz Nik Mat, stated that the Party was prepared to accept a non-Malay (and hence a non-Muslim) as Prime Minister. This is a significant departure from the Islamic theory of government, which bars non-Muslims from holding the highest position in the country. On this point the Party also differs from modern Muslim scholars such as Maududi and Muhammad Asad.[2] UMNO was quick to point out this shift, although not from a religious perspective but from that of maintaining Malay political control in Malaysia.[3]

PAS also allowed the building of the biggest 'Sleeping Buddha' in Malaysia in Kelantan and the rearing and slaughter of pigs in the state of Trengganu, thus lifting a ten-year ban imposed by UMNO-led governments to appease Muslims in the state. PAS has also agreed to allocate seats in municipal and district councils to non-Muslim representatives and promised that non-Muslims would be consulted in any matter affecting their interests. The Party has promised to elect more women candidates to its Central Working Committee and to field more women candidates for the 2004 general election. The PAS newspaper *Haraka* has also moderated its views. The Party appears to have stopped calling UMNO and its leaders 'unbelievers'. The targeted audience of the party has also widened. Its leaders do not miss any opportunity to meet foreign diplomats and officials. It is clear from this that PAS has evolved and in the process has deviated from some of its religious policies.

It could be argued that these reforms are due to the Party's desire to adopt a more moderate approach in order to become more electable. Since the last general election the Party has become the official Opposition in the country. The Party is aware that its policies are scrutinized not only by a nationwide audience but also by international governments, organizations and even by potential foreign investors. It would appear that Islam and an Islamic state are no longer the single aim and mantra of the Party. Words or phrases commonly heard are 'democracy'; 'justice'; 'fairness'; 'less corruption, cronyism and nepotism'; 'abolition of arbitrary laws'; 'economic development'; 'freedom of the press'; 'rule of law' as well as 'accountability' and 'transparency'. These indicate concerns similar to those of other opposition parties in the country. The transformation of conservative parties that hold a religious agenda is not new. In recent years we have seen a similar transformation of the Bharatiya Janata Party (BJP) of India. Several conservative politicians have been forced to change their tone and their stand once their political fortunes changed. In the 1960s and 1970s Dr Mahathir was a Malay nationalist with extreme ideas on non-Malays. His book *Malay Dilemma* was banned and he was expelled from the UMNO. But today non-Malays and non-Muslims hail him as the symbol of toleration.

An important question is: where will this moderation end? If PAS policies were so moderated as to lose their original content, then there would be very little difference between PAS and UMNO. In such a scenario PAS may be forced to fight its arch-rival on economic, social and national policy grounds, areas where the Party lacks, to some extent, the necessary expertise and experience. The more moderate the Party becomes the closer it may move towards UMNO in its religious views. This could give rise to dissatisfaction within the Party, leading to loss of support or even to the emergence of splinter parties. Further, if UMNO and PAS are forced to abandon their ideological differences and fight on a policy level, then UMNO is likely to benefit because of its close association with the independence movement. UMNO's earlier moderate views may also give assurance to non-Muslims, assuming that UMNO policies remain the same and only PAS continues to moderate its views. It is therefore necessary to see where UMNO is heading.

UMNO and its Islamization

It is not only PAS that is undergoing transformation. UMNO, too, is going through a period of soul-searching. As PAS modernizes and 'softens' its policies on various issues, UMNO is trying to become more Islamic in order to win back the support it has lost to PAS. Such political struggles are often represented as the Islamization of the country and publicized as the 'inculcation of Islamic values'.

This move can be traced back to the elevation to the leadership of Dr Mahathir in 1981. An important step in this process was UMNO's incorporation of influential religious figures to counter PAS's rise. These included Yusof Noor who was Dean of the Faculty of Islamic Studies at the University of Kebangsaan Malaysia and Zainal Abidin Kadir, the Director of the Islamic Centre (*Pusat Islam*). The latter was later upgraded into the Department of Islamic Development (Jakim). However, the star recruit was Anwar Ibrahim, a very vocal student with strong Islamic credentials. He was also the President of ABIM (Muslim Youth Movement of Malaysia) and a delegate to the World Assembly of Muslim Youth. Anwar and several other politicians profited from Islamization by making use of the political language of Islam.[4] As President of the International Islamic University, Anwar used his position to consolidate his own power-base within UMNO.

As part of the increasing Islamization of Malaysian society, the UMNO-led government has also introduced Islamic banking, insurance (*takaful*) and mortgage (*rahn*). There are increasing numbers of Islamic programmes on television, radio and other government-controlled media. Islamic festivals are given more coverage than in the past. As noted earlier, there are laws protecting Muslims from the influence of non-Muslim religions. A number of states within the federation have introduced, or are preparing, legislation prohibiting Muslims from renouncing Islam.

The question is where this Islamization process will lead. Will it lead to the establishment of an Islamic state or at least bring UMNO closer to that concept? One thing is clear: it has so far failed to neutralize PAS. In fact, as demands for Islamization grow on the part of groups such as PAS and *Arqam*, the UMNO-led government has been forced to react, for example by banning *Arqam*. However, the government also needs to maintain a delicate balance. Too strong a reaction against these religious groups could defeat the underlying objectives of Islamization: to neutralize PAS and attract more Malay supporters to UMNO. Further, the Malaysian government's standing among Muslim nations needs to be maintained. Were the government to do nothing at all, these pro-Islamization groups would soon be bold enough to challenge the very legitimacy of UMNO to represent Muslims, particularly Malays. This was clearly one of the reasons for banning *Arqam*.

UMNO, like any other political party, aims at maintaining political power. Islamization is a convenient tool to achieve this objective. In the 1999 general election UMNO lost significant ground to PAS among Malays. This was largely due to dissatisfaction with UMNO, especially because of the way the Anwar issue was handled.[5] UMNO must now find a way of winning back that support. One straightforward way would be to restore the status quo that existed before Anwar was sacked. However this is now impossible, especially under the present leadership. Another way would be more Islamization, which would be less costly in the present circumstances. In January 2000, Abdul Hamid Othman, Minister responsible for Islamic Affairs, suggested that more Islamization was the answer to counter the growing popularity of PAS. He advocated that more religious scholars and experts be given places in UMNO branches and divisions so that the party could project an Islamic face.[6]

Conclusion

Conflicting forces within each party, as well as the general conflict between UMNO and PAS, should ensure that Malaysia's religious policies remain moderate in the foreseeable future. There are other forces too that will ensure that strict Islamic penal laws such as the death penalty for apostasy are not introduced soon.

Strict Islamic penal laws cannot be implemented in Malaysia because of the multiracial and multi-religious nature of Malaysian society. Not only do non-Muslims and non-Malays form a significant percentage of the population, they also control much of the national wealth.[7] Were UMNO and PAS to make a collective attempt to implement *hudud* laws, establish an Islamic state or accelerate Islamization, various consequences would be likely. Non-Muslims (especially the more organized and more affluent Chinese) might well set aside their differences to form a united front. They would seek to protect their interests and ensure that an Islamic state was not established in Malaysia. Non-Malays across the political spectrum have as much, if not more, in common than do PAS and UMNO. There is also a very real likelihood that many of these wealthy people would migrate to Australia, New Zealand, Canada, the USA, Singapore or elsewhere, thereby jeopardizing economic development in Malaysia.

Attempts to enforce Islamic law could also give rise to separatist movements in some states, especially in those states where the non-Malays are in the majority. Separatist movements in the Borneo states of Sabah and Sarawak, for example, which are far away from the Malay Peninsula, could be hard to control. Establishment of an Islamic state would also mean that Malays might lose their constitutionally enshrined privileges because Islam does not recognize the right of any particular race.[8] Similarly, the royal families would also stand to lose. As Hussain Mutalib argued in 1990, Malaysia as an Islamic state would need to address the issue of *riba* (usury).[9] At the domestic level Malaysians currently have access to interest-free banking and even the interest-based banks in Malaysia provide interest-free banking services. However, it is quite another thing to base the entire national economy on the Islamic system. These elements within and outside UMNO and PAS are likely to ensure that the country remains as it is for the foreseeable future.

However, there does appear to be general consensus within the Malaysian Muslim community that some form of action ought to be taken to check the growing influence of Christianity in the region. The government may respond to these demands by introducing laws to curb apostasy. In recent years, Islam has become the main defining feature of Malay identity, and the preservation of religion – especially the government-sanctioned version – is seen as imperative for Malay dominance. Therefore 'minor' punishments coated with euphemisms such as 'rehabilitation' and 'education' are inevitable, despite the questionable legitimacy of such laws under the Malaysian Constitution. If the courts were to hold such laws unconstitutional it is likely the UMNO-led federal government would amend the Constitution in order to ensure their validity. This means that these 'minor' punishments for apostasy are likely to continue, at least in the short term.

PART III

Chapter 13

The Need to Rethink Apostasy Laws

Within the broad debate on human rights in the Muslim world, one of the rights targeted for criticism by Muslims is that of freedom of religion for fellow Muslims. These critics argue that freedom of religion for Muslims as conceptualized in international human rights instruments is not in line with Islamic norms, values and laws, and therefore should be rejected. Other Muslims argue that the right to freedom of religion is perfectly in line with Qur'anic and prophetic guidelines. This latter group of Muslims includes an increasing number of intellectuals, scholars and even prominent religious leaders.

A careful examination of the human rights discourse reveals that today the discourse is not necessarily a 'Western' one; it is a concern of the vast majority of Muslims as well. Most Muslim states, as members of the United Nations, accept in principle the Universal Declaration of Human Rights (UDHR) and some even have ratified major human rights conventions. Moreover, as a sign of the global participation in this discourse, some Muslims have developed what they consider to be 'Muslim' human rights documents. On the whole, these are modelled on the UDHR or similar human rights conventions but use Islamic ideas and terminology and are often justified on the basis of Qur'anic texts.

This book has explored a particular aspect of the right to freedom of religion and how this right was marginalized in pre-modern Islamic law through the law of apostasy and the death penalty associated with it. It has sought to demonstrate the background against which the law of apostasy was formulated, in particular the political context and the intra-Islamic intolerance that played a significant role in the development of that law. What is critical is the high degree of fluidity and diversity in understanding what constitutes apostasy, a state of affairs that has been utilized by political and religious figures alike to control, oppress, persecute or eliminate opponents. For that reason the potential misuse of laws on apostasy has always been considerable throughout Islamic history.

An important characteristic of this book is that it challenges the view that the punishment of apostasy by death is based on clear Qur'anic or prophetic instructions. Discussion in chapters 4 and 5 has demonstrated that there is nothing in the Qur'an to justify a temporal punishment for apostasy, and little to justify many of the apostasy laws associated with it. Much of this law was developed from certain isolated (*ahad*) *hadith* and interpretations of those *hadith*, or on the basis of analogy (*qiyas*) and *ijtihad*. Since none of these guarantee certainty of knowledge (*'ilm qat'i*) as understood in the principles of Islamic jurisprudence (*usul al-fiqh*), Muslims in the modern period have the opportunity to go back and rethink these laws. If these laws are no longer practicable or relevant for Muslims, there is a strong justification to reconsider them. The argument that these laws are backed by consensus (*ijma'*) should not deter Muslims from going along this path. Numerous other laws on which there was consensus at some point in Muslim history have been subject to revision and in some cases, as with those connected with slavery and the caliphate, dropped altogether.

An important function of this book is to highlight the nature of the debate on apostasy and apostasy laws in a multi-religious and multicultural nation-state, Malaysia, where Muslims are in the majority. Some apostasy laws are in place in several states of the Federation. The case study in chapters 9–12 indicates the political nature of the discourse on apostasy there, and serves to highlight some of the problems and challenges faced by the Malaysian legal system in dealing with apostasy cases. That the issue is political is demonstrated by the fact that both main political parties, PAS and UMNO, attempt to win votes by manipulating the debate on apostasy laws. Given that Malaysia is somewhat typical of other Muslim-majority nation-states in terms of religious pluralism, the difficulties and challenges that apostasy laws face there can be used as a basis for understanding what may happen elsewhere in the Muslim world if similar apostasy laws are put in place.

A number of issues emerge from the discussion in this book. On religious freedom, it is clear that the Qur'an supports the notion of religious freedom and religious faith as an individual choice. Religious freedom is presented in the Qur'an in a variety of contexts and ways. However, in interpreting these texts, Muslim scholars of the pre-modern period largely limited the scope of freedom available to a Muslim in choosing and adopting a religion or a belief system. They opted instead for a narrow definition of religious freedom, confining it to a freedom given to non-Muslims to either remain under Islamic rule as 'protected religious minorities' (*ahl al-dhimmah*) or to convert to Islam. As for Muslims, once they became Muslims, conversion from Islam was not permitted. To prevent conversion, Muslim jurists developed the apostasy laws with the death penalty as the ultimate punishment, which was doubtless justified on the basis of certain isolated *hadith*. This attitude of early jurists should not surprise us as they functioned at a time when religious freedom and individual human dignity were perhaps not related in the way they are today. Moreover, in that earlier time and social environment, an individual became a 'person' by being associated with a particular religion or tribe. In the case of Islam it was the religion rather than the tribe. In joining Islam, an individual automatically became part of the community of believers. This 'community of believers' also functioned as a political unit: the caliphate or emirate. Thus there was a conjunction between corporate religious identity rooted in the community and political identity. In general, as the concept developed in pre-modern Islamic law, if someone rejected the community of believers by converting to another religion, they were automatically excluded from the political community as well. This meant the complete loss of an individual's basic rights as a person (such as right to life, right to own property) which had been conferred on becoming a Muslim.

Since an individual's basic rights were dependent on being part of this community, the whole notion of apostasy and issues associated with it in the pre-modern period made good sense. By contrast, most Muslims today have moved away from this conjunction between religious community and political identity to a separation between the two. Today, a political community in the sense of a nation-state does not have to be based on a religious community and, in fact, most nation-states in the world, including the Muslim world, are not based on this strict identification. An individual can become a citizen of this political unit regardless of religious affiliation, which is the case in the majority of Muslim states, where modern constitutions guarantee religious freedom and equality before the law for all. Thus religious freedom, and freedom of belief in particular, has become a prima facie right in the modern period within the functioning of the nation-state. The pre-modern Islamic law of apostasy that depended on the meshing of religious identity and political community has therefore lost much of its meaning.

With few exceptions, today's societies are not 'closed'. People move from one area to another and from country to country in an unprecedented manner. Migration, travel and dual residence serve the purposes of education, business, recreation and employment in a world driven by highly developed communication networks. Muslims are migrating in large numbers to non-Muslim countries, and to a lesser extent the movement is the other way. Usually, even in the Muslim world, there are no ghettos or separate quarters for the followers of each religious tradition like those that existed in some regions in pre-modern times. Consequently people of all religious traditions in a given country may live side by side in the same neighbourhood, sharing the same space.

This unprecedented interaction and pluralism places substantial pressure on all Islamic scholars to offer new ideas about religious freedom relevant to today's multi-religious and multicultural world. The reaffirmation of pre-modern laws developed for a different time, place and circumstance is not particularly helpful or practical. In any event, many Muslims have abandoned aspects of the pre-modern apostasy laws, particularly punishment by death. It is only in a few Muslim states the law is still in force. Despite this, and despite the unrealistic nature of much of the debate, the question of apostasy is still discussed. It still finds its way into contemporary Islamic legal texts and current discourse, with many traditionalists continuing to argue for implementation of this outdated law.

The discussion in this book shows that apostasy laws today have a huge potential for abuse. There is a high degree of diversity in Muslim theological, legal or religio-political positions, and it is difficult to devise one set of creeds applicable to and accepted by all. In addition to pre-modern divisions, new divisions and groupings have emerged among Muslims today. Muslims from one group still accuse other groups of apostasy, heresy and unbelief. Similarly, in a number of Muslim countries, the government assumes the responsibility of 'protecting' local orthodoxies and those who do not adhere to the government-sanctioned orthodoxy can be branded as deviants, heretics or apostates. The potential for abuse is all the more real because governments in many Muslim countries are either semi-authoritarian or fully authoritarian, and civil, political and religious rights remain severely curtailed. Further, religion and religious institutions in these countries are often subordinated to the government. Such governments can use their authority to persuade or, if necessary, force religious officials and institutions to question the religious beliefs of political opponents and dissidents. The authoritarian tendencies inherent in these countries also mean that there are very few, if any, institutional safeguards, such as accountability through elected representatives of parliament, or via the courts, or through pressure from NGOs or the media, to check abuses.

For these reasons, it is essential to formulate an idea of religious freedom that is in harmony with existential realities and can take into account both Islamic belief and cultural diversity within nation-states. It is rather premature to believe that nation-states in the Muslim world are going to disappear or that a new single Muslim state will emerge with a caliphal system in which one caliph leads the faithful. Even a cursory look at the map of the Muslim world – with all its political, theological, economic and cultural differences – reveals that there are considerable divisions and differences among Muslims which would prevent the realization of such an idea. It is inconceivable that these Muslim states can be politically united under one umbrella, as some Muslims seem to believe, or that all Muslims will be residing in a *dar al-islam* that accommodates only Muslims as citizens.

If we are right about the way the world is moving, we will not be seeing more compartmentalization of the world into religious blocs. On the contrary, globalization will bring far more intensive linkages and mixes of people from a variety of religious backgrounds into the same space. With the increasing intensity of globalization, interaction and multiculturalism, many of the pre-modern ideas that Muslims inherited appear to be imprac-tical and unrealistic. Recognizing these new realities, many Muslim social systems have adopted modern ideas associated with religious freedom. However, tensions remain between the stated objectives and realities of life in a modern Muslim nation-state, and these tensions reflect the disjunction between the pre-modern and the postmodern world.

Today, almost all Muslim countries are multi-religious societies. Simi-larly there is no Muslim state with a population who follow the same legal and/or theological school. Even in Saudi Arabia, where all citizens are theoretically Muslim, there is a significant Shiʿi population. Several million Christians, Hindus and Buddhists are also long-term guest workers. The population of Yemen, for example, comprises Muslims (including Shafiʿis and Zaydis), and small numbers of Jews, Christians and even Hindus. The Kuwaiti population comprises Sunnis and Shiʿis, as well as Christians, Hindus and Parsis.

In addition, a substantial number of Muslims live as minorities else-where. Approximately 7 million Muslims live in the United States alone, and more than 15 million Muslims live in Europe as minorities. There are approximately 60 million Muslims in China and 140 million in India. Here apostasy laws have no meaning within the legal structures of these states. Muslims are free to convert or simply not to follow any religion at all, without detriment to their basic rights. In this context the pre-modern distinction between 'Muslim' territory and 'non-Muslim' territory is blurred. Categories in pre-modern Islamic law such as the 'abode of Islam' (*dar al-islam*) and 'the abode of war' (*dar al-harb*) are therefore not useful as categories that locate Muslims. Given globalization and increasing mobility, it is common for people of various faiths to live side by side. In a world of information exchange where proselytizing is widely practised, there is no doubt that conversions will occur across religious boundaries.

An important but rarely discussed challenge to laws on apostasy is the issue of 'silent apostasy'. In all Muslim communities there are what may be called both practising and non-practising (that is, nominal) Muslims. Practising Muslims themselves vary in their commitment to Islamic rituals, commandments and prohibitions. Some may be totally committed and devoted to both the fundamentals and non-fundamentals of the religion; others may adhere only to the fundamentals such as the five daily prayers, fasting, *zakat*, and pilgrimage. Some believers may practise many funda-mentals but ignore others and be irregular in their practice.

Besides those practising Islam at varying levels there are the merely nominal or 'cultural' Muslims; that is, those who have only a minimal affiliation with Islam. Nominal Muslims may carry a name of Muslim origin, live in a Muslim community, and identify themselves with Islam when asked about religious affiliation. They may have a superficial, distorted or vague familiarity with what Muslims 'do'. Nominal Muslims are not usually interested in observing religious practices apart from occasional attendance at ʿId prayer or participation in community religio-cultural activities. They have little commitment to Islam, and do not abide by its commandments or prohibitions. In all Muslim communities, there are numerous such nominal Muslims though there are no reliable studies in this area and even estimates of numbers are hard to find. Even if we estimate conservatively a quarter of the Muslim population to be nominal Muslims, this still represents at least 300 million Muslims.

Nominal Muslims present a major challenge to the law of apostasy. They profess Islam outwardly and perhaps incidentally, but have no commitment to it or its practices. From an Islamic legal perspective, one could argue that these nominal Muslims are akin to apostates if not actually apostates. In pre-modern Islamic law, it was widely held that anyone who did not, for instance, perform the obligatory requirements of the five daily prayers would fall into the category of apostate. According to Ibn Taymiyyah, the Muslim who does not pray (the five daily prayers) must be ordered to do so; if he refuses, he must be put to death. He will not be washed before burial, no prayer will be performed for him, and he will not be buried in a Muslim cemetery.[1] Ibn Taymiyyah's view is not isolated; as far as the fundamental religious obligations are concerned, many *ulama* would concur with him, at least in theory. In fact, many view Abu Bakr's (the first caliph) engagement in the so-called 'wars of apostasy' as fighting apostates whose crime was the refusal to pay *zakat*, a fundamental part of Islam like the prayers.

One reason why some Muslims and Muslim regimes feel the need to introduce apostasy laws today is to curtail conversions from Islam. However, Muslims also seek to convert non-Muslims. The fact that Islam is one of the fastest growing religions in the world is indicative of this. In countries like Malaysia the number of people converting to Islam is far greater than the number of Muslims who renounce Islam. Therefore, it follows that if states were to introduce apostasy laws, Muslims could be prevented from converting non-Muslims to Islam. It would be inequitable to suggest that only Muslims should have the right to proselytize. Further, forcing Muslims to adhere to their religion would categorize them as hypocrites in the eyes of the Qur'an. People who remain as Muslims under threat of force are unlikely to have anything beneficial to offer to Islam. Criminalizing apostasy does not address the real issue; it only gives the impression that Islam is an imposed religion. It may only succeed in offending the overwhelming majority of Muslims in the world who embrace Islam voluntarily, not by force. Therefore, a more effective and practical alternative needs to be found to prevent Muslims from renouncing Islam.

It seems that, with the exception of a vocal group of militants, ultra-conservatives and some extremists, a large number of Muslims throughout the Muslim world are moving away from the notion of an enforced religion to one of the profession of a religion as a covenant between an individual and God. This is closer to the Qur'anic idea of non-coercion in matters of faith and religion, which was so strongly emphasized in the Qur'an in a variety of contexts. Unlike the pre-modern period in which 'non-coercion in religion' was considered to have been 'abrogated', the modern view that is emerging among Muslims is that non-coercion remains a fundamental principle of Islam and that Islam guarantees religious freedom to all. Nevertheless, many Muslims have remained reluctant to take the logical step of examining apostasy laws and declaring them irrelevant to their life today. Others, although only a few, are arguing for doing away with apostasy laws that adversely affect the individual's basic rights as a person and are pressing for reform in this area. Given that the religio-political context in which apostasy laws were first put into effect in the post-prophetic period has lost its meaning and relevance in the modern period, it is important to rethink the law of apostasy and its punishment. The weak textual basis of the law of apostasy provides a strong Qur'anic justification for embarking on the task of reforming this law.

PART IV

Islamic *Aqidah* Protection (Perlis) Bill 2000[1]

ARRANGEMENT OF CLAUSES

A BILL

An Enactment to provide provisions for the protection, rehabilitation and determination of the *aqidah* of a Muslim and matters connected therewith.

ENACTED by the Legislature of the State of Perlis as follows:

Short title, application and commencement

1. (1) This Enactment may be cited as the Islamiah *Aqidah* Protection (the State of Perlis) Enactment 2000.

    (2) This Enactment shall come into operation on a date to be appointed by the Ruler by notification in the Gazette.

Interpretation

2. (1) In this Enactment, unless the context otherwise requires:–

'Administration Enactment' means the Administration of the Syariah Court Enactment 1991;

'attempt to change *aqidah*' means any act by a Muslim who is *mukallaf* on his own free will either by word, deed or by any means that may be interpreted as an attempt to change his *aqidah* and belief towards the religion of Islam;

'*Aqidah* Rehabilitation Centre' means any rehabilitation centre as determined under section 14 of this Act;

'Court' means Syariah High Court established under subsection 7(1) of the Administration Enactment;

'Hukum Syarak' means the laws of Islam as contained in the Al-Quran and the Sunnah Rasul Allah S.W.T.;

'Islamic Family Law' means the Islamic Family Law Enactment 1991;

'Judge' means a Syariah High Court Judge appointed under subsection 6B(1) of the Administration Enactment;

'Majlis' means the Majlis Agama Islam dan Adat Isti'adat Melayu Perlis established under subsection 4(1) of the Administration of Muslim Law Enactment 1963;

'Peguam Syarie' means a person appointed as Peguam Syarie under section 24 of the Administration Enactment;

'Syariah Enforcement Officer' means the officer appointed under section 29A of the Administration of Muslim Law Enactment, 1963 and includes the Chief Syariah Enforcement Officer;

'Secretary of the Majlis' means the Secretary of the Majlis Agama Islam appointed under subsection 4(6) of the Administration of Muslim Law Enactment, 1963.

    (2) All words and expressions used in this Enactment and not herein defined in this Enactment but defined in the Interpretation Acts 1948 and

1967 (Act 388), shall have the meaning thereby assigned to them respectively in the Acts to the extent that such meanings do not conflict with Hukum Syarak.

Jurisdiction of the Court to make declaration and order

3. The Court shall have jurisdiction to –

(a) declare that a person is no longer a Muslim;

(b) declare the religious status of a Muslim who has died; and

(c) make any other order as it deems fit in relation to the matters stated under paragraphs (a) and (b).

Acknowledgement as a Muslim

4. For the purposes of this Enactment and any other written law, a Muslim shall at all time, be acknowledged and treated as a Muslim, unless a declaration has been made by the Court under this Enactment that he is no longer a Muslim.

Information and investigation

5. If from information received or otherwise, a Syariah Enforcement Officer has reason to suspect the commission of an attempt to change *aqidah* by a Muslim, he shall as soon as possible investigate the matter.

Powers of Syariah Enforcement Officer in conducting investigation

6. In conducting an investigation under section 5, a Syariah Enforcement Officer shall have all the powers conferred on him under the Criminal Procedure in the Syarak Enactment 1991, as if he is conducting a criminal investigation under such Enactment.

Appearance in Court of the person who has attempted to change *aqidah*

7. (1) If at the end of his investigation under section 5, the Syariah Enforcement Officer is of the opinion that –

(a) there is sufficient evidence or reasonable ground of suspicion to justify the commencement of proceedings under this Enactment against the person; and

(b) the person against whom such investigation is conducted has attained the age of eighteen or more;

he shall make an application to the Court for a summons to be issued requiring the appearance of that person before the Court and that person shall appear as required.

(2) If the person who has been served with a summons under subsection

(1) is not present as required, the Syariah Enforcement Officer shall apply to the Court to issue a warrant of arrest to secure his attendance.

Powers of the Court against the person who has attempted to change his *aqidah*.

8. When a person appears or is brought before the Court under section 7, the Judge shall –

(a) advise such person to repent, and if the Judge is satisfied that he has repented according to Hukum Syarak, record his repentance and order his release; or

(b) if the person refuses to repent –

(i) order that he be detained at the *Aqidah* Rehabilitation Centre for a period not exceeding one year unless he has earlier repented under subsection 9(2); and

(ii) order the Syariah Enforcement Officer to submit a report to the Court and the officer in charge of the *Aqidah* Rehabilitation Centre, relating to the liabilities or obligations of that person under the Islamic Family Law not later than thirty days before the expiry of the period of his detention.

Procedure if the person repents

9. (1) If at any time, the person who has been ordered to be detained under subsection 8(b)(i) has repented, the officer in charge of the *Aqidah* Rehabilitation Centre shall prepare a report and, as soon as possible, produce that person before the Court.

(2) If the Judge is satisfied that the person brought before him under subsection (1) has repented in accordance with Hukum Syarak, he shall record the person's repentance and order his release.

Procedure if the person refuses to repent

10. (1) If the person under detention refuses to repent, the officer in charge of the *Aqidah* Rehabilitation Centre where he is detained shall, if –

(a) the report by the Syariah Enforcement Officer indicated that the person has no liability or obligation under the Islamic Family Law, produce him before the Court at the end of the period of his detention; or

(b) the report by the Syariah Enforcement Officer indicated that he has liabilities or obligations under the Islamic Family Law, produce him before the Court not less than thirty days before the expiry of the period of his detention.

(2) The officer in charge of the *Aqidah* Rehabilitation Centre shall at the time the person is produced before the Court, submit to the Judge a

progress report pertaining to the rehabilitation programmes which has been carried out on such person.

(3) When the person is brought before the judge under subsection 1(a) or (b), the Judge shall again advise such person to repent, and if –

(a) the Judge is satisfied that the person brought before him has repented in accordance with Hukum Syarak, he shall record the person's repentance and order his release; or

(b) the person still refuses to repent, the Judge shall, after examining the reports submitted to him and after hearing any explanation from such person, record his refusal to repent; and if –

(i) the Judge is satisfied that the person has no liability or obligation under the Islamic Family Law, declare that the person is no longer a Muslim and order his release; or

(ii) the Judge is satisfied that the person has any liability or obligation under the Islamic Family Law; section 11 shall apply.

Powers of the Court to order the settlement of liability, etc.

11. (1) In circumstances mentioned under subsection 10(3)(b)(ii), before the Judge makes a declaration against the person, he shall proceed to hear the liabilities or obligations of that person under the Islamic Family Law as if a divorce has occurred under this Enactment.

(2) In determining the liabilities or obligations under subsection (1), the Judge shall hear and decide the claims of all parties under the Islamic Family Law.

(3) When the Judge has decided on the liabilities or obligations of the parties, he shall in order –

(a) declare that the person is no longer a Muslim and dissolve his marriage;

(b) determine the person's liabilities or obligations under subsection (2); and

(c) release the person unless he has earlier been released upon the expiry of the detention.

(4) When an order made by the Judge is in respect of a liquidated sum such sum is recoverable as a Civil debt.

Reference for determination of the religious status of a deceased person

12. (1) A declaration to determine the religious status of a deceased person under section 3(b) shall be made by way of reference to the Court.

(2) No reference shall be made under this section unless by the Secretary

of the Majlis and only the Secretary of the Majlis may be a Party in that reference.

(3) The Secretary of the Majlis may on his own motion, or on the application of any person shall, as soon as possible, refer to the Judge for a declaration whether the deceased was a Muslim or otherwise at the time of his death.

(4) A reference shall be supported by –

(a) grounds of reference;

(b) an affidavit verifying the facts that are relied on for the reference; and

(c) a certificate of urgency.

(5) Where an application for a reference under subsection (3) to the Secretary of the Majlis is made by any person, he shall furnish the material facts of the case which must be supported by an affidavit to prove that he has an interest in that application.

(6) If the person making the application to the Secretary of the Majlis is a non-Muslim, he must file together with his application a statutory declaration made under the Statutory Declaration Act 1960 [Act 13].

(7) At the hearing of the reference, the Secretary of the Majlis shall have the right to be heard whether in person or by a Peguam Syarie and the Court may hear any other person on the matter to arrive at a just decision.

(8) If at the end of the hearing, the Judge is satisfied that –

(a) the deceased was a Muslim at the time of his death, he shall make a declaration of such fact and may order any person to do any act to give effect to the declaration and may specify the period in which such order is to be carried out; or

(b) the deceased was not a Muslim at the time of his death, he shall make a declaration of such fact and may make any other order that he deems fit.

Register of declaration and order

13. The Secretary of the Majlis shall keep and maintain or cause to be kept or maintained a register in any form as he deems fit for registration of the declaration and order made under this Enactment.

Determination of *Aqidah* Rehabilitation Centre

14. The Majlis may, by way of notification in the Gazette, determine any place or institution, as an *Aqidah* Rehabilitation Centre for the purposes of this Enactment.

Powers to make rules

15. (1) The Ruler, on the advice of the Majlis, may, by notification in the Gazette make rules as may be necessary or expedient for the purposes of carrying into effect the provisions of this Enactment.

(2) In particular and without prejudice to the generality of subsection (1), such rules may –

(a) make provisions for the control, isolation, detention, protection and rehabilitation of the person detained in any of the *Aqidah* Rehabilitation Centres;

(b) require the person responsible or the officer in charge of the *Aqidah* Rehabilitation Centre to submit to the Court reports and information in respect of the person detained at the centre;

(c) regulate the procedure of admission to or discharge from an *Aqidah* Rehabilitation Centre; and

(d) make the contravention of or a failure to comply with any regulation made under this Enactment an offence and may prescribe a fine not exceeding one thousand ringgit or imprisonment for a term not exceeding six months for such offence.

(ISHAK BIN SAHARI)
State Legal Adviser, Perlis

Appendix 2

Pakistan's Blasphemy Laws

Offences Relating to Religion: Pakistan Penal Code

295-B

Defiling, etc., of copy of Holy Quran. Whoever wilfully defiles, damages or desecrates a copy of the Holy Quran or of an extract therefrom or uses it in any derogatory manner or for any unlawful purpose shall be punishable for imprisonment for life.

295-C

Use of derogatory remarks, etc; in respect of the Holy Prophet. Whoever by words, either spoken or written or by visible representation, or by any imputation, innuendo, or insinuation, directly or indirectly, defiles the sacred name of the Holy Prophet Mohammed (PBUH) shall be punished with death, or imprisonment for life, and shall also be liable to fine.

298-A

Use of derogatory remarks, etc. . . . ., in respect of holy personages. Whoever by words, either spoken or written, or by visible representation, or by any imputation, innuendo or insinuation, directly or indirectly, defiles a sacred name of any wife (Ummul Mumineen), or members of the family (Ahlebait), of the Holy Prophet (PBUH), or any of the righteous caliphs (Khulafa-e-Rashideen) or companions (Sahaaba) of the Holy Prophet shall be punished by imprisonment of either description for a term which may extend to three years, or with fine, or with both.

298-B

Misuse of epithets, descriptions and titles, etc. reserved for certain holy personages or places.

1. Any person of the Qadiani group or the Lahori group (who call themselves Ahmadis or by any other name) who by words, either spoken or written or by visible representation:

    a. refers to or addresses, any person, other than a Caliph or companion of the Holy Prophet Mohammed (PBUH), as 'Ameerul Momneen', 'Khalifat-ul-Momneen', 'Khalifat-ul-Muslimeen', 'Sahaabi' or 'Razi Allah Anho';

    b. Refers to or addresses, any person, other than a wife of the Holy Prophet Mohammed (PBUH), as Ummul-Mumineen;

    c. refers to, or addresses, any person, other than a member of the family (Ahle-Bait) of the Holy Prophet Mohammed (PBUH), as Ahle-Bait; or

    d. refers to, or names, or calls, his place of worship as Masjid;

    shall be punished with imprisonment of either description for a term which may extend to three years, and shall also be liable to fine.

2. Any person of the Qadiani group or Lahori group, (who call themselves Ahmadis or by any other name), who by words, either spoken or written, or by visible representations, refers to the mode or form of call to prayers followed by his faith as 'Azan' or recites Azan as used by the Muslims, shall be punished with imprisonment of either description for a term which may extend to three years and shall also be liable to fine.

298-C

Person of the Qadiani group, etc, calling himself a Muslim or preaching or propagating his faith. Any person of the Qadiani group or the Lahori group (who call themselves Ahmadis or any other name), who directly or indirectly, poses himself as a Muslim, or calls, or refers to, his faith as Islam, or preaches or propagates his faith, or invites others to accept his faith, by words, either spoken or written, or by visible representation or in any manner whatsoever outrages the religious feelings of Muslims, shall be punished with imprisonment of either description for a term which may extend to three years and shall also be liable to fine.

Notes

Introduction

1. *The Message of the Qur'an*, trans. Muhammad Asad, Gibraltar: Dar-al-Andalus, 1980.

Chapter 1

1. Kevin Dwyer, *Arab Voices: The Human Rights Debate in the Middle East*, London: Routledge, 1991, pp. 1–7.
2. Chris Brown, 'Human Rights', *The Globalization of World Politics: An Introduction to International Relations*, 2nd edn, ed. John Baylis and Steve Smith, New York: Oxford University Press, 2001, p. 599.
3. Adrian Karatnycky, 'Religious Freedom and Democracy as Fundamental Human Rights', paper delivered at the International Coalition for Religious Freedom Conference on 'Religious Freedom and the New Millennium', Berlin: 29–31 May 1998, <http://www.religiousfreedom.com/conference/Germany/karatnycky.htm>, accessed 5 May 2002.
4. Quoted by Charles Canady, 'Religious Freedom and Democracy', paper delivered at the International Coalition for Religious Freedom Conference on 'Religious Freedom and the New Millennium', Berlin: 29–31 May 1998, <http://www.religiousfreedom. com/conference/Germany/canady.htm>, accessed 5 May 2002.
5. Article 9 of the ECHR states: 'Everyone has the right to freedom of thought, conscience and religion; this right includes freedom to change his religion or belief and freedom, either alone or in community with others and in public or private, to manifest his religion or belief, in worship, teaching, practice and observance.'
6. Arcot Krishnaswami,'Study of Discrimination in the Matter of Religious Rights and Practices, UN Doc. E/CN.4/Sub.2/200/Rev.1, UN Sales No.60.XIV.2 (1960), in *Religion and Human Rights: Basic Documents*, ed. Tad Stahnke and J. Paul Martin, New York: Center for the Study of Human Rights, Columbia University, 1998, p. 21.
7. Ben P. Vermeulen, 'International Agreements on Religious Freedom and their Implementation in Europe', paper delivered at the International Coalition for Religious Freedom Conference on 'Religious Freedom and the New Millenium', Berlin: 29–31 May 1998, <http://www.religiousfreedom.com/conference/Germany/vermeulen.htm>, accessed 6 May 2002.
8. General Comment No. 22 [ICCPR Article 18] Human Rights Committee, Forty-Eighth Session, 20 July 1993.
9. General Comment No. 22 [ICCPR Article 18] Human Rights Committee, Forty-Eighth Session, 20 July 1993.
10. Article 29(2), Universal Declaration of Human Rights.
11. Krishnaswami, 'Study of Discrimination in the Matter of Religious Rights and Practices', pp. 25–6.
12. Lee Boothby, 'Models of Religious Freedom', paper delivered at the International Coalition for Religious Freedom Conference on 'Religious Freedom and the New

Millennium', Berlin: 29–31 May 1998, <http://www.religiousfreedom.com/conference/ Germany/boothby.htm>, accessed 5 May 2002.

13. See Articles 2, 7, 18, 29.
14. Ann Elizabeth Mayer, *Islam and Human Rights: Tradition and Politics*, 2nd edn, Boulder and San Francisco: Westview Press; London: Pinter, 1995, pp. 1–18.
15. Mayer, *Islam and Human Rights*, p. 8.
16. Donna E. Arzt, 'Religious Human Rights in Muslim States of the Middle East and North Africa', in *Religious Human Rights in Global Perspective: Religious Perspectives*, ed. John Witte, Jr and Johan D. van der Vyver, The Hague: Martinus Nijhoff Publishers, 1996, pp. 387–454, and online at <http://www.law.emory.edu/EILR/volumes/spring96/arzt.html>, accessed 5 May 2002.
17. *Signatures to the United Nations Covenant on Civil and Political Rights*, <http://www.hrweb.org/legal/cprsigs.html>, accessed 24 January 2002.
18. US Department of State, *Annual Report on International Religious Freedom*, 1999, 2001, <http://www.state.gov/g/drl/rls/irf/2001/>, accessed 5 May 2002.
19. Muhammad al-Sadiq Afifi, *Al-Mujtama' al-Islami wa Huquq al-Insan*, Mecca: Muslim World League, 1987, p. 228.
20. Afifi, *Al-Mujtama' al-Islami wa Huquq al-Insan*, p. 244.
21. Sultanhussein Tabandeh, *A Muslim Commentary on the Universal Declaration of Human Rights*, London: F.T. Goulding, 1970, p. 70.
22. Tabandeh, *A Muslim Commentary*, p. 70.
23. Tabandeh, *A Muslim Commentary*, p. 71.
24. Tabandeh, *A Muslim Commentary*, p. 71.
25. Tabandeh, *A Muslim Commentary*, p. 71.
26. Hasan Ahmad Abidin, *Huquq al-Insan wa Wajibatuhu fi al-Qur'an*, Mecca: Rabitat al-Alam al-Islami, 1984, p. 137.
27. Abidin, *Huquq al-Insan wa Wajibatuhu fi al-Qur'an*, pp. 139–40.
28. Abidin, *Huquq al-Insan wa Wajibatuhu fi al-Qur'an*, p. 185.
29. Mohammad Hashim Kamali, *Islamic Law in Malaysia: Issues and Developments*, Kuala Lumpur: Ilmiah Publishers, 2000, pp. 203–19.
30. Mayer, *Islam and Human Rights*, pp. 141–61.
31. Mayer, *Islam and Human Rights*, pp. 61–78.
32. Article 12(a), UIDHR, for example.
33. The following information about specific countries is based on the US Department of State, *Annual Report on International Religious Freedom*.
34. Joint Decree of the Minister of Religion and the Minister of Home Affairs No.1 of 1979 on regulations for propagation of religion and overseas donations, quoted in Ahmad von Denffer, *Indonesia: Government Decrees on Mission and Subsequent Developments*, Leicester: Islamic Foundation, 1987, p. 27.

Chapter 2

1. Ahmad Amin, *Fajr al-Islam*, 12th edn, Cairo: Maktabat al-Nahdah al-Misriyyah, 1978, pp. 25–6.
2. Amin, *Fajr al-Islam*, p. 24.
3. The *Ka'bah* is a cube-shaped building within the precincts of the Great Mosque of Mecca. Muslims believe that the *Ka'bah* was built by Abraham and his son Ishmael, and that pilgrimage to the *Ka'bah* began at the time of Abraham.
4. Ibn Hisham, *Al-Sirah al-Nabawiyyah*, ed. Mustafa al-Saqqa, Ibrahim al-Abiyari and Abdul Hafiz Shalabi, vol. 2, Cairo: Mustafa al-Babi al-Halabi, 1955, p. 559.
5. Qur'an 5:68–86; 9:30.
6. Qur'an 2:75; 100–101; 146; 3:23; 78.

7.   Qur'an 2:89; 101; 3:81. In more than fifteen verses, the Qur'an states the concept of 'confirmation' of the previous revelations, Torah and Gospel.
8.   According to Muhammad Asad, this term is used here to 'describe the Qur'an as the determinant factor in deciding what is genuine and what is false in the earlier scriptures'. See footnote 64 in *The Message of the Qur'an*, p. 153.
9.   Qur'an 2:94.
10. Qur'an 5:73.
11. Qur'an 6:108.
12. Qur'an 9:1–13.
13. However, several events of the time can be taken to mean a harsher attitude on the part of some caliphs. This includes Caliph ʿUmar's decision to drive the Jews of Khaybar out of Arabia and settle them elsewhere. The Christians of Najran were sent to Kufa. The aim was to free the Arabian peninsula from non-Muslims. Jurji Zaydan, *Umayyads and ʿAbbasids: Being the Fourth Part of Jurji Zaydan's History of Islamic Civilization*, trans. D.S. Margoliouth, New Delhi: Kitab Bhavan, 1978, p. 29.
14. W. Montogomery Watt, *The Majesty that was Islam: The Islamic World 661–1100*, New York: Praeger, 1974, p. 65.
15. Watt, *The Majesty that was Islam*, p. 62.
16. Amin, *Fajr al-Islam*, pp. 258–61; ʿAbd al-Qahir al-Baghdadi, *Al-Farq Bayna al-Firaq*, Beirut: Dar al-Afaq al-Jadidah, 1980, p. 39.
17. Amin, *Fajr al-Islam*, pp. 258–9.
18. Amin, *Fajr al-Islam*, pp. 258–61.
19. Watt, *The Majesty that was Islam*, p. 69.
20. Watt, *The Majesty that was Islam*, pp. 70–71.
21. Amin, *Fajr al-Islam*, p. 280.
22. Richard K. Khuri, *Freedom, Modernity, and Islam*, New York: Syracuse University Press, 1998, p. 224.
23. Majid Fakhry, *Tarikh al-Falsafah al-Islamiyyah*, trans. Kamal al-Yazji, Beirut: al-Dar al-Muttahidah li al-Nashr, 1979, p. 77.
24. Ian Richard Netton, *A Popular Dictionary of Islam*, London: Curzon Press, 1997, p. 160.
25. Watt, *The Majesty that was Islam*, p. 250.
26. Muhammad Munir Adlabi, *Qatl al-Murtadd: al-Jarimah al-Lati Harramha al-Islam*, Dimashq: n.p., 1991, p. 37.
27. Adlabi, *Qatl al-Murtadd*, p. 37.
28. Adlabi, *Qatl al-Murtadd*, p. 38.
29. Netton, *A Popular Dictionary of Islam*, p. 94; Ibn al-Athir, *Al-Kamil fi al-Tarikh*, vol. 7, Beirut: Dar al-Kutub al-ʿIlmiyyah, 1998, pp. 5–6.
30. Netton, *A Popular Dictionary of Islam*, p. 72.
31. Annemarie Schimmel, *Mystical Dimensions of Islam*, Chapel Hill: University of North Carolina Press, 1975, p. 60.
32. Ibn al-Athir, *Al-Kamil fi al-Tarikh*, 7:6.
33. Adlabi, *Qatl al-Murtadd*, p. 39.
34. Adlabi, *Qatl al-Murtadd*, p. 39.
35. Adlabi, *Qatl al-Murtadd*, p. 40; Netton, *A Popular Dictionary of Islam*, p. 110.
36. Albert Hourani, *A History of the Arab Peoples*, London: Faber & Faber, 1991, p. 176.
37. Adlabi, *Qatl al-Murtadd*, p. 40.
38. Adlabi, *Qatl al-Murtadd*, p. 41.
39. Adlabi, *Qatl al-Murtadd*, p. 42.
40. Adlabi, *Qatl al-Murtadd*, pp. 42–3.
41. Fakhry, *Tarikh al-Falsafah al-Islamiyyah*, p. 136.
42. Sarah Stroumsa, *Freethinkers of Medieval Islam*, Leiden: Brill, 1999, pp. 37–86.
43. Stroumsa, *Freethinkers of Medieval Islam*, pp. 87–120.
44. Fakhry, *Tarikh al-Falsafah al-Islamiyyah*, p. 372.

45. Ibn Kathir, *Al-Bidayah wa al-Nihayah*, vol. 12, Beirut: Maktabat al-Ma'arif, 1995, p. 6.
46. The 'true community' is considered to be the pious ancestors who are the Companions, the Successors and those who followed them until the Day of Judgement. Muhammad b. Ibrahim al-Hamad, *'Aqidat Ahl al-Sunnah wa al-Jama'ah*, Riyadh: Dar Ibn Khuzaymah, 1998, p. 16.
47. Hamad, *'Aqidat Ahl al-Sunnah wa al-Jama'ah*, p. 17.
48. See for details, Hamad, *'Aqidat Ahl al-Sunnah wa al-Jama'ah*; 'Abd Allah b. Muhammad al-Qarni, *Dawabit al-Tafkir 'inda Ahl al-Sunnah wa al-Jama'ah*, Beirut: Mu'assasat al-Risalah, 1992.

Chapter 3

1. Deuteronomy 13:6–9, Revised Standard Version.
2. Leviticus 24:16.
3. Irving Hexham, *Concise Dictionary of Religion*, Downers Grove, IL: InterVarsity Press, 1993, pp. 20–21.
4. Qur'an 47:25.
5. Qur'an 5:54.
6. Qur'an 2:217.
7. Abd al-Rahman al-Jaziri, *Min Kitab al-Fiqh 'ala al-Madhahib al-Arba'ah*, vol. 5, Beirut: Dar al-Fikr, n.d., 422–3; Wahbah al-Zuhayli, *Al-Fiqh al-Islami wa Adillatuhu*, vol. 6, Dimashq: Dar al-Fikr, 1997, p. 184; Abu Bakr al-Jaza'iri, *Minhaj al-Muslim*, Cairo: Maktabat al-Kulliyat al-Azhariyyah, 1979, p. 535.
8. Jaziri, *Min Kitab al-Fiqh 'ala al-Madhahib al-Arba'ah*, 5:422–7.
9. Jaziri, *Min Kitab al-Fiqh 'ala al-Madhahib al-Arba'ah*, 5:422.
10. Jaza'iri, *Minhaj al-Muslim*, p. 535.
11. Zuhayli, *Al-Fiqh al-Islami wa Adillatuhu*, 6:183; Jaza'iri, *Minhaj al-Muslim*, p. 535; Jaziri, *Min Kitab al-Fiqh 'ala al-Madhahib al-Arba'ah*, 5:422–7.
12. Abu Muhammad Ali b. Ahmad b. Sa'id ibn Hazm, *Al-Muhalla*, ed. Ahmad Muhammad Shakir, vol. 11, Cairo: Maktabat Dar al-Turath, n.d, pp. 408–16.
13. However, in relation to God's attributes, there is a substantial amount of divergence among scholars about beliefs and apostasy, denial and doubt. This reflects the various theological controversies of early Islamic history.
14. Mohammad Hashim Kamali, *Freedom of Expression in Islam*, Kuala Lumpur: Berita Publishing, 1994, pp. 208–9.
15. Ibn Hazm, *Al-Muhalla*, 11:408–10; Jaziri, *Min Kitab al-Fiqh 'ala al-Madhahib al-Arba'ah*, 5:422–3.
16. Muhammad b. Ahmad al-Sarakhsi, *Kitab al-Mabsut*, vol. 10, Beirut: Dar al-Ma'rifah, n.d, pp. 100–110.
17. Qur'an 6:108.
18. For example, Ka'b b. al-Ashraf's killing as recorded in Muslim, 'Kitab al-Jihad wa al-Siyar', *Sahih Muslim*, trans. Abdul Hamid Siddiqi, Riyadh: International Islamic Publishing House, n.d.
19. Kamali, *Freedom of Expression in Islam*, pp. 223–4.
20. Kamali, *Freedom of Expression in Islam*, p. 224.
21. Kamali, *Freedom of Expression in Islam*, pp. 224–5.
22. 'Zindik', *Shorter Encyclopaedia of Islam*, ed. H.A.R. Gibb and J.H. Kramers, Leiden: Brill, 1991, p. 659.
23. 'Zindik', *Shorter Encyclopaedia of Islam*, p. 659.
24. 'Zindik', *Shorter Encyclopaedia of Islam*, p. 659.
25. Abd al-Rahman Badawi, *Min Tarikh al-Ilhad fi al-Islam*, 2nd edn, Cairo: Sina li al-Nashr, 1993, pp. 45–68.
26. Jaziri, *Min Kitab al-Fiqh 'ala al-Madhahib al-Arba'ah*, 5:428.

27. Muhammad Abu Zahrah, *Tarikh al-Madhahib al-Islamiyyah*, Cairo: Dar al-Fikr al-Arabi, n.d., pp. 141–2.
28. See Chapter 2 above, where many *ulama* who were accused of apostasy and heresy are listed.
29. Qur'an 2:8–10.
30. Qur'an 9:73.
31. Qur'an 9:68.
32. See, for instance, Jaziri's discussion of *zandaqah* with reference to the Maliki and Hanbali views, Jaziri, *Min Kitab al-Fiqh ʿala al-Madhahib al-Arbaʿah*, 5:428.
33. Philip Khuri Hitti, *History of the Arabs: From the Earliest Times to the Present*, London: Macmillan, 1986, pp. 358–60.
34. Watt, *The Majesty that was Islam*, pp. 70–71.
35. Watt, *The Majesty that was Islam*, pp. 62–5.
36. Watt, *The Majesty that was Islam*, pp. 69–71.
37. Ahmad b. Naqib al-Misri, *Reliance of the Traveller: A Classical Manual of Islamic Sacred Law*, trans. Nuh Ha Mim Keller, Evanston: Sunnah Books, 1994, pp. 596–8.
38. Jaza'iri, *Minhaj al-Muslim*, pp. 535–6.
39. ʿAli al-Tamimi, 'The Muslim's Belief – Some Causes that Lead to Apostasy from the Religion of Islam', *The Friday Report*, Makkah: Dar Makkah, August–September 1994, <http://www.islaam.com/sunnah/apostacy.htm>, accessed 18 February 2001.
40. Ibn Baz, *Ten Things Which Nullify One's Islam*, <http://thetruereligion.org/nullify.htm>, accessed 18 February 2001.
41. *Report of the Court of Inquiry Constituted under Punjab Act II of 1954 to Enquire into the Punjab Disturbances of 1953*, Lahore: Superintendent of Government Printing, 1954, p. 21.
42. *Report of the Court of Inquiry . . . into the Punjab Disturbances of 1953*, p. 218.
43. *Report of the Court of Inquiry . . . into the Punjab Disturbances of 1953*, p. 219.

Chapter 4

1. Sarakhsi, *Al-Mabsut*, 10:98.
2. Sarakhsi, *Al-Mabsut*, 10:98.
3. For a discussion on compulsion, see Sarakhsi, *Al-Mabsut*, 10:123; ʿAla' al-Din Abu Bakr b. Masʿud al-Kasani, *Badaʾiʿ al-Sanaʾiʿ fi Tartib al-Sharaʾiʿ*, vol. 7, Beirut: Dar al-Kutub al-ʿIlmiyyah, n.d., pp. 134, 177–8; Abu Muhammad ʿAbd Allah b. Ahmad b. Muhammad Ibn Qudama, *Al-Mughni*, vol. 8, Riyadh: Maktabat al-Riyad al-Hadithah, n.d., pp. 145–6.
4. Misri, *Reliance of the Traveller*, p. 595.
5. Misri, *Reliance of the Traveller*, p. 409; Kasani, *Badaʾiʿ al-Sanaʾiʿ fi Tartib al-Sharaʾiʿ*, 7:134; Ibn Qudama, *Al-Mughni*, 8:124–8.
6. Kasani, *Badaʾiʿ al-Sanaʾiʿ fi Tartib al-Sharaʾiʿ*, 7:134; Sarakhsi, *Al-Mabsut*, 10:123; Jaziri, *Min Kitab al-Fiqh ʿala al-Madhahib al-Arbaʿah*, 5:436–7.
7. Kasani, *Badaʾiʿ al-Sanaʾiʿ fi Tartib al-Sharaʾiʿ*, 7:134; Ibn Qudama, *Al-Mughni*, 8:134.
8. Jaziri, *Min Kitab al-Fiqh ʿala al-Madhahib al-Arbaʿah*, 5:435–6; Zuhayli, *Al-Fiqh al-Islami wa Adillatuhu*, 6:185.
9. Kasani, *Badaʾiʿ al-Sanaʾiʿ fi Tartib al-Sharaʾiʿ*, 7:134; Ibn Qudama, *Al-Mughni*, 8:135–6.
10. Jaziri, *Min Kitab al-Fiqh ʿala al-Madhahib al-Arbaʿah*, 5:435–6; Zuhayli, *Al-Fiqh al-Islami wa Adillatuhu*, 6:185.
11. Sarakhsi, *Al-Mabsut*, 10:108–9.
12. Sarakhsi, *Al-Mabsut*, 10:109; See also the discussion in Shihab al-Din Ahmad al-Qastallani, *Irshad al-Sari li Sharh Sahih al-Bukhari*, vol. 14, Beirut: Dar al-Fikr, 1990, pp. 393–5.

13. Sarakhsi, *Al-Mabsut*, 10:98ff.; Zuhayli, *Al-Fiqh al-Islami wa Adillatuhu*, 6:186–8.
14. Jaziri, *Min Kitab al-Fiqh ʿala al-Madhahib al-Arbaʿah*, 5:437.
15. Jaziri, *Min Kitab al-Fiqh ʿala al-Madhahib al-Arbaʿah*, 5:437.
16. Jaziri, *Min Kitab al-Fiqh ʿala al-Madhahib al-Arbaʿah*, 5:437.
17. See Kasani, *Badaʾiʿ al-Sanaʾiʿ fi Tartib al-Sharaʾiʿ*, 7:136; Ibn Qudama, *Al-Mughni*, 8:129 and other sources.
18. Sarakhsi, *Al-Mabsut*, 10:100.
19. Zuhayli, *Al-Fiqh al-Islami wa Adillatuhu*, 6:189; Sarakhsi, *Al-Mabsut*, 10:100; Jaziri, *Min Kitab al-Fiqh ʿala al-Madhahib al-Arbaʿah*, 5:429–31. For further details on this issue see also Zuhayli, *Al-Fiqh al-Islami wa Adillatuhu*, 6:188–92.
20. Kasani, *Badaʾiʿ al-Sanaʾiʿ fi Tartib al-Sharaʾiʿ*, 7:139.
21. Kasani, *Badaʾiʿ al-Sanaʾiʿ fi Tartib al-Sharaʾiʿ*, 7:139; Ibn Qudama, *Al-Mughni*, 8:137.
22. Ibn Qudama, *Al-Mughni*, 1:398–9.
23. Sarakhsi, *Al-Mabsut*, 10:99–100; Jaziri, *Min Kitab al-Fiqh ʿala al-Madhahib al-Arbaʿah*, 5:423–5; Zuhayli, *Al-Fiqh al-Islami wa Adillatuhu*, 6:186–8.
24. Sarakhsi, *Al-Mabsut*, 10:99–100; Jaziri, *Min Kitab al-Fiqh ʿala al-Madhahib al-Arbaʿah*, 5:423–5; Zuhayli, *Al-Fiqh al-Islami wa Adillatuhu*, 6:186–8.
25. Sarakhsi, *Al-Mabsut*, 10:99.
26. Jaziri, *Min Kitab al-Fiqh ʿala al-Madhahib al-Arbaʿah*, 5:423–4; Abu Ishaq al-Shirazi. *Al-Muhadhdhab fi Fiqh al-Imam al-Shafiʿi*, ed. Muhammad al-Zuhayli, vol. 5, Dimashq: Dar al-Qalam, 1996, pp. 208–9. Ibrahim al-Nakhaʿi and Sufyan al-Thawri's view is that the repentance should be sought for ever, that is, until the person reverts to Islam or dies.
27. For views related to this see Shams al-Din Muhammad b. Abu al-ʿAbbas Ahmad b. Hamzah b. Shihab al-Din al-Ramli, *Nihayat al-Muhtaj ila Sharh al-Minhaj*, vol. 7, Beirut: Dar al-Kutub al-ʿIlmiyyah, n.d., pp. 419–20; Ibn Qudama, *Al-Mughni*, 8:126; Kasani, *Badaʾiʿ al-Sanaʾiʿ fi Tartib al-Sharaʾiʿ*, 7:135.
28. Kasani, *Badaʾiʿ al-Sanaʾiʿ fi Tartib al-Sharaʾiʿ*, 7:135; Ibn Qudama, *Al-Mughni*, 8:126.
29. Ibn Qudama, *Al-Mughni*, 8:150.
30. Ibn Qudama, *Al-Mughni*, 8:150.
31. Misri, *Reliance of the Traveller*, p. 584; Sarakhsi, *Al-Mabsut*, 10:112.
32. Misri, *Reliance of the Traveller*, p. 593.
33. Jaziri, *Min Kitab al-Fiqh ʿala al-Madhahib al-Arbaʿah*, 5:8; See also Mohamed S. el-Awa, *Punishment in Islamic Law: A Comparative Study*, Indianapolis: American Trust Publications, 1982, p. 56.
34. Awa, *Punishment in Islamic Law*, p. 56.
35. Awa, *Punishment in Islamic Law*, p. 55 and references cited there.
36. Muhammad Salim al-Awa, 'Jaraʾim al-Hudud wa ʿUqubatuha', *Minbar al-Sharq*, No.10, 3 November 1993, pp. 21–2.
37. Awa, *Punishment in Islamic Law*, p. 56.
38. S.A. Rahman, *Punishment of Apostasy in Islam*, New Delhi: Kitab Bhavan, 1996, p. 10.
39. Rahman, *Punishment of Apostasy in Islam*, p. 10.
40. Qurʾan 9:11–12.
41. Verse 9:7 onwards is clear on this issue.
42. Muhammad b. ʿAli al-Shawkani, *Fath al-Qadir: al-Jamiʿ bayna Fannay al-Riwayah wa al-Dirayah min ʿIlm al-Tafsir*, vol. 2, Beirut: Dar al-Maʿrifah, [between 1980 and 1993], p. 438.
43. Qurʾan 5:33.
44. Shawkani, *Fath al-Qadir*, 2:44.
45. Shawkani, *Fath al-Qadir*, 2:44.
46. Qurʾan 16:106.
47. Qurʾan 22:11.
48. Shawkani, *Fath al-Qadir*, 3:546.

49. Shawkani, *Fath al-Qadir*, 3:546.
50. Muhammad b. ʿAli b. Muhammad al-Shawkani, *Nayl al-Awtar*, vol. 7, Beirut: Dar al-Kutub al-ʿIlmiyyah, n.d., p. 191; Qastallani, *Irshad al-Sari li Sharh Sahih al-Bukhari*, 14:396.
51. Qastallani, *Irshad al-Sari li Sharh Sahih al-Bukhari*, 14:395–6; see also Abu Bakr Ahmad b. al-Husayn b. ʿAli al-Bayhaqi, *Kitab al-Sunan al-Kubra*, reprinted Beirut: Dar al-Maʿrifah, 1986.
52. Shawkani, *Nayl al-Awtar*, 7:193.
53. Shawkani, *Nayl al-Awtar*, 7:193.
54. Bayhaqi, *Kitab al-Sunan al-Kubra*, 8:194.
55. Bayhaqi, *Kitab al-Sunan al-Kubra*, 8:195.
56. Bukhari, *Sahih al-Bukhari: The Translation of the Meanings of Sahih al-Bukhari, Arabic–English*, trans. Muhammad Muhsin Khan, rev. edn, Ankara: Hilal Yayinlari, 1976, p. 1012.
57. Shawkani, *Nayl al-Awtar*, 7:5–6.
58. Nawawi, *Sharh Sahih Muslim li al-Imam al-Nawawi*, vol. 11, Beirut: Dar al-Qalam, [between 1987 and 1993], p. 165.
59. Shawkani, *Nayl al-Awtar*, 7:151–63 regarding *al-muharibin wa qutta' al-turuq and qital al-khawarij wa ahl al-baghy.*
60. Qur'an, 8:72.
61. Qur'an 3:103.
62. Qur'an 4:59.
63. Bayhaqi, *Kitab al-Sunan al-Kubra*, 8:168.
64. Sarakhsi, *Al-Mabsut*, 10:109.
65. Bayhaqi, *Kitab al-Sunan al-Kubra*, 8:168–9.
66. Nawawi, *Sharh Sahih Muslim li al-Imam al-Nawawi*, 11:165.
67. Nawawi, *Sharh Sahih Muslim li al-Imam al-Nawawi*, 11:166.
68. Nawawi, *Sharh Sahih Muslim li al-Imam al-Nawawi*, 11:165.
69. Ibn Hisham, *Al-Sirah al-Nabawiyyah*, 2:409.
70. Ibn Hisham, *Al-Sirah al-Nabawiyyah*, 2:409.
71. Shawkani, *Nayl al-Awtar*, 7:136.
72. Poets, as we know, played the role that mass media play today. They were the mouthpieces of the tribe.
73. This ʿAbd Allah was killed by Saʿid b. Hurayth and Abu Barzah. Ibn Hisham, *Al-Sirah al-Nabawiyyah*, 2:410.
74. Ibn Hisham, *Al-Sirah al-Nabawiyyah*, 2:410.
75. Ibn Hisham, *Al-Sirah al-Nabawiyyah*, 2:410–11.
76. Ibn Hazm, *Al-Muhalla*, 11:189; Qastallani, *Irshad al-Sari li Sharh Sahih al-Bukhari*, 14:397 for a different version. See also Bayhaqi, *Kitab al Sunan al-Kubra*, 8:195.
77. See Book 38, No. 4348 in Abu Da'ud Sulayman b. al-Ashʿath al-Sijistani, *Sunan Abi Da'ud*, Beirut: Dar al-Kutub al-ʿIlmiyyah, 1997.
78. Rahman, *Punishment for Apostasy in Islam*, p. 79.
79. Shawkani, *Nayl al-Awtar*, 7:192.
80. Sarakhsi, *Al-Mabsut*, 10:110.
81. Ibn Hazm, *Al-Muhalla*, 11:190.
82. However, a number of Muslim scholars, prominent early figures as well as modern scholars, seem to have found difficulty in using this case. Tribes against whom the Caliph had to fight: Aswad al-Ansi, Banu Madlaj of Yemen; Musaylamah; Sajah; Tulayhah b. Khuwaylid (Banu Asad) and Laqit b. Malik Azdi.
83. See, for example, Khurshid Ahmad Fariq (ed.), *Tarikh al-Riddah: Gleaned from al-Iktifa of al-Balansi*, New Delhi: Asia Publishing House, 1970.
84. For details, see Fariq, *Tarikh al-Riddah.*

85. See, for instance, Abu Bakr's instructions to Khalid b. al-Walid in the case of the Asad and Ghatafan tribes: Fariq, *Tarikh al-Riddah*, pp. 29–30.
86. Fariq, *Tarikh al-Riddah*, pp. 16–17 regarding the Tay' tribe's position on this matter. In the case of the people of Daba, when Abu Bakr apparently intended to execute those fighters brought by Hudhayfah b. al-Yaman, 'Umar said to Abu Bakr, 'O Caliph of the Messenger of Allah. They are believers ... They are saying, "By God, we did not apostatize from Islam ...".', Fariq, *Tarikh al-Riddah*, p. 149.
87. Qastallani, *Irshad al-Sari li Sharh Sahih al-Bukhari*, 14:399.
88. Fariq, *Tarikh al-Riddah*, p. 2.
89. Sarakhsi, *Al-Mabsut*, 10:100.
90. Sarakhsi, *Al-Mabsut*, 10:110.
91. Sarakhsi, *Al-Mabsut*, 10:110.
92. '*Wa bi al-israr ʿala al-kufri yakunu muhariban li al-muslimin. Fa yuqtalu li dafʿi al-muharabah*', Sarakhsi, *Al-Mabsut*, 10:110.

Chapter 5

1.   Qur'an 91:7–8.
2.   Qur'an 17:15.
3.   Qur'an 18:29.
4.   Qur'an 6:104.
5.   Qur'an 88:21–2.
6.   Qur'an 10:99.
7.   Qur'an 13:31.
8.   Qur'an 16:9.
9.   Qur'an 6:149.
10. Qur'an 6:35.
11. Qur'an 24:54.
12. Qur'an 5:99. 'According to all the available evidence, this *surah* constitutes one of the last sections of the Qur'an revealed to the Prophet. The consensus of opinion places it in the period of his Farewell Pilgrimage, in the year 10AH': Asad, *The Message of the Qur'an*, p. 139.
13. Qur'an 64:12.
14. Qur'an 3:20. Revealed in Medina in 3AH; some verses were revealed in 10AH: Asad, *The Message of the Qur'an*, p. 65.
15. Qur'an 10:41.
16. Qur'an 109:1–6.
17. Qur'an 50:45.
18. Qur'an 10:108.
19. Qur'an 27:92.
20. Qur'an 6:66.
21. Qur'an 4:80.
22. Qur'an 88:21.
23. Qur'an 12:103.
24. Qur'an 28:56.
25. Qur'an 4:115.
26. Qur'an 6:48–9.
27. Qur'an 72:23.
28. Qur'an 7:13–18.
29. Qur'an 6:108.
30. Qur'an 5:43, 47.
31. Qur'an 7:35.
32. Qur'an 5:69.

33. Qur'an 49:13.
34. Qur'an 2:256.
35. Isma'il b. 'Umar Ibn Kathir, *Tafsir al-Qur'an al-'Azim*, vol. 1, Beirut: Dar al-Ma'rifah, 1987, p. 318.
36. Qur'an 9:123.
37. Qur'an 9:73; Jalal al-Din al-Suyuti, *Al-Durr al-Manthur fi al-Tafsir al-Ma'thur*, vol. 1, Beirut: Dar al-Kutub al-'Ilmiyyah, 1990, p. 584.
38. Suyuti, *Durr*, 1:583.
39. Suyuti, *Durr*, 1:583.
40. Suyuti, *Durr*, 1:583.
41. Suyuti, *Durr*, 1:582–5.
42. Suyuti, *Durr*, 1:583. See also Mahmoud Ayoub, *The Qur'an and its Interpreters: Volume I*, Albany: State University of New York Press, 1984, p. 252.
43. Qur'an 2:193.
44. Quoted in Ayoub, *The Qur'an and its Interpreters*, p. 254; Razi, *Tafsir*, 7:5.
45. Sayyid Qutb, *Fi Zilal al-Qur'an*, vol. 1, Cairo: Dar al-Shuruq, 1996, p. 291.
46. For some of these points, see Qutb, *Zilal*, 3:291–2.
47. Qutb, *Zilal*, 3:291.
48. Qutb, *Zilal*, 3:291.
49. Suyuti, *Durr*, 1:584.
50. Suyuti, *Durr*, 1:582–5.
51. Qur'an 2:191.
52. Qur'an 9:5, 8, 12, 13.
53. Qur'an 2:190–3.
54. Qur'an 8:38–40.
55. Qur'an 9:29.
56. Qur'an 9:4.
57. Qur'an 2:217.
58. Shawkani, *Fath al-Qadir*, 1:273.
59. Qur'an 3:144.
60. Qur'an 3:90.
61. Qur'an 3:91.
62. Shawkani, *Fath al-Qadir*, 1:452–3.
63. Hasan, Qatadah and 'Ata. See Shawkani, *Fath al-Qadir*, 1:452.
64. Shawkani, *Fath al-Qadir*, 1:452.
65. Qur'an 3:86–7.
66. Qur'an 3:106.
67. Qur'an 4:137.
68. See Shawkani's interpretation and a variety of reports related to this verse in Shawkani, *Fath al-Qadir*, 1:664–7.
69. Qur'an 9:74.
70. Shawkani, *Fath al-Qadir*, 2:490.
71. Qur'an 24:2; 5:38.
72. Rahman, *Punishment of Apostasy in Islam*, p. 39.
73. Awa, 'Jara'im al-Hudud wa 'Uqubatuha', p. 17.
74. Sarakhsi, *Al-Mabsut*, 10:100.
75. Qur'an 2:8–9.
76. Qur'an 2:10–13, 88, 19.
77. Qur'an 2:13–14.
78. Bayhaqi, *Kitab al-Sunan al-Kubra*, 8:196–7.
79. Bayhaqi, *Kitab al Sunan al-Kubra*, 8:196.
80. Shawkani, *Fath al-Qadir*, 2:496.
81. Ibn Hisham, *Al-Sirah al-Nabawiyyah*, 2:317.
82. W. Montgomery Watt, *Muhammad at Medina*, Oxford: Oxford University Press, 1956,

4th impression; Karachi: Oxford University Press, 1998, pp. 47–8. The phrases in square brackets have been added to clarify the meaning.
83. Sarakhsi, *Al-Mabsut*, 10:100; Bayhaqi, *Kitab al-Sunan al-Kubra*, 8:196.
84. Bayhaqi, *Kitab al Sunan al-Kubra*, 8:195.
85. Ibn Hazm, *Al-Muhalla*, 11:191.
86. Ibn Hazm, *Al-Muhalla*, 11:191.
87. Sarakhsi, *Al-Mabsut*, 10:110.

Chapter 6

1. Mohammad Hashim Kamali, *Punishment in Islamic Law: An Enquiry into the Hudud Bill of Kelantan*, Kuala Lumpur: Ilmiah Publishers, 1995, pp. 33–7.
2. From Islam Q & A, *Punishment of One who Leaves Islam*, <http://thetruereligion.org/apostatepunish.htm>, accessed 18 February 2001.
3. From Islam Q & A, *Why Death is the Punishment for Apostasy*, <http://thetruereligion.org/apostatedeath.htm>, accessed 18 February 2001.
4. Muhammad Mutawalli al-Sha'rawi, *Al-Jami' li al-Fatawa*, ed. Muhammad Hasan Muhammad, Cairo: Dar al-Jalil li al-Kutub wa al-Nashr, 1998, p. 12; Muhammad Mutawalli al-Sha'rawi, *Al-Fatawa*, Beirut: Dar al-'Awdah, 1983, p. 149.
5. 'Treason' can be defined in several ways. The principal forms now include: (a) causing the death or serious injury of the sovereign, his (or her) spouse or eldest son; (b) levying war against the sovereign in his (or her) realm, which includes any insurrection against the authority of the sovereign or of the government that goes beyond riot or violent disorder; (c) giving aid or comfort to the sovereign's enemies in wartime. The penalty for treason (fixed by law) is death, but the monarch may exercise the prerogative of mercy. Elizabeth A. Martin (ed.), *A Dictionary of Law*, Oxford: Oxford University Press, 1997, p. 473.
6. Albert Hourani, *Arabic Thought in the Liberal Age: 1798–1939*, Cambridge: Cambridge University Press, 1983, p. 237.
7. Abul A'la Maududi, *Murtadd ki Saza Islami Qanun Meyn*, Lahore: Islami Publications, 1963.
8. Ishtiaq Ahmed, *The Concept of an Islamic State: An Analysis of the Ideological Controversy in Pakistan*, London: Francis Pinter, 1987, pp. 103–4.
9. Ahmed, *The Concept of an Islamic State*, pp. 103–4.
10. Abul A'la Maududi, *Human Rights in Islam*, 2nd edn, Leicester: The Islamic Foundation, 1980.
11. Ahmed, *The Concept of an Islamic State*, p. 103.
12. Ismail R. al-Faruqi, *Islam*, Nile, IL: Argus Communications, 1984, p. 68.
13. Awa, *Punishment in Islamic Law*, p. 64.
14. Yusuf al-Qaradawi, *The Lawful and the Prohibited in Islam*, Kuala Lumpur: Islamic Book Trust, 1995, pp. 326–7.
15. Ahmed, *The Concept of an Islamic State*, pp. 78–9.
16. Al-Sadiq al-Nayhoum, *Islam Didd al-Islam: Shari'ah min Waraq*, Beirut: Riad al-Rayyes Books, 1995, pp. 137–9.
17. Nayhoum, *Islam Didd al-Islam*, pp. 137–9.
18. Rahman, *Punishment of Apostasy in Islam*, p. 54.
19. Rahman, *Punishment of Apostasy in Islam*, pp. 85–6.
20. Mahmud Shaltut, *Al-Islam: 'Aqidah wa Shari'ah*, Kuwait: Matabi' Dar al-Qalam, n.d., pp. 292–3.
21. Subhi Mahmassani, *Arkan Huquq al-Insan fi al-Islam*, Beirut: Dar al-'Ilm li al-Malayin, 1979, pp. 123–4.
22. Mohammad Hashim Kamali, *Islamic Law in Malaysia: Issues and Developments*, Kuala Lumpur: Ilmiah Publishers, 2000, p. 219.

23. Kamali, *Islamic Law in Malaysia*, p. 209.
24. Awa, *Punishment in Islamic Law*, p. 50.
25. Awa, *Punishment in Islamic Law*, p. 64.
26. Awa, *Punishment in Islamic Law*, p. 54.
27. Jamal al-Banna, 'Hurriyyat al-I'tiqad fi al-Islam', *Minbar al-Sharq*, **10** (3), November 1993, 30–38.
28. *The Grand Imams of Al-Azhar (Shuyukhul Azhar)*, <http://www.sunnah.org/history/Scholars/mashaykh_azhar.htm>, accessed 31 January 2002.
29. Shabbir Akhtar, *A Faith for All Seasons: Islam and Western Modernity*, London: Bellew Publishing, 1990, pp. 21–2; See also Shabbir Akhtar, *Be Careful with Muhammad!: The Salman Rushdie Affair*, London: Bellew Publishing, 1989, pp. 70–77 for the author's longer discourse on apostasy (and blasphemy and treason).
30. Sisters in Islam are a local NGO working on women's rights within Islam. Sisters in Islam, 'Islam, Apostasy and PAS', Press Release, <http://www.saksi.com/jul99/zainah.htm>, accessed 18 February 2001.
31. 'Interview on Apostasy with Dr. Hasan Al-Turabi'. <http://www.witness-pioneer.org/vil/Articles/shariah/interview_on_apostasy_hasan_turabi.htm>, accessed 18 March 2002.
32. 'Interview on Apostasy with Dr. Hasan Al-Turabi'.
33. Intra*View*: Interview 'Freedom of Thought and the Right to Apostasy' with Tunisian Sheikh Rashid Ghannoushi, 10 February 1998 <http://msanews.mynet.net/intra2.html#sect7>.
34. Intra*View*: Interview 'Freedom of Thought and the Right to Apostasy'.
35. Intra*View*: Interview 'Freedom of Thought and the Right to Apostasy'.
36. Intra*View*: Interview 'Freedom of Thought and the Right to Apostasy'.

Chapter 7

1. According to <http://www.religioustolerance.org/rt_pakis.htm> an old blasphemy law banning insults directed at any religion has been in place since 1927. In 1986 General Zia-ul-Haq amended the law so that it only applied to Islam.
2. In Pakistan, blasphemy provisions of the Penal Code in 1982 Section 295(b) were added, which stipulated a sentence of life imprisonment for 'whoever willfully defiles, damages, or desecrates a copy of the holy Koran'. In 1986 another amendment, Section 295(c), established the death penalty or life imprisonment for directly or indirectly defiling 'the sacred name of the holy Prophet Mohammed'. US Department of State, *Department of State Human Rights Report 2000*, February 2001, <http://www.humanrights-usa.net/reports/pakistan.html>, accessed 27 July 2001.
3. US Department of State, *Department of State Human Rights Report 2000*.
4. US Department of State, *Department of State Human Rights Report 2000*.
5. United States Commission on International Religious Freedom, *Report on International Religious Freedom: Pakistan*, released 1 May 2001.
6. United States Commission on International Religious Freedom, *Report on International Religious Freedom*.
7. International Christian Concern, 'A Climate of Fear in Pakistan', *Official Newsletter*, <http://www.persecution.org/concern/1996/09.html>, accessed 28 July 2001.
8. International Christian Concern, 'A Climate of Fear in Pakistan'.
9. International Christian Concern, 'A Climate of Fear in Pakistan'.
10. Nabil Megalli, 'Egyptian Leader Backs "Death Edict" for Opponents of Islamic Law', *Ottawa Citizen*, 31 July 1993.
11. Mary Anne Weaver, 'Revolution by Stealth', *New Yorker*, 8 June 1998, <http://www.dhushara.com/book/zulu/islamp/egy.htm>, accessed 4 February 2002.
12. Weaver, 'Revolution by Stealth'.

13. Quoted in Nadia Abou el-Magd, 'The Price of Freedom', *Al-Ahram Weekly Online*, No. 536, 31 May – 6 June 2001, <http://web1.ahram.org.eg/weekly/2001/536/eg7. htm>, accessed 21 April 2002.
14. Magd, 'The Price of Freedom'.
15. Magd, 'The Price of Freedom'.
16. BBC News, *Court to Hear Egypt Apostasy Case*, Monday 9 July 2001, <http://news.bbc.co.uk/hi/english/world/middle_east/newsid_1429000/1429415.stm>, accessed 21 April 2002.
17. Weaver, 'Revolution by Stealth'.
18. Weaver, 'Revolution by Stealth'.
19. In July 1993, the Shaykh of al-Azhar, Gad al-Haq Ali Gad al-Haq, sent a letter to the head of the *fatwa* and legislative section of the national administrative court requesting a clarification of al-Azhar's role regarding artistic works of a religious nature. In February 1994 Tariq al-Bishri responded and issued an opinion that al-Azhar was the sole authority to which the Ministry of Culture must refer Islamic matters, and that it was to issue licences for films, books and tapes that discussed religion. Richard Engel, 'Book Ban Exposes Azhar Censorship', *Middle East Times*, 31 August 1997, <http://www.metimes.com/cens/35ban.htm>, accessed 21 April 2002.
20. Engel, 'Book Ban Exposes Azhar Censorship'.
21. Jailan Halawi, 'Prison Limelight', *Al-Ahram Weekly Online*, No. 519, 1–7 February 2001, <http://www.ahram.org.eg/weekly/2001/519/eg6.htm>, accessed 21 April 2002.
22. Weaver, 'Revolution by Stealth'.
23. Max Rodenbeck, 'Witch Hunt in Egypt', *The New York Review of Books*, 16 November 2000, <http://www.nybooks.com/articles/13904>, accessed 21 April 2002.
24. Rodenbeck, 'Witch Hunt in Egypt'.
25. *Director Youssef Chahine*, <http://www.sfjff.org/sfjff16/d0722a.htm>, accessed 21 April 2002.
26. Weaver, 'Revolution by Stealth'.
27. Weaver, 'Revolution by Stealth'.
28. Weaver, 'Revolution by Stealth'.
29. Lazhari Labter, *Journalistes Algeriens: Entre le Baillon et les Balles*, Paris: L'Harmattan, 1995.
30. I am indebted to Redha Ameur, a PhD candidate under my supervision, for this translation from French. Ali Merad, *Le Reformisme Musulman en Algerie: de 1925 à 1940: Essai d'Histoirie Religieuse et Sociale*, Paris: Mouton, 1967, pp. 404–9.
31. Jubilee Campaign Press Release, *Muslim Extremists Seek Death of Prominent Christians*, 12 July 1994, <http://www.jubileecampaign.co.uk/world/pak13.htm>, accessed 31 January 2002.

Chapter 8

1. Frithjof Schuon, *Stations of Wisdom*, London: John Murray, 1961, p. 64. In dealing with the general theme of this chapter, I have benefited from the work of Amal Qarami, Qadiyyat al-Riddah fi al-Fikr al-Islami al-Hadith, Tunis: Dar al-Janub Iil-Nashr, 1996.
2. On 'Westoxication' see ʿAbdolkarim Soroush, *Reason, Freedom and Democracy in Islam: Essential Writings of ʿAbdolkarim Soroush*, trans., ed. and intro. Mahmoud Sadri and Ahmad Sadri, New York: Oxford University Press, 2000, pp. 160–1.
3. Soroush, *Reason, Freedom and Democracy in Islam*, p. 160.
4. Mayer, *Islam and Human Rights*, pp. 143–4.
5. Mayer, *Islam and Human Rights*, p. 144.
6. Mayer, *Islam and Human Rights*, p. 144.
7. David Pearl and Werner Menski, *Muslim Family Law*, 3rd edn, London: Sweet & Maxwell, 1998, p. 131.

8. Human Rights Watch, 'V. Discrimination Against Women', *Kuwait Promises Betrayed: Denial of Rights of Bidun, Women and Freedom of Expression*, **12** (2) (E), October 2000, <http://www.hrw.org/reports/2000/kuwait/kuwait-05.htm>, accessed 31 January 2002.
9. ISIS, *Testimonies: Why I Left Islam*, <http://www.isisforum.com/testimonies/index.htm>, accessed 28 July 2001.
10. ISIS, *Testimonies*, <http://www.isisforum.com/testimonies/testimonies.htm>.
11. ISIS, *Testimonies*, <http://www.isisforum.com/testimonies/testimonies2.htm>.
12. ISIS, *Testimonies*, <http://www.isisforum.com/testimonies/index.htm>.
13. ISIS, *Testimonies*, <http://www.isisforum.com/testimonies/index.htm>.
14. ISIS, *Testimonies*, <http://www.isisforum.com/testimonies/index.htm>.
15. ISIS, *Testimonies*, <http://www.isisforum.com/testimonies/testimonies.htm>.
16. ISIS, *Testimonies*, <http://www.isisforum.com/testimonies/index.htm>.
17. I am again indebted to Redha Ameur for translating these texts from Merad, *Le Reformisme Musulman en Algerie*, pp. 404–9.
18. Quoted in Merad, *Le Reformisme Musulman en Algerie*, p. 407.
19. Quoted in Merad, *Le Reformisme Musulman en Algerie*, p. 407.
20. Merad, *Le Reformisme Musulman en Algerie*, p. 407.
21. Quoted in Merad, *Le Reformisme Musulman en Algerie*, p. 407.
22. Quoted in Merad, *Le Reformisme Musulman en Algerie*, p. 408, n. 1.
23. Analogously this relates to honour-killing in relation to women engaging in extra-marital affairs in some communities. In fact, apostates are dealt with quietly often by family members who cannot bear the fact that one of their family members has brought dishonour upon the family or clan by conversion to another religion.
24. It is reported that: 'In Lebanon, one of the most westernized countries of the region, an average of one woman per month is killed by a close male relative who says she has soiled the honour of the family by committing adultery or engaging in pre-marital sexual relations.' BBC News, *Beirut Hosts 'Honour Killing' Conference*, Sunday 13 May 2001, <http://news.bbc.co.uk/hi/english/world/middle_east/newsid_1328000/1328238.stm>, accessed 4 February 2002.
25. According to an Amnesty International report: 'Every year hundreds of women are known to die as a result of honour killings.' Amnesty International, *Honour Killing of Girls and Women*, 22 September 1999, <http://www.amnesty.ca/library/1999/asa3318.htm>, accessed 4 February 2002.

Chapter 9

1. The governor is referred to as *Yang di-Pertua Negeri*.
2. Constitution, Malaysia, Article 38(1) read with Fifth Schedule (1).
3. Constitution, Article 32(3). The king is called *Yang-di-Pertuan Agong*.
4. Constitution, Article 38(2)(b).
5. Constitution, Article 4.
6. For details see Chapter 11 below, on jurisdiction.
7. *Ramah v. Laton* [1927] 6 FMSLR 128.
8. See M.B. Hooker, *Islamic Law in South-East Asia*, Singapore: Oxford University Press, 1984, ch. 3.
9. *Che Omar bin Che Soh v. Public Prosecutor* [1988] 2 MLJ 55.
10. L.A. Sheridan, 'The Religion of the Federation', *Malayan Law Journal*, **2**, 1988, xiii.
11. *Report of the Federation of Malaysia Constitutional Commission, 1956–57*, Kuala Lumpur: Government Printer, 1957, para. 169.
12. Constitution, Article 3(2).
13. Hussin Mutalib, *Islam in Malaysia from Revivalism to Islamic State*, Singapore: Singapore University Press, 1993, p. 17.

14. The Constitution required Parliament to retain English as the official language for a period of ten years following independence.

15. Judith A. Nagata, *The Reflowering of Malaysian Islam: Modern Religious Radicals and Their Roots*, Vancouver: University of British Columbia Press, 1984, p. 57.

16. Philip Koh Tong Ngee, *Freedom of Religion in Malaysia – The Legal Dimension*, Petaling Jaya: Graduate Christian Fellowship, 1987, p. 20.

17. Kua Kia Soong (ed.), *Malaysian Cultural Policy and Democracy*, Selangor: The Resource and Research Centre, 1990, pp. 209–41.

18. Constitution, Article 12(1). This should be read in the light of Article 153, which allows preferential treatment in favour of Malays. 'Malay' in turn has been defined as one who habitually speaks the Malay language, practises Malay custom and is a follower of Islam. See Constitution, Article 160(2).

19. However, it is lawful for the federal and the state governments to establish or maintain or assist in establishing or maintaining Islamic institutions or to provide or assist in providing instruction in the religion of Islam and incur such expenditure as may be necessary for the purpose. Constitution, Article 12(3).

20. Constitution, Article 12(3).

21. Constitution, Article 12(4).

22. Constitution, Article 150 enables the king to proclaim a state of emergency if he is satisfied that a grave emergency exists whereby the security or economic life of the nation is threatened.

23. Other protections that cannot be violated are Islamic law, Malay customs, native law or customs of Sabah or Sarawak, citizenship and language. See Constitution, Article 150(6).

24. Constitution, Article 9.

25. Constitution, Article 11.

26. Constitution, Article 12.

27. Constitution, Article 11(5).

28. Constitution, Article 11(4).

29. See, for instance, Control and Restriction (The Propagation of Non-Islamic Religions Among Muslims) (Negeri Sembilan) Bill, 1991; Non-Islamic Religions (Control of Propagation Amongst Muslims) (Selangor) Enactment, 1988; Control and Restriction of the Propagation of Non-Islamic Religions to Muslims (Malacca) Enactment, 1988; Control and Restriction of the Propagation of Non-Islamic Religions (Kelantan) Enactment, 1981.

30. Section 4, Control and Restriction (The Propagation of Non-Islamic Religions Among Muslims) (Negeri Sembilan) Bill, 1991; Section 4, Non-Islamic Religions (Control of Propagation Amongst Muslims) (Selangor) Enactment, 1988; Section 4, Control and Restriction of the Propagation of Non-Islamic Religions to Muslims (Malacca) Enactment, 1988; Section 4, Control and Restriction of the Propagation of Non-Islamic Religions (Kelantan) Enactment, 1981.

31. Section 5, Control and Restriction (The Propagation of Non-Islamic Religions Among Muslims) (Negeri Sembilan) Bill, 1991; Section 5, Non-Islamic Religions (Control of Propagation Amongst Muslims) (Selangor) Enactment, 1988; Section 5, Control and Restriction of the Propagation of Non-Islamic Religions to Muslims (Malacca) Enactment, 1988; Section 5, Control and Restriction of the Propagation of Non-Islamic Religions (Kelantan) Enactment, 1981.

32. Section 7, Control and Restriction (The Propagation of Non-Islamic Religions Among Muslims) (Negeri Sembilan) Bill, 1991; Section 7, Non-Islamic Religions (Control of Propagation Amongst Muslims) (Selangor) Enactment, 1988; Section 7, Control and Restriction of the Propagation of Non-Islamic Religions to Muslims (Malacca) Enactment, 1988 Section 7, Control and Restriction of the Propagation of Non-Islamic Religions (Kelantan) Enactment, 1981.

33. Section 8, Control and Restriction (The Propagation of Non-Islamic Religions Among

Muslims) (Negeri Sembilan) Bill, 1991; Section 8, Non-Islamic Religions (Control of Propagation Amongst Muslims) (Selangor) Enactment, 1988; Section 8, Control and Restriction of the Propagation of Non-Islamic Religions to Muslims (Malacca) Enactment, 1988; Section 8, Control and Restriction of the Propagation of Non-Islamic Religions (Kelantan) Enactment, 1981.

34.	Violation of this could lead to a fine up to RM1000. Section 9(1) and (3), Control and Restriction of the Propagation of Non-Islamic Religions (Kelantan) Enactment, 1981.

35.	See, for instance, Schedule, Parts I and II, Control and Restriction (The Propagation of Non-Islamic Religions Among Muslims) (Negeri Sembilan) Bill, 1991; Schedule, Parts I and II, Control and Restriction of the Propagation of Non-Islamic Religions (Kelantan) Enactment, 1981.

36.	Ahmad F. Yousif, *Religious Freedom, Minorities and Islam – An Inquiry into the Malaysian Experience*, Selangor: Thinker's Library, 1998, p. 97.

37.	See, for instance, Section 157(2), Administration of Muslim Law (Penang) Enactment, 1959; and Section 160(2), Administration of Muslim Law (Kedah) Enactment, 1962.

38.	Section 125, Administration of Muslim Law (Perlis) Enactment, 1964; Section 156, Administration of Muslim Law (Malacca) Enactment, 1959; Section 201, Administration of Islamic Religious Affairs (Trengganu) Enactment, 1986; Section 158, Administration of Muslim Law (Penang) Enactment, 1959; Section 141, Administration of Muslim Law (Kedah) Enactment, 1962; Section 91, Council of the Religion of Islam and Malay Custom (Kelantan) Enactment, 1994; Section 166, Administration of Muslim Law (Selangor) Enactment, 1952.

39.	Identical provisions are found in Section 159, Administration of Muslim Law (Malacca) Enactment, 1959 and Section 160, Administration of Muslim Law (Penang) Enactment, 1959.

40.	Section 26, Administration of Islamic Religious Affairs (Trengganu) Enactment, 1986; Section 35, Administration of Islamic Law (Negeri Sembilan) Enactment, 1991; Section 39, Administration of Islamic Law (Federal Territories) Act, 1993. Section 37, Administration of Muslim Law (Penang) Enactment, 1959 also requires prior approval by the king.

41.	SUARAM (Malaysia), *Abolish ISA Movement*, <http://www.suaram.org/isa/list_detainees.htm>, accessed 13 May 2001.

42.	Section 8, Internal Security Act, 1960.

43.	Generally state laws use the phrase 'false doctrine'. Section 167, Administration of Muslim Law (Selangor) Enactment, 1952; Section 204, Administration of Islamic Religious Affairs (Trengganu) Enactment, 1986; Section 119, Council of the Religion of Islam and Malay Custom (Kelantan) Enactment, 1994; Section 157, Administration of Muslim Law (Malacca) Enactment, 1959; Section 161, Administration of Muslim Law (Kedah) Enactment, 1962. Section 158, Administration of Muslim Law (Pahang) Enactment, 1959; Section 13, Crimes (Syariah) (Perak) Bill, 1992 uses the word 'apostasy', while Section 102, Council of the Religion of Islam and Malay Custom (Kelantan) Enactment, 1994 uses the word *murtad*.

44.	*Bernama*, 17 November 1998 (Online Lexis, 9 December 2000).

45.	Raymond L.M. Lee and Susan E. Ackerman, *Sacred Tensions: Modernity and Religious Transformation in Malaysia*, Columbia, SC: University of South Carolina Press, 1997, p. 48.

46.	*Straits Times (Singapore)*, 8 March 1995, p. 17 (Online Lexis, 9 December 2000).

47.	The breakdown of the 51 deviationist groups were Selangor 15, Kelantan 6, Pahang 5, Federal Territory and Perak 4 each, Kedah, Johor and Trengganu 3 each, Pulau Piang and Malacca 2 each and Sabah, Sarawak, Negeri Sembilan and Perlis 1 each. See *Bernama*, 17 November 1998 (Online Lexis, 9 December 2000).

48.	*Bernama*, 10 August 1998 (Online Lexis, 9 December 2000).

49.	Nagata, *The Reflowering of Malaysian Islam*; Chandra Muzaffar, *Islamic Resurgence in Malaysia*, Petaling Jaya: Fajar Bakti Sdn. Bhd., 1987 and Mohamed Abu Bakar,

'Islamic Revivalism and the Political Process in Malaysia', *Asian Survey*, **21** (10), 1981, 1040–59.

50. For details see Lee, *Sacred Tensions*, pp. 49–51 and Abdullahi Ahmed An-Naʻim, 'Culture and Human Rights', in *The East Asian Challenge for Human Rights*, eds Joanne Bauer and Daniel A. Bell, Cambridge: Cambridge University Press, 1999, pp. 147–68.
51. *Newsweek*, 14 September 1994, p. 23; *The Economist*, 10 September 1994, p. 17; and *Asian Survey*, **35** (2), February 1995, 186 (8).
52. An-Naʻim, 'Culture and Human Rights', p. 161.
53. Nagata, *The Reflowering of Malaysian Islam*, pp. 64–9.
54. Lee and Ackerman, *Sacred Tensions*, pp. 51–3.

Chapter 10

1. PAS's general approach to *hudud* laws is summarized in Rose Ismail (ed.), *Hudud in Malaysia: The Issues at Stake*, Kuala Lumpur: Sisters in Islam, 1995, pp. 51–3.
2. *New Straits Times (Malaysia)*, 21 November 1994 (Online Lexis, 9 December 2000).
3. *Bernama*, 25 October 1999 (Online Lexis, 9 December 2000).
4. Islam in the Federal Territories is regulated by the Parliament in the same way as state legislatures regulate it in their respective states.
5. Syariah Criminal Code (II) (Kelantan) Enactment, 1993, Section 48.
6. Syariah Criminal Code (II) (Kelantan) Enactment, 1993, Section 23(1).
7. Syariah Criminal Code (II) (Kelantan) Enactment, 1993, Section 23(2).
8. Syariah Criminal Code (II) (Kelantan) Enactment, 1993, Section 23(3).
9. Syariah Criminal Code (II) (Kelantan) Enactment, 1993, Section 23(4).
10. Kamali, *Punishment in Islamic Law*, p. 33.
11. Kamali, *Punishment in Islamic Law*, p. 33.
12. Kamali, *Punishment in Islamic Law*, pp. 33–7.
13. *Teoh Eng Huat v. Kadhi, Pasir Mas & Anor* [1986] 2 MLJ 228.
14. *New Straits Times*, 12 August 1992, p. 17 (Online Lexis, 9 December 2000).
15. Syariah Criminal Code (II) (Kelantan) Enactment, 1993, Section 23(4).
16. Syariah Criminal Code (II) (Kelantan) Enactment, 1993, Section 11(1).
17. Constitution, Federal List, Item 4(h).
18. For an interesting article on the constitutionality of the Code, see Mohammed Imam, 'Syariah/Civil Courts? Jurisdiction in Matters of Hukum Syara: A Persisting Dichotomy', *Current Law Journal*, 1, 1995, lxxxi.
19. Constitution, State List, Item 1.
20. Syariah Criminal Code (II) (Kelantan) Enactment, 1993, Section 56(2).
21. Hussin Mutalib and Taj ul-Islam Hashmi (eds.), *Islam, Muslims and the Modern State: Case-Studies of Muslims in Thirteen Countries*, Basingstoke: Macmillan Press, 1994, p. 159.
22. Hussin Mutalib, *Islam and Ethnicity in Malay Politics*, Singapore: Oxford University Press, 1990, p. 35.
23. *Malaysiakini*, 9 October 2001, <http://www.malaysiakini.com>, accessed 23 April 2002.
24. *Straits Times*, 19 May 1992, p. 14 (Online Lexis, 9 December 2000).
25. *Bernama*, 10 July 1999 (Online Lexis, 9 December 2000).
26. *Straits Times (Singapore)*, 20 May 1994, p. 22 (Online Lexis, 9 December 2000).
27. *Straits Times*, 19 May 1992, p. 14 (Online Lexis, 9 December 2000).
28. *Bernama*, 11 July 1999 (Online Lexis, 9 December 2000).
29. *Bernama*, 10 July 1999 (Online Lexis, 9 December 2000).
30. *Bernama*, 9 July 1999 (Online Lexis, 9 December 2000).
31. *Straits Times (Singapore)*, 20 May 1994, p. 22 (Online Lexis, 9 December 2000).

32. *Bernama*, 10 July 1999 (Online Lexis, 9 December 2000).
33. *Straits Times (Singapore)*, 30 March 1994, p. 15 (Online Lexis, 9 December 2000).
34. *New Straits Times (Malaysia)*, 15 May 1998, p. 6 (Online Lexis, 9 December 2000).
35. *Bernama*, 17 November 1998 (Online Lexis, 9 December 2000).
36. *Straits Times (Singapore)*, 30 March 1994, p. 15 (Online Lexis, 9 December 2000).
37. *Straits Times*, 19 May 1992, p. 14 (Online Lexis, 9 December 2000).
38. *Straits Times*, 19 May 1992, p. 14 (Online Lexis, 9 December 2000).
39. *Straits Times (Singapore)*, 13 January 1994, p. 18 (Online Lexis, 9 December 2000).
40. *Straits Times (Singapore)*, 23 August 1998, p. 14 (Online Lexis, 9 December 2000).
41. *New Straits Times (Malaysia)*, 22 August 1998, p. 5 (Online Lexis, 9 December 2000).
42. *Straits Times (Singapore)*, 8 March 1995, p. 17 (Online Lexis, 9 December 2000).
43. *Straits Times (Singapore)*, 23 August 1998, p. 14 (Online Lexis, 9 December 2000).
44. Section 90A(1), Administration of Islamic Law (Negeri Sembilan) Enactment, 1991; Section 102(1), Council of the Religion of Islam and Malay Custom (Kelantan) Enactment, 1994.
45. See, for instance, Section 205, Administration of Islamic Religious Affairs (Trengganu) Enactment, 1986.
46. Syariah Offences (Malacca) Enactment, 1991, Section 66.
47. Syariah Offences (Malacca) Enactment, 1991, Section 66(2) (1(a) and (b).
48. Syariah Offences (Malacca) Enactment, 1991, Section 66(3).
49. Council of the Religion of Islam and Malay Custom (Kelantan) Enactment, 1994, Section 102(3); Syariah Criminal Offences (Sabah) Enactment, 1995, Section 63(1).
50. Section 28, Crimes (Syariah) (Perak) Enactment, 1992; Section 127, Council of the Religion of Islam and Malay Custom (Kelantan) Enactment, 1994; Section 3, Syariah Criminal Offences (Johor) Enactment, 1997.
51. Section 11, Crimes (Syariah) (Perak) Enactment, 1992; Section 126, Council of the Religion of Islam and Malay Custom (Kelantan) Enactment, 1994; Section 6, Syariah Criminal Offences (Johor) Enactment, 1997.
52. Section 14, Crimes (Syariah) (Perak) Enactment, 1992; Section 209, Administration of Islamic Religious Affairs (Trengganu) Enactment, 1986; Section 130, Administration of Muslim Law (Perlis) Enactment, 1964; Section 120 and 122, Council of the Religion of Islam and Malay Custom (Kelantan) Enactment, 1994; Section 7, Syariah Criminal Offences (Johor) Enactment, 1997.
53. Section 17, Crimes (Syariah) (Perak) Enactment, 1992; Section 172, Administration of Muslim Law (Selangor) Enactment, 1952.
54. Section 22, Crimes (Syariah) (Perak) Enactment, 1992; Section 169, Administration of Muslim Law (Selangor) Enactment, 1952; Section 128, Administration of Muslim Law (Perlis) Enactment, 1964.
55. Section 14, Crimes (Syariah) (Perak) Enactment, 1992; Section 203, Administration of Islamic Religious Affairs (Trengganu) Enactment, 1986.
56. Section 136, Council of the Religion of Islam and Malay Custom (Kelantan) Enactment, 1994; Section 206, Administration of Islamic Religious Affairs (Trengganu) Enactment, 1986; Section 161, Administration of Muslim Law (Penang) Enactment, 1959; Section 170, Administration of Muslim Law (Selangor) Enactment, 1952; Section 129, Administration of Muslim Law (Perlis) Enactment, 1964; Section 8, Syariah Criminal Offences (Johor) Enactment, 1997.
57. Section 90A(2), Administration of Islamic Law (Negeri Sembilan) Enactment, 1991.
58. Section 90A(4)(a), Administration of Islamic Law (Negeri Sembilan) Enactment, 1991.
59. Section 90A(4)(b), Administration of Islamic Law (Negeri Sembilan) Enactment, 1991.
60. Section 90(6) and (7), Administration of Islamic Law (Negeri Sembilan) Enactment, 1991.
61. *Straits Times (Singapore)*, 8 March 1995, p. 17 (Online Lexis, 9 December 2000).
62. For details see Chapter 11 on jurisdiction.
63. See Santha Oorjithanm, 'A Matter of Personal Faith', *Asiaweek*, 26 (40), 13

October 2000, <http://www.asiaweek.com/asiaweek/magazine/2000/1013/nat.malaysia. html>, accessed 13 May 2001.

64. Section 5, Islamic *Aqidah* Protection (Perlis) Bill, 2000.
65. Section 2(1), Islamic *Aqidah* Protection (Perlis) Bill, 2000.
66. Section 5, Islamic *Aqidah* Protection (Perlis) Bill, 2000.
67. Section 5, Islamic *Aqidah* Protection (Perlis) Bill, 2000.
68. Section 6, Islamic *Aqidah* Protection (Perlis) Bill, 2000.
69. Section 7(1), Islamic *Aqidah* Protection (Perlis) Bill, 2000.
70. Section 7(2), Islamic *Aqidah* Protection (Perlis) Bill, 2000.
71. Section 8(a), Islamic *Aqidah* Protection (Perlis) Bill, 2000.
72. Section 8(b), Islamic *Aqidah* Protection (Perlis) Bill, 2000.
73. Section 14 read with section 2(1), Islamic *Aqidah* Protection (Perlis) Bill, 2000.
74. Section 15, Islamic *Aqidah* Protection (Perlis) Bill, 2000.
75. Section 11, Islamic *Aqidah* Protection (Perlis) Bill, 2000.
76. Section 11(3), Islamic *Aqidah* Protection (Perlis) Bill, 2000.
77. *Straits Times (Singapore)*, 23 August 1998, p. 14 (Online Lexis, 9 December 2000).
78. *Straits Times (Singapore)*, 25 August 1992, p. 17 (Online Lexis, 9 December 2000).
79. Lee Min Choon, *Freedom of Religion in Malaysia*, Kuala Lumpur: Kairos Research Centre, 1999, p. 52.
80. Section 102, Council of the Religion of Islam and Malay Custom (Kelantan) Enactment, 1994; Section 90A, Administration of Islamic Law (Negeri Sembilan) Enactment, 1991.
81. Section 46, Islamic Family Law (Sabah) Enactment, 1992; Section 46, Islamic Family Law (Perlis) Enactment, 1991; Section 46, Islamic Family Law (Selanagor) Enactment, 1984; Section 45, Islamic Family Law (Johor) Enactment, 1990; Section 46, Islamic Family Law (Federal Territories) Act, 1984; Section 46, Islamic Family Law (Negeri Sembilan) Enactment, 1983; Section 39, Islamic Family Law (Kedah) Enactment, 1979; Section 46, Islamic Family Law (Pahang) Enactment, 1987; Section 33, Islamic Family Law (Malacca) Enactment, 1983; Section 34, Islamic Family Law (Kelantan) Enactment, 1987.
82. Section 130, Islamic Family Law (Amendment) (Negeri Sembilan) Enactment No. 4, 1991.
83. Section 89(d), Islamic Family Law (Sabah) Enactment, 1992; Section 83(d), Islamic Family Law (Perlis) Enactment, 1991; Section 83d, Islamic Family Law (Selanagor) Enactment, 1984; Section 84(d), Islamic Family Law (Johor) Enactment, 1990; Section 83(d), Islamic Family Law (Negeri Sembilan) Enactment, 1983; Section 83(d), Islamic Family Law (Kedah) Enactment, 1979; Section 84(d); Islamic Family Law (Pahang) Enactment, 1987; Section 72(d), Islamic Family Law (Malacca) Enactment, 1983.
84. Section 81, Islamic Family Law (Negeri Sembilan) Enactment, 1983.
85. *Dalip Kaur v. Pegawai Polis Daerah, Balai Polis Daerah, Bukit Mertajam & Anor* [1991] 1 MLJ 1.
86. Oorjithanm, 'A Matter of Personal Faith'.
87. *Bernama*, 18 June 1998 (Online Lexis, 9 December 2000).
88. *Straits Times (Singapore)*, 19 June 1998, p. 43 (Online Lexis, 9 December 2000).
89. *Straits Times (Singapore)*, 17 April 1998 (Online Lexis, 9 December 2000).
90. *Straits Times*, 6 July 1992 (Online Lexis, 9 December 2000).
91. *Mohamed Habibullah Bin Mahmood v. Faridah Bte Dato Talib* [1992] 2 MLJ 793.
92. Section 102(1), Council of the Religion of Islam and Malay Custom (Kelantan) Enactment, 1994. Section 209(2), Administration of Islamic Religious Affairs (Trengganu) Enactment, 1986 provides that a Muslim who says he is no longer a Muslim treats the religion with contempt, which is punishable by a fine not exceeding RM3000 or imprisonment not exceeding one year, or both. See also Section 102(2), Council of the Religion of Islam and Malay Custom (Kelantan) Enactment, 1994.
93. *Bernama*, 8 February 1998 (Online Lexis, 9 December 2000).
94. Section 11(1), Islamic *Aqidah* Protection (Perlis) Bill, 2000.

Chapter 11

1. Constitution, Article 74(1).
2. Constitution, Article 74(2).
3. Constitution, Article 75.
4. Constitution, Ninth Schedule, Federal List, Item 4.
5. Constitution, State List, Item 1.
6. The effect of this removal is not clear because in a parliamentary democracy based on separation of powers, which Malaysia is, judicial powers and functions even if explicitly taken away from the judiciary still cannot be exercised by the other two organs, that is the Parliament and the government. The end result would be that the judicial powers would always vest in the courts unless a radically different system of government were adopted.
7. Removal of a case from a lower court to a higher court or other ways of reviewing decisions of subordinate courts by superior courts. See Courts of Judicature Act, 1964.
8. *Mohd Hanif bin Farikulah v. Bushra Chaudari* [2001] 5 MLJ 533.
9. Section 2, Syariah Courts (Criminal Jurisdiction) Act, 1965.
10. *Lim Chan Seng v. Pengarah Jabatan Agama Islam Pulau Pinang & Anor* [1996] 3 CLJ 231. This case was quoted with disapproval in *Md Hakim Lee v. Majlis Agama Islam Wilaya Persekutuan, Kuala Lumpur* [1998] 1 MLJ 681.
11. *Shaik Zolkaffily bin Shaik Natar & Ors v. Majlis Agama Islam Pulau Penang* [1997] 3 MLJ 281.
12. *Shaik Zolkaffily bin Shaik Natar & Ors v. Majlis Agama Islam Pulau Penang* [1997] 3 MLJ 293.
13. *Mohamed Habibullah bin Mahmood v. Faridah bte Dato Talib* [1992] 2 MLJ 793 at 800.
14. *Md Hakim Lee v. Majlis Agama Islam Wilayah Persekutuan, Kuala Lumpur* [1998] 1 MLJ 681.
15. *Md Hakim Lee v. Majlis Agama Islam Wilayah Persekutuan, Kuala Lumpur* [1998] 1 MLJ 688–9.
16. *Soon Singh a/l Bikar Singh v. Pertubuhan Kebajkan Islam Malaysia (PERKIM) Kedah & Anor* [1999] 1 MLJ 489.
17. *Soon Singh a/l Bikar Singh v. Pertubuhan Kebajkan Islam Malaysia (PERKIM) Kedah & Anor* [1999] 1 MLJ 502.
18. *Dalip Kaur v. Pegawai Polis Daerah, Balai Polis Daerah, Bukit Mertajam & Anor* [1991] 1 MLJ 1.
19. Section 90(3), Administration of Islamic Law (Negeri Sembilan) Enactment, 1991 provides that a convert who later decides to renounce Islam shall report the said decision to the Registrar of the Converts (Registrar of *Saudara Baru*) who shall register the said decision in the prescribed form. The Administration of Islamic Law (Federal Territories) Act, 1993 does not deal explicitly with renunciation of Islam. However, Section 91 provides that a person who has converted to Islam and has been registered in the Register of *Mukallafs* shall, for the purposes of any federal or state law and for all time, be treated as a Muslim.
20. Explanation to Section 102, Council of the Religion of Islam and Malay Custom (Kelantan) Enactment, 1994.
21. Section 102(2), Council of the Religion of Islam and Malay Custom (Kelantan) Enactment, 1994.
22. See *Mohamed Habibullah bin Mahmood v. Faridah bte Dato Talib* [1992] 2 MLJ 793, where the respondent tried to invoke the jurisdiction of the civil court by allegedly renouncing Islam apparently because she believed that she could get more appropriate remedies in the civil court.
23. Ahmad Mohamed Ibrahim, *The Administration of Islamic Law in Malaysia*, Kuala Lumpur: Institute of Islamic Understanding, 2000, p. 598.

24. *Soon Singh a/l Bikar Singh v. Pertubuhan Kebajikan Islam Malaysia (PERKIM) Kedah & Anor* [1999] 1 MLJ 489.
25. *Teoh Eng Huat v. Kadhi, Pasir Mas & Anor* [1986] 2 MLJ 228. See also Constitution, Article 12(4).
26. Constitution, Article 4.
27. *Daud Mamat & Ors v. Majlis Agama Islam/Adat & Anor* [2001] 2 CLJ 161.
28. *Adelaide Company of Jehovah's Witnesses Inc v. Commonwealth* (1943) CLR 116.
29. *Adelaide Company of Jehovah's Witnesses Inc v. Commonwealth* (1943) CLR 123.
30. Since 1957 the Chinese population has dropped from 37 per cent to 26 per cent, while the Indian population has dropped from 10.3 per cent to 7.7 per cent. Census Reports of 1957 and 2000, Department of Statistics, Malaysia. Census Report 2000 is also available online at: <http://www.statistics.gov.my/English/pageCS.htm>, accessed 25 May 2002.
31. *New Straits Times (Malaysia)*, 12 August 1992 (Online Lexis, 9 December 2000).
32. A writ issued by the court to bring before it a person who is allegedly held in unlawful custody. The objective of the exercise is to release them.
33. *Nor Kursiah bte Baharuddin v. Shahril bin Lamin & Anor* [1997] 1 MLJ 537.
34. *Mad Yaacob Ismail v. Kerajaan Negeri Kelantan & Anor and Other Applications* [2001] 2 CLJ 647.
35. Section 102(3), Council of the Religion of Islam and Malay Custom (Kelantan) Enactment, 1994.
36. See *Daud Mamat & Ors v. Majlis Agama Islam/Adat & Anor* [2001] 2 CLJ 161, *Mad Yaacob Ismail v. Kerajaan Negeri Kelantan & Anor and Other Applications* [2001] 2 CLJ 647.
37. *Nor Kursiah bte Baharuddin v. Shahril bin Lamin & Anor* [1997] 1 MLJ 537.
38. *Re Gurbachan Singh's Application* [1967] 1 MLJ 74; *Gurdit Singh v. Public Prosecutor* [1933] MLJ 224.

Chapter 12

1. *Bernama*, 23 July 1999 (Online Lexis, 9 December 2000).
2. Muhammad Asad, *The Principles of State and Government in Islam*, Berkeley: University of California Press, 1961, pp. 39–41; Sayyid Abul A'Ala Maududi, *The Islamic Law and Constitution*, 9th edn, Lahore: Islamic Publications, 1986, pp. 262–3.
3. *Utusan Malaysia*, the country's top-selling Malay-language newspaper, described Nick Aziz's statement as 'irresponsible and disturbs the political calm in this country'. It added that: 'The consequences of a lack of Malay dominance can only be grave for the Malays because it will destroy the country and damage racial ties ... it raises serious concerns because it could generate fears, worries and unrest in society.' See *Straits Times Interactive*, 10 November 1999, <http://straitstimes.asia1.com>, accessed 10 November 1999.
4. Kamarulnizam Abdullah, 'National Security and Malay Unity: The Issue of Radical Religious Elements in Malaysia', *Contemporary Southeast Asia*, **21** (2), August 1999, 256.
5. Anwar, the former Deputy Prime Minister as well as UMNO Vice President, was sacked from office in 1998 and was subsequently convicted on corruption charges. He and his supporters maintain that he is a victim of political conspiracy.
6. *Straits Times Interactive*, 21 January 2000, < http://straitstimes.asia1.com>, accessed 21 January 2000.
7. According to the latest census, Malay and other indigenous peoples constitute 65.5 per cent of Malaysia's total population of 23.27 million; Chinese: 26 per cent; Indian: 7 per cent; Others: 9 per cent. Source: Department of Statistics, Malaysia <http://www.statistics.gov.my/English/pageCS.htm>, accessed 25 May 2002.

8. See Qur'an 49:13.
9. Mutalib, *Islam and Ethnicity in Malay Politics*, p. 168.

Chapter 13

1. Ibn Taymiyyah, *Majmuʿ Fatawa Shaykh al-Islam Ahmad b. Taymiyyah*, vol. 35, Mecca: Maktabat al-Nahdah al-Hadithah, 1404AH, pp. 105–6.

Appendix 1

1. This is an unofficial copy provided by the Human Rights Commission of Malaysia.

Glossary

ahad (hadith)	solitary or isolated *hadith*; a *hadith* which has not been narrated by a large number of people.
ahl al-dhimmah	a non-Muslim minority under the protection of the Islamic state.
ahl al-hadith	those who follow *hadith*.
ahl al-ittiba‘	those who follow the way of the *salaf* or pious ancestors.
ahl al-jama‘ah	a term used to refer to the Sunnis.
ahl al-ra'y	people who emphasize reason in constructing Islamic law.
ahl al-sunnah	those who follow the *sunnah*.
ahl al-sunnah wa al-jama‘ah	Sunnis.
alhamdulillah	'praise be to God'. An expression used by Muslims on various occasions.
‘alim (pl. *ulama*)	scholar of Islam.
Allah	God.
allahu akbar	'God is the Greatest'. Phrase used to praise God.
al-salaf al-salih	the pious ancestors; earliest Muslims.
al-ta'ifah al-mansurah	the group of Muslims supported by God and the Prophet.
‘amal	actions or deeds.
ansar	Muslims of Medina who believed in the Prophet Muhammad and provided support for his mission.
‘aqidah (pl. *aqaa'id*)	belief; creed; faith
‘aqil	a person who is sane (as opposed to insane, *majnun*).
‘aql	reason.
‘asr	the late afternoon prayer.
astaghfirullahal azim	'I seek forgiveness of God'
awliya'	saints; often used for *sufi* masters.
baligh	age of majority in accordance with Islamic law.
bayt al-mal	the public purse.
bid‘ah	innovation.

bulugh	reaching puberty or maturity under Islamic law.
da'wah	the preaching of Islam.
dar	abode; place.
dar al-harb	abode or domain of war.
dar al-islam	abode or domain of Islam; region under the control of Muslims.
dar al-jaza'	abode of reward and punishment; the Hereafter.
dar al-kufr	abode or domain of unbelief; region under the control of non-Muslims.
daruriyyan	by necessity.
diyah	blood money, compensation.
faraq	judicial separation of a marriage (term used in Malaysia).
faridah	an Islamic obligation such as prayer, charity, fasting, pilgrimage, etc.
fasakh	annulment of a marriage for reasons permitted by Islamic law, such as when the husband's whereabouts is unknown for a specific period, or failure to provide maintenance, etc. (term used in Malaysia).
fasiq	one who commits grave sins.
fatwa	a religious edict or scholarly opinion on a point of Islamic law.
fay'	booty; spoils of war.
fiqh	Islamic jurisprudence; Islamic law.
firqah najiyah	the group of Muslims that will be saved from Hell on the Day of Judgement.
fisq	engaging in sin.
fitrah	nature; human nature.
fuqaha'	jurists in Islamic law.
hadd	an obligatory punishment fixed by God or the Prophet.
hadhanah	custody of children (term used in Malaysia).
hadith	reports relating to the sayings and deeds of the Prophet Muhammad.
hajj	annual pilgrimage to Mecca. It is obligatory for those who are both physically and materially capable of undertaking the journey.
halal	what is permissible in Islamic law.
haqq adamiyy	right of Man (as opposed to right of God).
haqq al-'abd	same as *haqq adamiyy*; right of Man (as opposed to right of God).

haqq allah	right of God.
haram	what is prohibited in Islamic law.
harta sepencarian	property jointly acquired by husband and wife during the continuation of marriage (term used in Malaysia).
hijab	veil; head or face cover for Muslim women.
hirabah	brigandage.
hisbah	religious institution under the authority of the state that appoints people to carry out the responsibility of enjoining what is right and forbidding what is wrong.
hudud (pl. of *hadd*)	literally 'limits'; fixed punishments specified in the Qur'an and *sunnah* (as opposed to discretionary punishment, *ta'zir*).
huquq (pl. of *haqq*)	rights.
i'tiqad	conviction.
'ibadah	various forms of worship and rituals in Islam.
'id	day of the feast. There are two such days in the Muslim calendar: *'id al-fitr* which occurs immediately after the month of Ramadan, and *'id al-adha* which occurs during the month of pilgrimage.
'inad	stubbornness.
iblis	Satan.
ijma'	consensus of Muslim jurists on a point of Islamic law.
ijtihad	exercise of individual judgement to arrive at a solution to a problem in Islamic law.
ilahi	'my God'.
ilhad	freethinking.
imam	leader in prayer; leader of the Muslim community.
imamah	imamate; leadership of the Muslim community.
iman	faith; belief. There are six pillars of *iman*: belief in God, His angels, His revealed books, His messengers, the Day of Judgement and belief in Fate and Divine Decree.
injil	the Gospel; what was revealed to Jesus.
insha' allah	'if God wills'. Muslims are discouraged from saying 'I will do such and such tomorrow' without the use of the phrase *insha' allah*.

irtadda	to turn back, to renounce (Islam).
irtidad	see *riddah*.
islahi	reformist.
israr	persistence.
istihza'	mockery.
jabriyyah	Jabris; determinists.
jahili	ignorant; non-Islamic (as opposed to Islamic, with reference to societies, laws, ethical and moral issues).
jaza'	punishment or reward.
jihad	struggle; often used for war in defence of Islam and Muslims.
jizyah	polltax paid by non-Muslims under the protection of the Islamic state.
ka'bah	the sacred building in Mecca, to which all Muslims turn in their daily prayers.
kadi	*shari'ah* court judge (term used in Malaysia).
kafir (pl. *kafirun*)	unbeliever.
kalam	Islamic theology.
khalifah	caliph.
khalq al-qur'an	creation of the Qur'an; the famous debate over whether the Qur'an is created or not, which occurred during the Abbasid period.
kharaj	a special tax levied on land holdings.
khawarij	Kharijis; an early Islamic group who rebelled against the state.
khilafah	caliphate.
kitabiyyah	a female member of the People of the Book (*ahl al-kitab*).
kuffar	unbelievers.
kufr	unbelief.
madhahib (pl. of *madhhab*)	schools of law.
madrasah	school; religious education institution.
mahdi	the guided one.
majnun	legally insane, mad.
mamak	derogatory reference to Indian Muslims (term used in Malaysia).
marad al-maut	terminal illness where the person is likely to die in that condition (term used in Malaysia).
mawali	clients.
mihnah	inquisition.
Misr	Egypt.
mu'min	believer in God.

mubaligh	one who has reached the age of puberty or *baligh* (term used in Malaysia).
mufawadah	a form of partnership contract in Islam.
mufti	an official who can issue Islamic legal rulings.
muharabah	brigandage; rebellion.
muharib (pl. *muharibun*)	an individual who is in a state of war (against Muslims).
mujahid (pl. *mujahidin*)	a person engaged in *jihad* including military action.
mukallaf	one who is legally responsible for their actions.
munafiq (pl. *munafiqun*)	hypocrite; one who outwardly professes Islam but in reality does not believe in it.
murji'ah	a theological trend in Islam according to which judgement about the grave sinner is postponed until the Day of Judgement.
murtadd	apostate; a Muslim who commits an offence that takes them away from Islam; one who rejects Islam and professes another religion or atheism.
mushrik (pl. *mushrikun*)	polytheist.
muslim	Muslim; one who surrenders to God; a believer in God and the Prophet Muhammad.
mutakallimun	those engaged in *kalam* (Islamic theology).
mu'tazilah	mu'tazlis; those who belong to the Islamic theological school of the *mu'tazilah*.
nabi	prophet.
nazir	mosque supervisors appointed by state authorities (term used in Malaysia).
nifaq	hypocrisy.
nusyuz	the refusal of a wife to obey the lawful wishes or commands of her husband (term used in Malaysia).
Pusat Islam	Islamic Centre – a federal body responsible for co-ordinating and overseeing Islamic activities (term used in Malaysia).
qadariyyah	Qadaris; a theological trend which held to human freedom.
qadhf	slander; accusation of a Muslim of illegal sexual intercourse, fornication or adultery.
qadi	a judge.
qasir	legal minor, under-age person.
qatl	killing.

qiblah	direction in which Muslims face when performing their obligatory prayers.
qital	killing; fighting.
ra'y	opinion, view.
rahn	mortgage.
rashidun	four rightly guided caliphs: Abu Bakr, ʿUmar, ʿUthman and ʿAli; those who succeeded as rulers of the Muslims after the death of the Prophet.
rasul	messenger of God.
riba	usury, interest or unlawful addition or gain.
riddah	apostasy.
ru'asa'	leaders (of a community).
rujuʿ	a return to the original married state.
rukn (pl. *arkan*)	pillar.
sabb	reviling; slander; use of foul language.
sabb allah	reviling God; blasphemy.
sabb al-rasul	reviling the Prophet; blasphemy.
sahib al-kabirah	one who commits a major (or grave) sin.
sahih	authentic; a *hadith* which is considered authentic.
salafi	a person who belongs to the *salafiyyah* school; one who follows the pious ancestors of the early period of Islam.
salat	the five daily obligatory prayers.
sariqah	theft.
shahadah	profession of faith; declaration that there is no deity but God and that Muhammad is the messenger of God.
Sham	Syria.
sharʿi	legal (according to Islamic law).
shariʿah	Islamic law; law based on the Qur'an and *sunnah* of the Prophet.
shaykh	a term used to refer to an elderly, religious or wise person.
shiʿah	a religio-political group in Islam (as opposed to *sunni*).
shibr	span.
shirk	idolatry; polytheism.
shurub	drinking liquor or intoxicating drinks (term used in Malaysia).
silat	form of self-defence (term used in Malaysia).
sirah	biography; biography of the Prophet.
subhanallah	'glory be to God'.

sufi	a person engaged in practising Sufism (Islamic mysticism).
sunnah	the normative behaviour of the Prophet. It is used sometimes to refer to *hadith*.
sunni	a religio-political group in Islam (as opposed to *shi'ah*); mainstream Muslims.
syariah	see *shari'ah* (term used in Malaysia).
ta'zir	discretionary punishment (as opposed to obligatory fixed punishments, *hudud*, specified in the Qur'an).
tafsir	interpretation of the Qur'an; commentaries on the Qur'an.
taghut	despot.
tahkim	arbitration; arbitration between 'Ali and Mu'awiyah.
takaful	insurance based on Islamic principles.
tawhid	monotheism; declaration that God is one.
tawrah	the Torah; what was revealed to Moses.
ulama	scholars.
ummah	community; Muslim community.
wahy	revelation.
wahyu	revelation from Allah to the heart or mind of prophets (term used in Malaysia).
wakaf	permanent dedication (usually non-moveable property) for charity or for religious objectives (term used in Malaysia).
wali	one who is said to have become a 'friend' of God through spiritual exercises.
warathah	heirs.
zakat	charity tax, one of the five pillars of Islam.
zandaqah	heresy.
zina	adultery, fornication.
zindiq (pl. *zanadiqah*)	heretic.

Bibliography

Abdullah, Kamarulnizam, 'National Security and Malay Unity: The Issue of Radical Religious Elements in Malaysia', *Contemporary Southeast Asia*, 21 (2), August 1999, 256.

Abidin, Hasan Ahmad, *Huquq al-Insan wa Wajibatuhu fi al-Qur'an*, Mecca: Rabitat al-Alam al-Islami, 1984.

Abu Zahrah, Muhammed, *Tarikh al-Madhahib al-Islamiyyah*, Cairo: Dar al-Fikr al-Arabi, n.d.

Adlabi, Muhammad Munir, *Qatl al-Murtadd: al-Jarimah al-Lati Harramaha al-Islam*, Dimashq: n.p., 1991.

Afifi, Muhammad al-Sadiq, *Al-Mujtama' al-Islami wa Huquq al-Insan*, Mecca: Muslim World League, 1987.

Ahmed, Ishtiaq, *The Concept of an Islamic State: An Analysis of the Ideological Controversy in Pakistan*, London: Francis Pinter, 1987.

Akhtar, Shabbir, *A Faith for All Seasons: Islam and Western Modernity*, London: Bellew Publishing, 1990.

Akhtar, Shabbir, *Be Careful with Muhammad! The Salman Rushdie Affair*, London: Bellew Publishing, 1989.

Amin, Ahmad, *Fajr al-Islam*, 12th edn, Cairo: Maktabat al-Nahdah al-Misriyyah, 1978.

An-Na'im, Abdullahi Ahmed, *Toward an Islamic Reformation: Civil Liberties, Human Rights and International Law*, New York: Syracuse University Press, 1990.

An-Na'im, Abdullahi Ahmed, 'Culture and Human Rights', in *The East Asian Challenge for Human Rights*, ed. Joanne Bauer and Daniel A. Bell, Cambridge: Cambridge University Press, 1999, pp. 147–68.

An-Na'im, Abdullahi Ahmad, 'The Islamic Law of Apostasy and its Modern Applicability: A Case from Sudan'. *Religion*, 16, 1986, 197–224.

Arzt, Donna E., 'Religious Human Rights in Muslim States of the Middle East and North Africa', in *Religious Human Rights in Global Perspective: Religious Perspectives*, ed. John Witte, Jr and Johan D. van der Vyver, The Hague: Martinus Nijhoff Publishers, 1996, pp. 387–454.

Asad, Muhammad, *The Principles of State and Government in Islam*, Berkeley: University of California Press, 1961.

Awa, Mohammed S. el-, *Punishment in Islamic Law: A Comparative Study*, Indianapolis: American Trust Publications, 1982.

214

Awa, Muhammad Salim el-,'Jara'im al-Hudud wa 'Uqubatuha', *Minbar al-Sharq*, No. 10, 3 Nov. 1993, 15–29.

Ayoub, Mahmoud, *The Qur'an and its Interpreters: Volume 1*, Albany: State University of New York Press, 1984.

Badawi, Abd al-Rahman, *Min Tarikh al-Ilhad fi al-Islam*, 2nd edn, Cairo: Sina li al-Nashr, 1993.

Baghdadi, 'Abd al-Qahir al-, *Al-Farq Bayna al-Firaq*, Beirut: Dar al-Afaq al-Jadidah, 1980.

Bakar, Mohamed Abu, 'Islamic Revivalism and the Political Process in Malaysia', *Asian Survey*, 21 (10), 1981, 1040–59.

Banna, Jamal al-, 'Hurriyyat al-I'tiqad fi al-Islam', *Minbar al-Sharq*, No. 10, 3 Nov. 1993, 30–38.

Bayhaqi, Abu Bakr Ahmad b. al-Husayn b. Ali al-, *Kitab al-Sunan al-Kubra*, Beirut: Dar al-Ma'rifah, reprint of 1354 Hijri edition, 1986.

Boothby, Lee, 'Models of Religious Freedom', paper delivered at the International Coalition for Religious Freedom Conference on 'Religious Freedom and the New Millennium', Berlin: 29–31 May 1998.

Brown, Chris, 'Human Rights', *The Globalization of World Politics: An Introduction to International Human Relations*, 2nd edn, ed. John Baylis and Steve Smith, New York: Oxford University Press, 2001.

Bukhari, *Sahih al-Bukhari: The Translation of the Meanings of Sahih al-Bukhari, Arabic–English*, trans. Muhammad Muhsin Khan, rev. edn, Ankara: Hilal Yayinlari, 1976.

Canady, Charles, 'Religious Freedom and Democracy', paper delivered at the International Coalition for Religious Freedom Conference on 'Religious Freedom and the New Millennium', Berlin: 29–31 May 1998.

Choon, Lee Min, *Freedom of Religion in Malaysia*, Kuala Lumpur: Kairos Research Centre, 1999.

Dalacoura, Katerina, *Islam Liberalism and Human Rights*, London and New York: I.B. Tauris, 1998.

Dwyer, Kevin, *Arab Voices: The Human Rights Debate in the Middle East*, London: Routledge, 1991.

Fakhry, Majid, *Tarikh al-Falsafah al-Islamiyyah*, trans. Kamal al-Yazji, Beirut: al-Dar al-Muttahidah li al-Nashr, 1979.

Fariq, Khurshid Ahmad (ed.), *Tarikh al-Riddah*, New Delhi: Asia Publishing House, 1970.

Faruqi, Ismail R. al-, *Islam*, Nile, IL: Argus Communications, 1984.

Ghannushi, Rashid al-, *Huquq al-Muwatanah: Huquq Ghayr al-Muslim fi al-Mujtama' al-Islami*, Herndon: International Institute of Islamic Thought, 1993.

Gibb, H.A.R. and J.H. Kramers (eds), *Shorter Encyclopaedia of Islam*, Leiden: Brill, 1991.

Hamad, Muhammad b. Ibrahim al-, *'Aqidat Ahl al-Sunnah wa al-Jama'ah*, Riyadh: Dar Ibn Khuzaymah, 1998.

Hasan, Ahmad, *The Early Development of Islamic Jurisprudence*, Islamabad: Islamic Research Institute, 1970.

Hexham, Irving, *Concise Dictionary of Religion*, Downers Grove, IL: InterVarsity Press, 1993.

Hitti, Philip Khuri, *History of the Arabs: From the Earliest Times to the Present*, London: Macmillan, 1986.

Hooker, M.B., *Islamic Law in South-East Asia*, Singapore: Oxford University Press, 1984.

Hourani, Albert, *Arabic Thought in the Liberal Age: 1798–1939*, Cambridge: Cambridge University Press, 1983.

Hussain, S. Showkat, *Minorities, Islam and the Nation State*, Kuala Lumpur: Islamic Book Trust, 1997.

Hussain, Sheikh Shukat, *Human Rights in Islam*, 2nd edn, New Delhi: Kitab Bhavan, n.d.

Ibn al-Athir, *Al-Kamil fi al-Tarikh*, Beirut: Dar al-Kutub al-'Ilmiyyah, 1998.

Ibn Hazm, Abu Muhammad 'Ali b. Ahmad b. Sa'id, *Al-Muhalla*, ed. Ahmad Muhammad Shakir, Cairo: Maktabat Dar al-Turath, n.d.

Ibn Hisham, *Al-Sirah al-Nabawiyyah*, ed. Mustafa al-Saqqa, Ibrahim al-Abiyari and 'Abd al-Hafiz Shalabi, Cairo: Mustafa al-Babi al-Halabi, 1955.

Ibn Kathir, Isma'il b. 'Umar, *Tafsir al-Qur'an al-'Azim*, Beirut: Dar al-Ma'rifah, 1987.

Ibn Qudama, Abu Muhammad 'Abd Allah b. Ahmad b. Muhammad, *Al-Mughni*, Riyadh: Maktabat al-Riyad al-Hadithah, n.d.

Ibn Rushd, *The Distinguished Jurist's Primer: A Translation of Bidayat al-Mujtahid*, trans. Imran Ahsan Khan Nyazee, Reading: Centre for Muslim Contribution to Civilization, Garnet Publishing, 1996.

Ibrahim, Ahmad Mohamed, *The Administration of Islamic Law in Malaysia*, Kuala Lumpur: Institute of Islamic Understanding, 2000.

Ismail, Rose (ed.), *Hudud in Malaysia: The Issues at Stake*, Kuala Lumpur: Sisters in Islam, 1995.

Jaza'iri, Abu Bakr al-, *Minhaj al-Muslim*, Cairo: Maktabat al-Kulliyyat al-Azhariyyah, 1979.

Jaziri, Abd al-Rahman al-, *Min Kitab al-Fiqh 'ala al-Madhahib al-Arba'ah*, Beirut: Dar al-Fikr, n.d.

Kamali, Mohammad Hashim, *Islamic Law in Malaysia: Issues and Developments*, Kuala Lumpur: Ilmiah Publishers, 2000.

Kamali, Mohammad Hashim, *Punishment in Islamic Law: An Enquiry into the Hudud Bill of Kelantan*, Kuala Lumpur: Ilmiah Publishers, 1995, 2000.

Kamali, Mohammad Hashim, *Freedom of Expression in Islam*, Kuala Lumpur: Berita Publishing, 1994.

Karatnycky, Adrian, 'Religious Freedom and Democracy as Fundamental Human Rights', paper delivered at the International Coalition for

Religious Freedom Conference on 'Religious Freedom and the New Millennium', Berlin: 29–31 May 1998.

Kasani, ʿAla' al-Din Abu Bakr b. Masʿud al-, *Bada'iʿ al-Sana'iʿ fi Tartib al-Shara'iʿ*, Beirut: Dar al-Kutub al-ʿIlmiyyah, n.d.

Khuri, Richard K., *Freedom, Modernity, and Islam*, New York: Syracuse University Press, 1998.

Koh Tong Ngee, Philip, *Freedom of Religion in Malaysia – The Legal Dimension*, Petaling Jaya: Graduate Christian Fellowship, 1987.

Krishnaswami, Arcot, 'Study of Discrimination in the Matter of Religious Rights and Practices', UN Doc. E/CN.4/Sub.2/200/Rev.1, UN Sales No.60.XIV.2 (1960), in *Religion and Human Rights: Basic Documents*. ed. Tad Stahnke and J. Paul Martin, New York: Center for the Study of Human Rights, Columbia University, 1998.

Labter, Lazhari, *Journalistes Algeriens: Entre le Baillon et les Balles*, Paris: L'Harmattan, 1995.

Lee, Raymond L.M. and Susan E. Ackerman, *Sacred Tensions: Modernity and Religious Transformation in Malaysia*, Columbia, SC: University of South Carolina Press, 1997.

Mahmassani, Subhi, *Arkan Huquq al-Insan fi al-Islam*, Beirut: Dar al-ʿIlm li al-Malayin, 1979.

Martin, Elizabeth A. (ed.), *A Dictionary of Law*, Oxford: Oxford University Press, 1997.

Maududi, Abul Aʿla, *The Islamic Law and Constitution*, trans. and ed. Kurshid Ahmad, 4th edn, Lahore: Islamic Publications, 1969 (9th edn, 1986).

Maududi, Abul Aʿla, *Human Rights in Islam*, Leicester: Islamic Foundation, 1980.

Maududi, Abul Aʿla, *Murtadd ki Saza Islami Qanun Meyn*, Lahore: Islami Publications, 1963.

Mayer, Ann Elizabeth, *Islam and Human Rights: Tradition and Politics*, 2nd edn, Boulder and San Francisco: Westview Press; London: Pinter, 1995.

Merad, Ali, *Le Reformisme Musulman En Algerie de 1925 à 1940: Essaie d'Histoire Religieuse et Sociale*, Paris: Mouton, 1967.

Misri, Ahmad b. Naqib al-, *Reliance of the Traveller: A Classical Manual of Islamic Sacred Law*, trans. Nuh Ha Mim Keller, Evanston: Sunnah Books, 1994.

Muslim, *Sahih Muslim*, trans. Abdul Hamid Siddiqi, Riyadh: International Islamic Publishing House, n.d.

Mutalib, Hussin, *Islam and Ethnicity in Malay Politics*, Singapore: Oxford University Press, 1990.

Mutalib, Hussin, *Islam in Malaysia from Revivalism to Islamic State*, Singapore: Singapore University Press, 1993.

Mutalib, Hussin and Taj ul-Islam Hashimi (eds), *Islam, Muslims and the Modern State: Case-Studies of Muslims in Thirteen Countries*, Basingstoke: Macmillan Press, 1994.

Muzaffar, Chandra, *Islamic Resurgence in Malaysia*, Petaling Jaya: Fajar Bakti Sdn. Bhd, 1987.

Nagata, Judith A., *The Reflowering of Malaysian Islam: Modern Religious Radicals and Their Roots*, Vancouver: University of British Columbia Press, 1984.

Nawawi, Muhy al-Din Abu Zakariyya Yahya b. Sharaf al-, *Sharh Sahih Muslim*, Beirut: Dar al-Qalam, [between 1987 and 1993].

Nayhoum, al-Sadiq al-, *Islam Didd al-Islam: Shari'ah min Waraq*, Beirut: Riad al-Rayyes Books, 1995.

Netton, Ian Richard, *A Popular Dictionary of Islam*, London: Curzon Press, 1997.

Pearl, David and Werner Menski, *Muslim Family Law*, 3rd edn, London: Sweet & Maxwell, 1998.

Peters, Rudolph, *Jihad in Classical and Modern Islam*, Princeton: Markus Wiener Publications, 1996.

Qaradawi, Yusuf al-, *The Lawful and the Prohibited in Islam*, Kuala Lumpur: Islamic Book Trust, 1995.

Qaradawi, Yusuf al-, ''Uqubat al-Riddah wa Muwaajahat al-Murtaddin', *Minbar al-Sharq*, No. 10, 3 Nov. 1993, 5–14.

Qarami, Amal, Qadiyyat al-riddah fi al-Fikr al-Islami al-Hadith, Tunis: Dar al-Junub Iil-Nashr, 1996.

Qarni, Abd Allah b. Muhammad al-, *Dawabit al-Tafkir 'inda Ahl al-Sunnah wa al-Jama'ah*, Beirut: Mu'assasat al-Risalah, 1992.

Qastallani, Abu al-'Abbas Shihab al-Din Ahmad al-, *Irshad al-Sari li Sharh Sahih al-Bukhari*, Beirut: Dar al-Fikr, 1990.

Qutb, Sayyid, *Fi Zilal al-Qur'an*, Cairo: Dar al-Shuruq, 1996.

Rahman, S.A., *Punishment of Apostasy in Islam*, New Delhi: Kitab Bhavan, 1996.

Ramli, Shams al-Din Muhammad b. Abu al-'Abbas Ahmad b. Hamzah b. Shihab al-Din al-, *Nihayat al-Muhtaj ila Sharh al-Minhaj*, Beirut: Dar al-Kutub al-'Ilmiyyah, n.d.

Report of the Court of Inquiry Constituted under Punjab Act II of 1954 to Enquire into the Punjab Disturbances of 1953, Lahore: Superintendent of Government Printing, 1954.

Report of the Federation of Malaysia Constitutional Commission, 1956–57, Kuala Lumpur: Government Printer, 1957.

Sachedina, Abdulaziz A., 'Freedom of Conscience and Religion in the Qur'an', *Human Rights and the Conflict of Cultures: Western and Islamic Perspectives on Religious Liberty*, ed. David Little, J. Kelsay and A.A. Sachedina, Columbia, SC: University of South Carolina Press, 1988.

Safwat, S.M., 'Offences and Penalties in Islamic Law', *Islamic Quarterly*, 26, 1987, 149–79.

Sarakhsi, Muhammad b. Ahmad al-, *Kitab al-Mabsut*, Beirut: Dar al-Ma'rifah, n.d.

Sarakhsi, Shams al-Din al-, *Al-Mabsut*, Beirut: Dar al-Maʿrifah, 1989. [4n12]

Shaʿrawi, Muhammad Mutawalli al-, *Al-Jamiʿ li al-Fatawa*, ed. Muhammad Hasan Muhammad, Cairo: Dar al-Jalil li al-Kutub wa al-Nashr, 1998.

Shaltut, Mahmud, *Al-Islam: ʿAqidah wa Shariʿah*, Kuwait: Matabiʿ Dar al-Qalam, n.d.

Shawkani, Muhammad b. ʿAli al-, *Fath al-Qadir: al-Jamiʿ bayna Fannay al-Riwayah wa al-Dirayah min ʿIlm al-Tafsir*, Beirut: Dar al-Maʿrifah, [between 1980 and 1993].

Shawkani, Muhammad b. ʿAli b. Muhammad al-, *Fath al-Qadir*, Beirut: Dar al-Kutub al-ʿIlmiyyah, n.d.

Shawkani, Muhammad b. ʿAli b. Muhammad al-, *Nayl al-Awtar*, Beirut: Dar al-Kutub al-ʿIlmiyyah, n.d.

Sheridan, L.A., 'The Religion of the Federation', *Malayan Law Journal*, 2, 1988, xiii.

Shirazi, Abu Ishaq al-, *Al-Muhadhdhab fi Fiqh al-Imam al-Shafiʿi*, ed. Muhammad al-Zuhayli, Dimashq: Dar al-Qalam, 1996.

Sijistani, Abu Daʾud Sulayman b. al-Ashʿath al-, *Sunan Abi Daʾud*, Beirut: Dar al-Kutub al-ʿIlmiyyah, 1997.

Soong, Kua Kia (ed.), *Malaysian Cultural Policy and Democracy*, Selangor: The Resource and Research Centre, 1990.

Soroush, ʿAbdolkarim, *Reason, Freedom and Democracy in Islam: Essential Writings of ʿAbdolkarim Soroush*, trans., ed. and intro. Mahmoud Sadri and Ahmad Sadri, Oxford: Oxford University Press, 2000.

Stroumsa, Sarah, *Freethinkers of Medieval Islam*, Leiden: Brill, 1999.

Suyuti, Jalal al-Din al-, *Al-Durr al-Manthur fi al-Tafsir al-Maʾthur*, Beirut: Dar al-Kutub al-ʿIlmiyyah, 1990.

Suyuti, Jalal al-Din al-, *Tarikh al-Khulafaʾ*, ed. Muhammad Muhy al-Din ʿAbd al-Hamid, n.p, n.d.

Tabandeh, Sultanhussein, *A Muslim Commentary on the Universal Declaration of Human Rights*, London: F. T. Goulding, 1970.

Tamimi, ʿAli al-. 'The Muslim's Belief – Some Causes that Lead to Apostasy from the Religion of Islam', *The Friday Report*, Makkah: Dar Makkah, August–September 1994.

Tarabishi, George, *Min al-Nahdah ila al-Riddah*, London: Dar al-Saqi, 2000.

United States Commission on International Religious Freedom, *Report on International Religious Freedom: Pakistan*, released on 1 May 2001.

US Department of State, *Annual Report on International Religious Freedom*, 1999, 2001.

Vermeulen, Ben P., 'International Agreements on Religious Freedom and their Implementation in Europe', paper delivered at the International Coalition for Religious Freedom Conference on 'Religious Freedom and the New Millennium', Berlin: 29–31 May 1998.

Von Denffer, Ahmad, *Indonesia: Government Decrees on Mission and Subsequent Developments*, Leicester: Islamic Foundation, 1987.

Watt, W. Montgomery, *Muhammad at Medina*, 4th impression, Karachi: Oxford University Press, 1998.

Watt, W. Montgomery, *The Majesty that was Islam: The Islamic World 661–1100*, New York: Praeger, 1974.

Yousif, Ahmad F., *Religious Freedom, Minorities and Islam – An Inquiry into the Malaysian Experience*, Selangor: Thinker's Library, 1998.

Zuhayli, Wahbah al-, *Al-Fiqh al-Islami wa Adillatuhu*, Dimashq: Dar al-Fikr, 1997.

Cases

Adelaide Company of Jehovah's Witnesses Inc v. Commonwealth (1943) CLR 116.

Che Omar bin Che Soh v. Public Prosecutor [1988] 2 MLJ 55.

Dalip Kaur v. Pegawai Polis Daerah, Balai Polis Daerah, Bukit Mertajam & Anor [1991] 1 MLJ 1.

Daud Mamat & Ors v. Majlis Agama Islam/Adat & Anor [2001] 2 CLJ 161.

Gurdit Singh v. Public Prosecutor [1933] MLJ 224.

Lim Chan Seng v. Pengarah Jabatan Agama Islam Pulau Pinang & Anor [1996] 3 CLJ 231.

Mad Yaacob Ismail v. Kerajaan Negeri Kelantan & Anor and Other Applications [2001] 2 CLJ 647.

Md Hakim Lee v. Majlis Agama Islam Wilaya Persekutuan, Kuala Lumpur [1998] 1 MLJ 681.

Mohamed Habibullah Bin Mahmood v. Faridah Bte Dato Talib [1992] 2 MLJ 793.

Mohd Hanif bin Farikulah v. Bushra Chaudari [2001] 5 MLJ 533.

Nor Kursiah bte Baharuddin v. Shahril bin Lamin & Anor [1997] 1 MLJ 537.

Ramah v. Laton [1927] 6 FMSLR 128.

Re Gurbachan Singh's Application [1967] 1 MLJ 74.

Shaik Zolkaffily bin Shaik Natar & Ors v. Majlis Agama Islam Pulau Penang [1997] 3 MLJ 281.

Soon Singh a/l Bikar Singh v. Pertubuhan Kebajkan Islam Malaysia (PERKIM) Kedah & Anor [1999] 1 MLJ 489.

Teoh Eng Huat v. Kadhi, Pasir Mas & Anor [1986] 2 MLJ 228.

Statutes (Malaysia)

Administration of Islamic Law (Federal Territories) Act, 1993.

Administration of Islamic Law (Negeri Sembilan) Enactment 1991.

Administration of Islamic Religious Affairs (Trengganu) Enactment, 1986.
Administration of Muslim Law (Kedah) Enactment, 1962.
Administration of Muslim Law (Malacca) Enactment, 1959.
Administration of Muslim Law (Pahang) Enactment, 1959.
Administration of Muslim Law (Penang) Enactment, 1959.
Administration of Muslim Law (Perlis) Enactment, 1964.
Administration of Muslim Law (Selangor) Enactment, 1952.
Administration of Syariah Court (Kelantan) Enactment, 1982
Control and Restriction (The Propagation of Non-Islamic Religions Among Muslims) (Negeri Sembilan) Bill, 1991.
Control and Restriction of the Propagation of Non-Islamic Religions (Kelantan) Enactment, 1981.
Control and Restriction of the Propagation of Non-Islamic Religions to Muslims (Malacca) Enactment, 1988.
Council of the Religion of Islam and Malay Custom (Kelantan) Enactment, 1994.
Courts of Judicature Act, 1964.
Crimes (Syariah) (Perak) Enactment, 1992.
Federal Constitution, 1957.
Internal Security Act, 1960.
Islamic *Aqidah* Protection (Perlis) Bill, 2000.
Islamic Family Law (Amendment) (Negeri Sembilan) Enactment No. 4, 1991.
Islamic Family Law (Federal Territories) Act, 1984.
Islamic Family Law (Johor) Enactment, 1990.
Islamic Family Law (Kedah) Enactment, 1979.
Islamic Family Law (Kelantan) Enactment, 1987.
Islamic Family Law (Malacca) Enactment, 1983.
Islamic Family Law (Negeri Sembilan) Enactment, 1983.
Islamic Family Law (Pahang) Enactment, 1987.
Islamic Family Law (Perlis) Enactment, 1991.
Islamic Family Law (Sabah) Enactment, 1992.
Islamic Family Law (Selangor) Enactment, 1984.
Non-Islamic Religions (Control of Propagation Amongst Muslims) (Selangor) Enactment, 1988.
Syariah Courts (Criminal Jurisdiction) Act, 1965.
Syariah Criminal Code (II) (Kelantan) Enactment, 1993.
Syariah Criminal Offences (Johor) Enactment, 1997.
Syariah Criminal Offences (Sabah) Enactment, 1995.
Syariah Offences (Malacca) Enactment, 1991.

Index